DIVERSE VOICES IN PUBLIC LAW

Diverse Voices

Series Editors: **Se-shauna Wheatle**, Durham University and **Jonathan Herring**, University of Oxford

---

As law faculties, academics and students increasingly realize that their reading lists are dominated by white, male, hetero-normative perspectives, the Diverse Voices series gives students an opportunity to engage with voices that have so often been silenced: the voices of black and racialized people, women, disabled, LGBTQI, working class and neuroatypical people. Diverse Voices presents a ground-breaking platform for critiquing the law from the perspective of minoritized and marginalized groups and debating and understanding the impact of the law on these different groups.

Forthcoming

Diverse Voices in Tort Law
Edited by **Kirsty Horsey**

Advisory board

Find out more at
bristoluniversitypress.co.uk/diverse-voices

DIVERSE VOICES IN PUBLIC LAW

Edited by
Se-shauna Wheatle and Elizabeth O'Loughlin

BRISTOL
UNIVERSITY
PRESS

First published in Great Britain in 2023 by

Bristol University Press
University of Bristol
1–9 Old Park Hill
Bristol
BS2 8BB
UK
t: +44 (0)117 374 6645
e: bup-info@bristol.ac.uk

Details of international sales and distribution partners are available at bristoluniversitypress.co.uk

British Library Cataloguing in Publication Data
A catalogue record for this book is available from the British Library

ISBN 978-1-5292-2073-5 hardcover
ISBN 978-1-5292-2074-2 paperback
ISBN 978-1-5292-2075-9 ePub
ISBN 978-1-5292-2076-6 ePdf

Cover design: Nicky Borowiec
Front cover image: stock.adobe.com/IzzetNoyan
Bristol University Press use environmentally responsible print partners.
Printed and bound in Great Britain by CPI Group (UK) Ltd, Croydon, CR0 4YY

FSC
www.fsc.org
MIX
Paper | Supporting responsible forestry
FSC® C013604

Contents

Table of Cases, Statutes, Statutory Instruments and Other Jurisdictions

Cases

Statutes

Statutory instruments

Other jurisdictions

Notes on Contributors

Alysia Blackham is Associate Professor at the Melbourne Law School, University of Melbourne.

Ben Bowling is Professor of Criminology and Criminal Justice at King's College London.

Tufyal Choudhury is Associate Professor at Durham Law School and Senior Research Fellow at the Bingham Centre for the Rule of Law.

Donal K. Coffey is Assistant Professor/Lecturer at the National University of Ireland, Maynooth.

Ciara Fitzpatrick is Lecturer in Law at Ulster University.

Shruti Iyer is a DPhil candidate at the Centre for Socio-Legal Studies, University of Oxford.

Elizabeth O'Loughlin is Assistant Professor of Public Law and Human Rights at Durham Law School.

Alex Powell is Lecturer in Law at Oxford Brookes University.

Devyani Prabhat is Professor of Law at the University of Bristol Law School.

Paul F. Scott is Senior Lecturer in Law at University of Glasgow.

Kanika Sharma is Senior Lecturer in Law at the School of Law, SOAS University of London.

Alexandra Sinclair is Research Fellow at the Public Law Project and a Doctoral student at the London School of Economics.

Coree Brown Swan is Lecturer in Comparative Politics at Queen's University Belfast.

Se-shauna Wheatle is Associate Professor in Law at Durham Law School.

Series Editors' Preface

Se-shauna Wheatle and Jonathan Herring

Law is dominated by a select range of actors: the wealthy, the white, the male and the enabled. Their prevalence among those who appear before the courts, whether as litigants or legal representatives, and those who judge the cases is inescapable.

This is true in much academic discourse too. The privileged dominate the practice of law, the law reports and the legal academy. *Diverse Voices* is an attempt to engage with a wider range of voices and perspectives than are typically encountered within the legal academy and legal studies. What are the stories that are not told in traditional law courses? Whose values are permitted and who is ignored? Who is rendered visible and who is subjected to the legal gaze? Who is controlled and who is empowered by the law?

Inevitably this series will not capture all the voices that need to be heard. It cannot capture the depth of nuance that a deep intersectional analysis requires. What the series does do is to disrupt the dominant discourse and to highlight those marginalised, silenced or misrepresented by the law. It seeks to start a listening process and begin a journey. It is certainly not the last word or the final destination. It is a beginning.

Introduction

Se-shauna Wheatle and Elizabeth O'Loughlin

Public law teaching is in a perpetual state of flux. Public law issues dominate the news cycle, raising public consciousness of norms and conventions that are normally solely the purview of the most expert of lawyers and academics.[1] A prolonged period of political upheaval and public policy reforms have highlighted the importance of the principles and actors that guide public law and the impact that this field has on the state at large, as well as the lives of individuals. This instability in UK public law has coincided with a move towards rethinking educational practices at UK law schools. There is increasing awareness of the inequality that undergirds and is reflected in the law we teach, the sources we marshal in teaching that law, and the voices and perspectives that are represented in course content and delivery.

Gender disparity in scholarly influence, measured both in gendered publication patterns and differential citations of academic work, has been widely documented in the social sciences, and is also reflected in course syllabi.[2] Similar observations have been made about legal academia specifically[3] and have prompted some leading journals to host information sessions aimed at female academics.[4] In UK public law, almost all of the main

---

1 For example, the inner workings of Erskine May's authoritative reference book on parliamentary procedure became a common talking point among general commentators and the public during a series of key Brexit votes in 2019: Walker, P. (2019) 'What Has John Bercow Done Now?', *The Guardian* [online], 18 March. Available from: https://www.theguardian.com/politics/2019/mar/18/what-has-john-bercow-done-now [Accessed 25 July 2022].

2 A recent confirmation of the persistence of these patterns can be found in: Dion, M., Sumner, J. and Mitchell, S. (2018) 'Gendered Citation Patterns across Political Science and Social Science Methodology Fields', *Political Analysis*, 26(3): 312–27.

3 Pant, S. (2020) 'Calculating the Gender Gap in Legal Scholarship: An Empirical Study', *Saint Louis University Law Journal*, 65(1): 199–226.

4 *Modern Law Review* (2020) 'Modern Law Review Information Session for Female Academics'. Available from: https://onlinelibrary.wiley.com/page/journal/14682230/homepage/zoom_info_session [Accessed 25 July 2022].

textbooks are written by male academics and they contain only a very brief discussion of issues of diversity in the field.[5] There is even less diversity in relation to race and sexual orientation. Public law publications are dominated by the perspectives of white British (and usually English) writers. This book aims to create a space for less represented voices. By developing a UK public law text that centres marginalised and excluded perspectives, we seek to cement the idea that such voices ought to be viewed as part of the standard curriculum and discourse.

This book aims to amplify the voices of scholars who are underrepresented in the field, and to acquaint students with a range of underexplored perspectives on the main topics of public law. To further these aims, the book includes chapters addressing citizenship and belonging, colonialism in constitutional law, judicial diversity, and minority critiques of human rights and administrative law. The majority of the chapters are written by racialised or minoritised persons, women and LGBTQI persons. Further, a significant number of the contributors are early career researchers. Accordingly, the book explicitly seeks to offer diversity of voices as well as diversity of topical perspectives and issues. A key objective of the book is to enrich students' understanding of the complex dynamics that emerge within public law, the impact of historical and societal inequities on public law norms, and the ways in which these norms may impact minorities and perpetuate inequalities. The embrace of both topical and authorship diversity encourages critical reflection on the traditional approach to, and commentary on, UK public law topics. Further, from a practical point of view, including a wider range of voices and views within a core public law book provides a useful resource for students and academics seeking to engage with more critical and diverse perspectives on their reading lists.

The book and the series in which it sits adopt the label of 'diversity'. However, several of the chapters also complement approaches that seek to 'decolonise' legal studies. Colonialism has been powerfully described by Ania Loomba as 'the conquest and control of other people's land and goods', through processes that 'locked the original inhabitants and newcomers into the most complex and traumatic relationships in human history'.[6] Relatedly, the concept of coloniality captures the longstanding frameworks of power, forms of domination and exploitation that resulted from colonialism, and

[5] Rare examples of UK public law texts authored by women can be found in: Young, A. (2021) *Turpin and Tomkins' British Government and the Constitution: Texts and Materials* (8th edn), Cambridge: Cambridge University Press; Webley, L. and Samuels, H. (2021) *Complete Public Law: Texts, Cases, and Materials* (5th edn), Oxford: Oxford University Press; Dennett, A. (2021) *Public Law Directions* (2nd edn), Oxford: Oxford University Press.

[6] Loomba, A. (1998) *Colonialism/Postcolonialism*, London: Routledge, 2.

identifies their coexistence with modernity.[7] Conscious that decolonising discourse should not be overused or misused,[8] it should be made clear that this book does not take as its central aim the decolonisation of public law education.[9] Nonetheless, several chapters in the book identify the 'persistence of colonialism', understood as the continuity of structures and systems of domination and subordination, emerging from the domination of the European metropole over subjugated territories.[10] Therefore, while decolonising work includes critically examining and expanding the demographic profile of authors and commentators featured on a module,[11] it also requires the recognition of structures that maintain coloniality. In law, this involves examining the effects of empire and colonial structures on UK law, and acknowledging the impact of colonisation and the legal and political controls that sustained it in shaping the institutions of the UK constitution and administrative state.[12] The book also squarely engages with legacies of racism and racialisation in the development and implementation of administrative laws and policies. Colonialism involves 'the oppression of one racialised group by another' and includes the very construction of race and what it means to be Black or Brown.[13] The continuity of the concept of 'race' – the intellectual elaboration of which occurred in parallel with

---

7 Quijano, A. (2000) 'Coloniality of Power and Eurocentrism in Latin America', *International Sociology*, 15(2): 215–32.

8 Important works have identified patterns of the 'easy adoption' of decolonising discourse in educational advocacy and scholarship: Tuck, E. and Yang, K. (2012) 'Decolonization is Not a Metaphor', *Decolonization: Indigeneity, Education & Society*, 1(1): 1–40.

9 Such an aim should be an ongoing process of conceptual thinking and concrete action, which will mean different things in different contexts. See Bhambra, G.K., Gebrial, D. and Nişancıoğlu, K. (eds) (2018) *Decolonising the University*, London: Pluto Press. There are already important thinkers and actors in this area in the UK legal academy. See, for example: Jivraj, S. (2020) 'Decolonising the Academy: Between a Rock and a Hard Place', *Interventions*, 22(4): 552–73; Adebisi, F. (2020) 'Decolonising the Law School: Presences, Absences, Silences … and Hope', *Law Teacher*, 54(4): 471–4 and other contributions in the issue; and Cullen, A. (2021) 'Decolonizing Public Law', in D. Tran (ed) *Decolonizing University Teaching and Learning: An Entry Model for Grappling with Complexities*, London: Bloomsbury, 139–43.

10 Yusuf, H.O. and Chowdhury, T. (2019) 'The Persistence of Colonial Constitutionalism in British Overseas Territories', *Global Constitutionalism*, 8(1): 157–90, at 160–1.

11 Decolonising SOAS Working Group (2018) 'Decolonising SOAS Learning and Teaching Toolkit for Programme and Module Convenors'. Available from: https://blogs.soas.ac.uk/decolonisingsoas/files/2018/10/Decolonising-SOAS-Learning-and-Teaching-Toolkit-AB.pdf [Accessed 25 July 2022], at 9.

12 Please see contributions to the special journal issue 'The Constitutional Legacies of Empire': Scott, P.F. (2020) 'Introduction: The Constitutional Legacies of Empire', *Northern Ireland Legal Quarterly*, 71(2): 99–107.

13 Black, L. and Solomos, J. (eds) (2022) *Theories of Race and Racism: A Reader* (3rd edn), Abingdon: Routledge, 475.

the expansion of the European colonial project – is interwoven with the persistence of racism.[14] Decolonisation must therefore acknowledge and confront such oppression and its racialised bases, and examine its continuing manifestation in existing laws, institutions and structures. The content of this collection makes a step in this direction by reflecting awareness of the racialised construction of authority and knowledge, and how this inevitably impacts the formulation and application of legal rules, and the assessment of the quality and effectiveness of constitutional and administrative norms and institutions.

In addition to addressing the construction of power in public law and its intersection with historical, racial and social inequalities, the collection also adopts a critical approach to topics of general import in the field. Public law textbooks cover important topics such as the branches of government, individual rights and judicial review. They typically include the following core topics: (1) the nature and sources of the UK constitution; (2) the principles and concepts of the constitution, including the rule of law, separation of powers and parliamentary sovereignty; (3) the relationship between the UK and international legal orders, including the European Union (EU); (4) the structure and powers of the Westminster Parliament; (5) the structure and powers of central government; (6) devolution arrangements and the relationship between the devolution settlement and Westminster; (7) parliamentary accountability; (8) the courts, including the foundations and grounds of judicial review; and (9) rights, including common law freedoms and the Human Rights Act 1998.[15]

Current UK public law texts provide students with a formative grounding in the fundamentals of UK constitutional and administrative law, and equip students with some essential tools for critical analysis of the development and direction of the law. However, they tend to omit perspectives that interrogate the usual framing and foundations of the UK's institutional and juridical structures. For instance, little attention is paid to the impact of empire and

---

[14] Quijano's theory of social classification depicts the category of race as 'a mental construction that expresses the basic experience of colonial domination and pervades the more important dimensions of global power, including its specific rationality: Eurocentrism': Quijano, A. (2000) 'Coloniality of Power, Eurocentrism, and Latin America', *Nepantla: Views from South*, 1(3): 533–80, at 533.

[15] The core texts considered are Elliott, M. and Thomas, R. (2020) *Public Law* (4th edn), Oxford: Oxford University Press; Masterman, R. and Murray, C. (2022) *Constitutional and Administrative Law* (3rd edn), Cambridge: Cambridge University Press; Stanton, J. and Prescott, C. (2022) *Public Law* (3rd edn), Oxford: Oxford University Press; Young, A. (2021) *Turpin and Tomkins' British Government and the Constitution: Text and Materials* (8th edn), Cambridge: Cambridge University Press. Some texts also cover alternative means of administrative justice, including 'ombudsmen' (ombudspersons) and inquiries.

British imperial activities on the shape of governmental power in the UK. This is coupled with inattention to the ways in which public law concepts and institutions have been employed to further the project of colonial control in other territories. Similarly, while there is traditionally a discussion of individual rights and the relationship between the individual and the state, there is little analysis of the impact of state administrative policies and powers in perpetuating disadvantage. The importance of governmental agencies in administering central tenets of the administrative state, such as immigration or welfare, is acknowledged in major textbooks, but largely through the lens of jurisprudential debates regarding the political or legal nature of the constitution and the role of courts in moderating administrative power. Such discourse is important, but there is a need for students to be better acquainted with people's lived experiences with state policies – typically enforced by frontline decision makers – and to understand how these experiences relate to the public law topics they study. To that end, this book will cover important core UK public law material in a way that examines the impact of the administrative state on disadvantage and inequality.

Detailed synopsis

This book covers the main topics in UK public law from critical perspectives and from the point of view of underrepresented voices. It consists of two parts: (I) constitutional structures and concepts; and (II) the individual and the state. As such, the book to some extent mirrors the framing commonly adopted by other core texts in the area. It is, however, distinguished by the focus it gives to underexplored and critical approaches to the key features of UK public law. To that end, we have selected chapter authors based on their expertise in areas that shed greater light on the complex framing of contemporary power relations in the UK constitution, and the impact this has on disempowered groups in their interactions with the everyday machinery of the state.

In Part I, 'Constitutional Structures and Concepts', this collection offers students a critical perspective on fundamental principles such as the rule of law and parliamentary supremacy, and the changing roles of the executive and Parliament, especially in their capacity to impact the daily lives of individuals. Kanika Sharma's chapter 'The Rule of Law and Racial Difference in the British Empire' examines the use of the rule of law to establish and perpetuate patterns of domination and subjugation in colonial territories. Sharma challenges the positive, aspirational presentation of the rule of law. Her chapter considers how the British conceptualisation(s) of the concept was influenced by British attempts to rule distant territories, and how the doctrine was utilised to establish and legitimise British rule over colonies. Fundamentally, she invites us to consider whether, considering the instantiation of racial difference and domination, the rule of law could ever be fully realised in the Empire. These questions and challenges resonate today, in light of the use of rule of law concepts and objectives in setting and implementing the agenda of international development. This chapter therefore encourages continued interrogation of the history of the rule of law and its use in past and continuing power structures.

The critical analysis of principles entwined with a Diceyan legacy continues in Donal K. Coffey's 'Parliamentary Supremacy and the People'. Coffey critiques the development of the doctrine through the lens of the constitution's unsettled and uncomfortable relationship with democracy. Repeatedly, the question arose whether a democratic vote of the public was required to provoke fundamental constitutional change. Coffey surveys historical evidence to argue in favour of a convention that 'if parliamentary supremacy itself is to be altered … then the wishes of the people must first be ascertained'. For Coffey, it is this thinking that justifies the doctrine of constitutional statutes and modifies the normal rule that the will of a subsequent Parliament will prevail over that of an earlier Parliament. He contends that statutes that are properly designated 'constitutional' are those which are underpinned by referendums; it is the consent of the populace that justifies their special constitutional treatment. Coffey's insights, which challenge the Diceyan construction of parliamentary sovereignty, will remain useful in understanding the contours of the doctrine in the future use of referendums in the UK.

In 'Strong Executive, Weak Parliament?', Paul F. Scott seeks to understand the scope and source of executive power in the modern constitution. Scott's chapter is largely concerned with arguments that seek to assert an executive 'right to govern' that derives directly from the electorate. This chapter questions the constitutional salience of this argument and maintains that the executive draws its legitimacy from Parliament, and that the exercise of governmental power is contingent on the confidence and support of the House of Commons. Scott argues that the executive should be understood beyond an identification of ministers and central government, and as encompassing the civil servants, agencies and other bodies that comprise the 'administrative state'. For Scott, this understanding of the composition of the executive ought to impact arguments for a strong(er) executive. Moreover, he cautions against the use of powers of the Crown to evade Parliament's attempts to exercise its will. Considering the breadth of the modern administrative state, it is crucial to continue to articulate and defend Parliament's role in legitimating and determining the boundaries of executive power.

Executive power is also central to Alexandra Sinclair's chapter, 'Legislating for Seismic Events: An Examination of the Role of Delegated Legislation'. The chapter charts the expanded use of delegated legislation over the past

100 years, particularly in moments of crisis. Sinclair starkly explains that delegated legislation has become the main method of law making in the UK and considers some of the constitutional implications of this development. The chapter explores in detail the use of delegated legislation to make laws in response to Brexit and COVID-19, and argues that these two seismic events were largely legislated by the executive, with limited parliamentary oversight. Sinclair explains that the modern role of delegated legislation, with the expanded and heightened law-making power of the executive, undermines the fundamental constitutional principles of the separation of powers and parliamentary sovereignty. Sinclair cautions that current mechanisms for oversight of delegated legislation are deficient and must be buttressed to redress the 'current democratic deficit'.

Questions around power distribution also arise in Coree Brown Swan's chapter, 'Scotland, Devolution and Independence: A Union at its Limits?'. Brown Swan discusses the political and social motivations behind Scottish devolution and the continued debates regarding Scottish independence. The chapter demonstrates that while the devolution settlement enabled a dispersal of power away from the centre, mechanisms for intergovernmental cooperation were – and remain – unsettled. Brown Swan explains that the Brexit vote and process of leaving the EU exposed and exacerbated the inadequacies of intergovernmental relations between Scotland and Westminster. The limited role afforded to devolved governments in the negotiations highlighted the contingent and vulnerable nature of Scotland's consultative role, particularly in fields that arguably straddle devolved powers (to Scotland) and reserved powers (of Westminster). The Brexit process has revealed the instability and unsettled nature of devolution, re-ignited the independence debate and strengthened views that the status quo is ultimately untenable. Brown Swan questions whether the debates occasioned by devolution and Brexit mean that the flexibility of the UK constitution has finally been exhausted.

Part I ends with an exploration of the meaning and importance of 'Diverse Voices in the Judiciary'. In this chapter, Alysia Blackham conceives of diversity as a broad concept encompassing personal characteristics and professional pathways. Blackham defends the importance of judicial diversity on the grounds that a judiciary which is more reflective of the population appears more accessible and legitimate, and is ultimately more representative of an ethos of equality. Blackham suggests a fundamental reconceptualisation of the idea of 'merit', which takes account of listening skills, empathy and problem solving, alongside legal knowledge and advocacy skills. The chapter details recent initiatives and progress towards judicial diversity, and provides a frank assessment of the gaps that remain. In response, Blackham proposes 'a fundamental rethink of judicial careers'. This would encompass not only approaches to judicial appointment, but also the support provided to judges throughout their career and post-retirement. Blackham advises that improving judicial diversity will also require improvement of diversity within the legal profession and legal academia, as institutions that contribute to the judicial pool. The chapter therefore proposes a broader conception of both judicial diversity and efforts to improve diversity in the judiciary.

Part II explores the parameters of the relationship between 'The Individual and the State'. As with the previous section, there is a degree of overlap with other public law textbooks. However, other texts commonly introduce students to the ways in which public law regulates what the state can and cannot do to individuals, principally through an exposition of judicial review and the Human Rights Act 1998. This part distinguishes itself both in terms of its subject matter, with a particular focus on the impact of state policies on vulnerable groups, and in giving students more insight into individuals' everyday experiences of state administrative power. Devyani Prabhat's chapter on 'The *Begum* Case, Discretion and Parliamentary Sovereignty: Unmaking the Constitutional Subject' examines the powers of the British state to cancel citizenship as a counterterrorism measure. The chapter outlines the legislative provisions at the disposal of the Home Secretary to cancel the British citizenship status of citizens and underlines that the present approach puts those with migrant connections but without another nationality at risk of statelessness. The *Begum* case shows that any British citizen with other national connections is at a greater risk of being stripped of their citizenship and being rendered stateless, and reveals that racialised hierarchies of citizenship status are embedded in British nationality law. Further, Prabhat argues that the approach of the courts to review of cancellation cases renders British minority ethnic nationals 'voiceless' in the legal system. Prabhat identifies that the *Begum* case sits in a wider trend of deference by the courts to ministerial decision making, even in instances where the courts have greater institutional competence, such as where fundamental rights are engaged. Prabhat's important analysis reveals the risk that those with multiple nationality connections will be treated as 'accidental citizens'. Should their citizenship be stripped, they are not entitled to re-enter the country to access legal remedies: the 'constitutional subject is expelled from constitutional protection and becomes a non-entity for the state'.

Counterterrorism measures are also the topic of Tufyal Choudhury's chapter, 'Racialisation in UK Counterterrorism Law and Policy'. Choudhury examines the embeddedness of processes of racialisation in the development and implementation of these laws in response to the violent actions of ISIS and Al-Qaeda. His analysis covers four aspects of counterterrorism in the UK state that cumulatively contribute to racialisation. First, the broad legal definition of terrorism gives executive decision makers significant discretion to determine what falls within the scope of counterterrorism laws, giving rise to a greater risk of discriminatory practices that may be difficult to detect and challenge in the national security context. Second, 'pre-emptive' terrorism offences were inscribed with racialised tropes from their inception, designed primarily to respond to 'Islamist extremism', and led to the criminalisation of otherwise neutral activities 'knitted together' to show intention to commit a terrorist act. Third, the use of radicalisation as the primary framework for understanding terrorism encourages counter-radicalisation policies that develop and use 'indicators' to identify individuals who might be at risk of radicalisation. Fourth, Choudhury shows how the development of the Prevent strategy, which now involves frontline public-sector workers in the identification of individuals vulnerable to radicalisation, reveals processes of racialisation. Choudhury's work underlines the sweeping nature of the powers and responsibilities at the heart of counterterrorism measures, generating 'unjust spaces for discretionary and selective enforcement' that are very difficult to challenge.

Ben Bowling and Shruti Iyer's chapter on 'Racism, Law and the Police: Over 50 Years of Anti-discrimination Law and Policing' also highlights the limits of public law protections for racialised minorities. The chapter examines the historical relationship between policing and anti-discrimination law to demonstrate that the protective capacity of public law is in practice shaped by a range of extra-legal forces. Bowling and Iyer introduce Grimshaw and Jefferson's 'environmental model' for understanding policework as affected by three environmental elements: law, work and democracy. The chapter then charts the historical link between immigration law and 'race relations' law, tracing the development of increasingly harsh immigration control laws alongside strengthened powers of enforcement for police officers. While successive 'race relations' legislation sought to tackle overt forms of discrimination in the 1960s and indirect discrimination in the 1976 Race Relations Act, police powers remained exempt from the reach of anti-discrimination legislation. The chapter then turns to the 'working environment' of the police, revealing that racial stereotypes shaped police practice and the occupational culture of policing in the 1970s and 1980s. Bowling and Iyer's exploration of Grimshaw and Jefferson's third element of environmental theory – the democratic relationship with the public – charts the incremental erosion of the justification for exempting the police from the gaze of anti-discrimination legislation. Despite these developments, the chapter concludes with a frank assessment of the capacity of anti-discrimination legislation to tackle racial discrimination in policing, highlighting the difficulties of constructing a racial discrimination claim in court. Bowling and Iyer's analysis serves as an important reminder that there are large gaps between law 'in the books', and the structural and cultural forces that continue to perpetuate racism.

In 'The Administration of Social Security Benefits: Gendered Implications', Ciara Fitzpatrick examines the ways in which women's full access to social citizenship rights has been limited since the inception of the post-war social security system. The chapter demonstrates that recent social security reforms have disproportionately disadvantaged women. Aspects of the 'male breadwinner model', Fitzpatrick argues, persist in key aspects of social security, such as the delivery of a single household payment, tethering a woman's financial status to their partner. At the same time, 'welfare conditionality' undermines the flexibility that people with caring responsibilities – usually women – need. The benefit cap (limiting household income received through the social security system) and the two-child limit (limiting benefits to the first two children born on or after 6 April 2017) have a clearly disproportionate impact on women and their children. Fitzpatrick provides an overview of recent unsuccessful judicial review challenges mounted against these policies, arguing that the measures indirectly discriminate against women. Her analysis reveals the failure of the UK Supreme Court to engage with the gendered consequences of government policy and demonstrates that public law redress mechanisms will not necessarily prevent the serious erosion of the social rights of women and children in the face of clear parliamentary intent.

The volume concludes with further reflection on the impact of the administrative state upon the lives of individuals. Alex Powell's 'Administrative Violence: First-Instance Decision Making in Sexual Diversity Asylum Claims' presents a case study of asylum claims made by sexually diverse people. Powell introduces a novel 'administrative violence' framework that captures the way in which administrative systems operate at a level of abstraction, limiting individual decision makers' recognition of, or accountability for, the human impact of their decisions, and causing day-to-day administrative processes to be potential sites of harm. The chapter sets out the legal and policy framework for refugee status determination in the UK, outlining the lack of guidance that exists for decision makers to determine whether a claimant is a sexually diverse person, and the factors that ensure claimants have poor access to appeal routes. Powell then draws upon eight semi-structured interviews with people who were granted refugee status in the UK based on their sexual diversity. Participants' experience of the UK asylum process reveals how instances of delays, the perceived preconceptions of decision makers about sexual diversity, and the use of repeat questioning to test the veracity of asylum seekers' accounts led to significant distress for asylum claimants. Powell powerfully argues that such experiences are demonstrative of the capacity for the administrative state to produce administrative violence. Such analysis has implications for other areas of administrative practice and underlines the significance of first-instance decision making as the primary site of engagement with public law for individuals.

The authors in this collection challenge received wisdom and assumptions in constitutional law. Their chapters confront the orthodox meaning and limitations of fundamental concepts such as the rule of law and parliamentary sovereignty, and question the assumptions surrounding merit in the context public appointments and citizenship in the context of immigration and nationality law. Several key themes run though the contributions to this collection. First, the long shadow that the frameworks of power which sustained the British Empire has cast upon our legal system is made evident. Coffey's and Sharma's chapters show the pivotal role that empire and developments within the British Empire have had in shaping the evolution of UK constitutional doctrines and principles such as the rule of law and parliamentary supremacy. Bowling and Iyer's chapter also reveals how the legacy of empire and the politics of decolonisation left an indelible print on the development of immigration laws. Relatedly, the hangover of colonialism's justifying of racial hierarchies is made clear in Prabhat's exploration of the contingent nature of citizenship for British citizens with migrant connections, Choudhury's uncovering of processes of racialisation in counterterrorism, and Bowling and Iyer's mapping of systemically discriminatory policing.

Questions about the extent and legitimacy of executive power also recur throughout the book. The chapters by Sinclair and Scott point to the constitutional dissonance occasioned by expanding and overweening executive power. The tension between the desire for swift action, particularly in the face of crises and political changes, and the need for legitimation and accountability produce debates about the source and breadth of executive power. Powell's chapter shows the importance of engaging with the influence wielded by frontline decision makers within the executive, while Choudhury's contribution highlights the broad discretionary powers granted to security officials in counterterrorism policy. Sinclair and Fitzpatrick identify one key source for the growth of executive power as the expanded role and influence of secondary legislation.

The chapters on racialisation and counterterrorism, policing, and asylum law all show the woolly line between public law and criminal law. They challenge us to examine the criminalisation of the actions and experiences of marginalised groups, and prompt reflections on identity-based variations in individuals' experience and interaction with the state. These variations can – and perhaps should be – reflected in analyses of public law rules and their constitutional impact. They underline the importance of engaging with other disciplines and methods to examine and understand the everyday coercive power of the British state through the eyes of those who experience it.

Finally, many of the authors remind us of the limits of the reach of public law. Present political conditions have placed the fine balance between constitutional institutions – such as the relationship between the executive and Parliament – under strain. Brown Swan highlights that the intergovernmental cooperation required for the effective functioning of devolution arrangements is buckling under the political upheaval of the moment, calling into question the stability of the Union. In areas where we might hope that the remedial capacity of public law will bite, several contributions shine a light on the inability, particularly of anti-discrimination legislation, to blunt the sharpest edges of individuals' discriminatory experiences with public power. Choudhury's contribution on racialisation and counterterrorism, and Bowling and Iyer's chapter on race and police powers speak of the limited effects of equality reforms and the need to fundamentally reshape institutions, structures and societal attitudes. Powell's work emphasises the limited meaningful access to appeal routes for asylum claimants. Fitzpatrick and Prabhat both show the highly deferential approach taken by the courts to reviewing executive decision making in the areas of national security and social and economic policy. Such judicial reasoning is shown to give little weight to the realisation of important rights, and to allow the persistence of policies that undermine fair trial rights and push certain groups below the poverty line. This illustrates the significance of Blackham's call for increased judicial diversity, and ways to greater realise and sustain diversity on the bench, if we are to see greater judicial engagement with, for example, the gendered impacts of state policies. The chapters in this book remind us of the power and limits of public law, and that law is not the only, or even the most effective, tool available to us for effecting social change.

PART I

Constitutional Structures and Concepts

1

The Rule of Law and Racial Difference in the British Empire

Kanika Sharma[1]

Introduction

The concept of the rule of law and its utility remain hotly debated in public law. The only thing that scholars agree on is the fact that there is no universal definition of the concept. Imagined positively, the rule of law is depicted as an aspirational ideal, one that is often linked to ideas of justice, equality and – from the 20th century onwards – democracy. When viewed negatively, the same rule of law 'is seen as an ideological mask of oppression',[2] that is, a tool that helps to facilitate the oppressive and unequal nature of the law while allowing the latter to conceal this inequality. In fact, to call the rule of law 'ideological' is to admit that the concept helps to hide and supress the activities that happen in its name.[3]

---

1 I wish to thank Paul O'Connell, Laura Lammasniemi, Elizabeth O'Loughlin, Se-shauna Wheatle and the anonymous reviewer for their comments and feedback on this chapter. Thanks are also due to the past and present students on my Legal Systems of Asia and Africa module at SOAS, University of London for the opportunity to refine many of the ideas discussed here.

2 Peerenboom, R. (2004) 'Varieties of rule of law: an introduction and provisional conclusion', in R. Peerenboom (ed) *Asian Discourses on Rule of Law: Theories and Implementation of Rule of Law in Twelve Asian Countries, France and the US*, London: RoutledgeCurzon, 1–53, at 1.

3 McBride, K. (2016) *Mr Mothercountry: The Man Who Made the Rule of Law*, Oxford: Oxford University Press, 12.

The rule of law is often studied alongside the two other key constitutional principles in the UK: the separation of powers and parliamentary sovereignty. The historic development of the doctrine in the UK, including the influential works of A.V. Dicey, the distinction between formal and substantive ideas of the rule of law, and the contributions of scholars such as Joseph Raz, Richard Dworkin and Tom Bingham, are all well-traversed grounds. What scholars in the genre have ignored, however, is the centrality of the rule of law doctrine to Britain's colonial project in centuries past, and the ways in which ideas of law and, indeed, the rule of law, have long been used to shore up the moral legitimacy of British colonialism while hiding its exploitative nature.

In this chapter we will examine the history of the doctrine of the rule of law and its relation to the British Empire through three interrelated concerns. First, as it developed in the heyday of the Empire, how was the modern British idea of the rule of law as put forward by theorists such as Dicey impacted by British attempts to rule far and distant lands? Second, how was the doctrine itself used to establish and legitimise British colonial rule? And third, considering the policy of colonial and racial difference that was inherent to the process of colonisation, could the rule of law ever be fully established in the Empire?

A short history of the rule of law

The earliest conceptions of the rule of law can be traced back to Greek civilisation, where as early as the 5th century BCE there was an idea of democracy and equality before the law.[4] However, this was a limited equality, and women, children and enslaved people were excluded from its domain. Central to this imagination of the rule of law was its opposition to the rule of the despot (that is, rule of a single ruthless human being), and this figure was essentialised by Greek authors such as Aristotle as the 'Oriental despot'.[5]

The idea of the rule of law as we know it today began to coalesce in Europe in the Middle Ages. In Britain its earliest conception is linked to the Magna Carta (1215),[6] particularly the section stating that no one could be deprived of property except in accordance with the 'law of the land'.[7] However, it is important to note that many of these protections were only afforded to the propertied classes, and most of the population was excluded from its remit.

[4] For a discussion of the classical European origins of the rule of law, see Tamanaha, B.Z. (2004) *On the Rule of Law: History, Politics, Theory*, Cambridge: Cambridge University Press, chapter 1.

[5] Venturi, F. (1963) 'Oriental despotism', *Journal of the History of Ideas*, 24(1): 133–42, at 133.

[6] Dallmayr, F. (1990) 'Hermeneutics and the rule of law', *Cardozo Law Review*, 11: 1449–69, at 1452.

[7] Magna Carta 1215, Cl 39.

This conception of the rule of law slowly evolved to become an integral part of modern liberalism (and, as critics argue, modern capitalism)[8] and is the basis of the current doctrine of the rule of law.

Today, the rule of law is most closely associated with the works of the British jurist A.V. Dicey (1835–1922), who articulated, though he did not coin,[9] the modern idea of the rule of law at the end of the 19th century.[10] Dicey argued that the supremacy of law had been a characteristic of the English constitution ever since the Norman Conquest,[11] and was distinguished by three features that he used to formulate his definition of the rule of law: first, the absence of arbitrary powers of the state, that is, no person was punishable except for a distinct breach of the law; second, legal equality among people of all classes, that is, every person is subject to ordinary courts administered by ordinary tribunals; and, lastly, that the general principles of constitutional law had developed as part of common law rather than being attributed to a written constitution.[12]

Dicey was writing at a time when the British Empire was rapidly expanding,[13] and many of its moral and legal claims were being debated in Britain and in the colonies. Dicey himself was a frequent participant in these debates, and in some of his writings he recognised that the rule of law when imposed by one society on another may itself be 'arbitrary and oppressive'.[14] However, for him, the problem did not lie with the rule of law doctrine, but was based on his assumption that certain civilisations were too 'backward' to appreciate the benefits of the doctrine.[15] Despite these reservations, he held a positive view of the British Empire and its commitment to the rule of law, even noting that: 'The one permanent, certain, indisputable effect of English government in the East has been the establishment of the rule of law.'[16]

---

8 For instance, see Unger, R.M. (1976) *Law in Modern Society: Toward a Criticism of Social Theory*, New York: The Free Press; and Tamanaha, B.Z. (2008) 'The dark side of the relationship between the rule of law and liberalism', *NYU Journal of Law and Liberty*, 3: 516–47.

9 Simpson, A.W.B. (2002) *Human Rights and the End of Empire: Britain and the Genesis of the European Convention*, Oxford: Oxford University Press, 25–6.

10 See Dicey, A.V. (1889) *Introduction to the Study of the Law of the Constitution* (3rd edn), London: Macmillan & Co.

11 Dicey (1889) 171.

12 Dicey (1889) chapter 4.

13 The British Empire established its earliest colonies in the 16th century in North America. The Empire expanded rapidly in the 19th century before peaking in the early 20th century, covering a quarter of the world and ruling over more than 450 million people.

14 Lino, D. (2018) 'The rule of law and the rule of empire: A.V. Dicey in imperial context', *Modern Law Review*, 81(5): 739–64, at 743.

15 Ibid.

16 Dicey, A.V. (1880) 'Wheeler's short history of India', quoted in Lino (n 14) 762.

Thus, we see that not only did Dicey popularise the rule of law doctrine, but he was also instrumental in 'identif[ying] it with the English way of life'.[17] However, scholars such as Judith Shklar are critical of Dicey's intervention, have labelled it 'an unfortunate outburst of Anglo-Saxon parochialism' and have blamed him for both traditionalising and formalising the concept.[18] In other words, Dicey's intervention cemented the claim that the rule of law doctrine had emerged out of British tradition and that only particular procedures or practices, such as the common law system that developed in Britain, were suitable for its development. Dicey's exposition on the subject coincided with the accelerated expansion of the British Empire, with the rule of law ideology subsequently being projected as a necessary companion and exemplary benefit of this Empire as it spread across the globe.

As Hugh Tulloch notes in his critique of Dicey and the latter's attitude towards demands for greater rights by the Irish: '[I]t is impossible not to detect in Dicey's own writing an air of narrow and stultifying paternalism, and a rigid adherence to the letter rather than to the spirit of the law.'[19] In fact, Dicey's attitude towards the movement for Irish Home Rule shows that he was even willing to forgo his commitment to the letter of the law in order to oppose greater rights for colonised people. Dicey remained steadfastly opposed to Irish Home Rule and any break-up of the Union, going so far as to champion armed rebellion by the Irish Unionists.[20]

Here, Dicey's thoughts are in keeping with most British jurists and philosophers of his time. The idea that colonial rule was not about the economic and racial exploitation of the colonised people, but about something else 'was a persistent theme in the rhetoric of colonial rule itself'.[21] This something else was the 'civilizing mission', which included the supposed transfer of state and legal institutions (including ideas of the rule of law, justice and liberty) from 'civilised' Britain to the 'savage' colonies. This was usually accompanied by physical signs of civilisational 'progress', that is, the expansion of infrastructure – of trains and roads and other signifiers of 'development' that allowed for the rapid transport of goods and humans, and further deepened the exploitation of colonial hinterlands. However, as

17 Weiner, M.J. (2009) *An Empire on Trial: Race, Murder, and Justice under British Rule, 1870–1935*, Cambridge: Cambridge University Press, 8.

18 Shklar, J. (1987) 'Political theory and the rule of law', in A. Hutchinson and P.J. Monahan (eds) *The Rule of Law: Ideal or Ideology*, Toronto: Carswell, 1–16, at 5. See also Kirby, J. (2019) 'AV Dicey and English constitutionalism', *History of European Ideas*, 45(1): 33–46.

19 Tulloch, H. (1980) 'AV Dicey and the Irish Question: 1870–1922', *Irish Jurist*, 15(1): 137–65, at 145.

20 Dicey's letter to St Loe Strachey, 13 July 1913, quoted in Tulloch (n 19) 145.

21 Chatterjee, P. (1993) *The Nation and its Fragments: Colonial and Postcolonial Histories*, Princeton: Princeton University Press, 14.

we shall see in this chapter, despite these promises of transplanting 'good governance' and the rule of law in the colony, the British colonial legacy was one of ingrained inequality between the coloniser and the colonised, and an entrenchment of colonial and racial difference within the legal systems of the colonies.

Modern conceptions of the rule of law

The rule of law doctrine developed significantly over the 20th century. In addition to Dicey's formal or procedural idea of the rule of law,[22] later developed by F.A. Hayek and Joseph Raz, today we also understand the substantive nature of the rule of law found in the works of scholars such as Richard Dworkin, John Laws, Tom Bingham and T.R.S. Allan. Scholars who support a formal or thin understanding of the rule of law argue that it should be concerned with the procedure and form of the law, and not its content. If a law is public, prospective, intelligible and consistently applied, it meets the criteria of the rule of law, even if the content of the law in question is reprehensible and against human rights. As Raz famously noted: '[A] non-democratic legal system, based on the denial of human rights, or extensive poverty, on racial segregation, sexual inequalities, and religious persecution may, in principle, conform to the requirements of the rule of law better than any of the legal systems of the more enlightened Western democracies.'[23] Within this category, the thinnest conception of the rule of law takes the form of rule *by* law. Rule *by* law is the idea that law is the means by which the state conducts its affairs and, thus, easily collapses into the notion of the 'rule by the government'.[24] In fact, such an idea of the rule of law offers minimal limitations on state power and little protection to citizens and communities against the state.

In contrast, substantive theories of the rule of law associate the doctrine with ideas of 'good', that is, democratic government, the protection of human dignity and rights, and notions of liberty. In response to Raz, Bingham has noted:

> While … one can recognize the logical force of Professor Raz's contention, I would roundly reject it in favour of a 'thick' definition, embracing the protection of human rights within its scope. A state

---

22 For a discussion of Dicey as a formalist, see Craig, P.P. (1997) 'Formal and substantive conceptions of the rule of law: an analytical framework', *Public Law*: 467–87, at 470–4.

23 Raz, J. (1979) *The Authority of Law: Essays on Law and Morality*, Oxford: Oxford University Press, 211.

24 Tamanaha (n 4) 92.

> which savagely represses or persecutes sections of its people cannot in my view be regarded as observing the rule of law, even if the transport of the persecuted minority to the concentration camp or the compulsory exposure of female children on the mountainside is the subject of detailed laws duly enacted and scrupulously observed.[25]

Despite the differences between the formalist and substantive conceptions of the rule of law, 'all non-trivial accounts of the rule of law conceive equality and freedom as intimately related'[26] – that is, all ideas of the rule of law have some idea of equality and liberty at their core. As we shall see below, the rule of law espoused under British colonialism was the formalist version of the doctrine; however, even this thin conception was not properly upheld and principles of equality were frequently discarded to maintain the efficiency of the Empire.

Law, the rule of law and the British Empire

Law in the colony

Colonialism, simply put, is the process through which one society seeks to rule and transform another.[27] It typically involves an overhaul of the colonised legal system, often accompanied by the transfer of laws from the metropole to the colony. However, it is important to recognise that there is/was no universal experience of colonialism or colonial law. Colonialism differs by coloniser, by colony,[28] by location within the colony (popular port cities and urban areas had a different experience of colonialism and colonial law from the hinterland) and by time (for instance, early and later European colonialism differed in both purpose and intensity). What is common across all forms of colonialism is that such empires are based on coercion and not consent, and that law plays a legitimising role in both establishing and maintaining the empire.

Thus, law was central to the British colonial project to subjugate the colonised population and maximise its exploitation. However, it was perceived and projected instead as a 'gift' from the British to the colonised peoples in order to facilitate the latter's civilisational and cultural development. For

[25] Bingham, T. (2010) *The Rule of Law*, London: Allen Lane, 67.

[26] Bellamy, R. (2003) 'The rule of law', in R. Bellamy and A. Mason (eds) *Political Concepts*, Manchester: Manchester University Press, 118–30, at 120.

[27] Merry, S.E. (1991) 'Law and colonialism', *Law and Society Review*, 25(4): 889–922, at 890.

[28] For instance, British colonies could be classified as Crown colonies, self-governing dominions, protectorates, mandates or condominium territories. For an explanation, see Birnhack, M.D. (2012) *Colonial Copyright: Intellectual Property in Mandate Palestine*, Oxford: Oxford University Press, 28–9.

instance, in 1833, Robert Miller, a member of the Legislative Council of the Governor-General of India, was adamant that the very notion of law was introduced to India by Englishmen:

> When we came to this country did we find equitable law courts in which Englishmen and Natives could alike obtain equal justice? … There was no such thing as law and justice. The land was a land of violence, of systematic and periodical marauding, of constant blackmail [and] … many forms of anarchy and misrule and lawlessness. … It was for us, a mere handful of strangers, to introduce law and order, and to import into this country as much justice as was possible under the circumstances.[29]

Four decades later, writing in the context of Africa, F.D. Lugard, the first Governor-General of Nigeria (and previously Governor of Hong Kong), summed up the benefits of European imperialism in Africa as follows:

> Europe benefited by the wonderful increase in the amenities of life for the mass of her people which followed up the opening of Africa at the end of the nineteenth century. Africa benefited by the influx of manufactured goods, and the substitution of law and order for the methods of barbarism.[30]

These quotes reveal the popular European colonial stance that colonised territories on other continents did not usually contain any indigenous laws before the advent of European colonialism.[31] In its most extreme form this manifested as a claim of *terra nullius* – or nobody's land – where the coloniser believed that the indigenous population lacked any form of political organisation or system of land rights. Therefore, not only did the land not belong to any individual, but in the absence of political organisation there was also no community leader with whom a treaty could be signed. Thus, whole countries and, in the case of Australia, a whole continent was declared to be *terra nullius* and the British colonisers were able to claim ownership of it. Antony Anghie notes that while Africa may not have been explicitly

[29] Robert Miller speaking during the debate on the Ilbert Bill 1883, quoted in Kolsky, E. (2010) *Colonial Justice in British India: White Violence and the Rule of Law*, Cambridge: Cambridge University Press, 100.

[30] Lugard, F.D. (1922) *The Dual Mandate in British Tropical Africa*, Edinburgh: William Blackwood and Sons, 615.

[31] See Banner, S. (2005) 'Why terra nullius? Anthropology and property law in early Australia', *Law and History Review*, 23(1): 95–131; and Idowu, W. (2004) 'African philosophy of law: transcending the boundaries between myth and reality', *EnterText*, 4(2): 52–93.

labelled *terra nullius* in the way that Australia was, it was undeniably treated in similar ways:

> [The] exclusion [of Africans from the Berlin Conference][32] was reiterated and intensified in a more complex way by the [legal] positivist argument that African tribes were too primitive to understand the concept of sovereignty to cede it by treaty. … [I]ts effect was to transform Africa into a conceptual terra nullius; as such, only dealings between European states with respect to those territories could have decisive legal effect.[33]

By using a self-referential definition of what constituted law, the British were able to overthrow indigenous law in the colonies or marginalise it to the sphere of personal laws, that is, laws relating to marriage, succession and inheritance.[34] Three key developments further bolstered the spread and entrenchment of colonial law: first, the use of repugnancy clauses to restrict the application of precolonial laws that were deemed to be 'repugnant' by the coloniser; second, establishing a dual system of law, that is, different laws and adjudicating courts for the colonisers and the colonised; and last, the codification of colonial laws. Thus, while most indigenous law remained unrecognised as 'law', any indigenous law that was 'discovered' was usually found to be lacking. It was either repealed on the grounds of repugnancy or was seen to be fit only for the colonised population within the dual system of law. The biggest impact on colonial legal systems, however, was wrought by the colonial strategy of legal codification, under whose guise indigenous laws were swiftly replaced by colonial law. As McBride notes, this process of codification was particularly central to ideas of the rule of law, especially positivist ideas of the doctrine,[35] because codification (that is, the process of writing down laws) gave the impression that these laws were open and transparent and applicable to all, though they were far from any such thing. For instance, under the openly biased section 72 of the Indian Criminal Procedure Code 1872, European British subjects could only be tried by judges, magistrates or justices of the peace of their own race,[36] and, as we shall see later, the proposal to remove this privilege was robustly challenged.

---

32 The Berlin Conference (1884–85) was attended by 13 European states (including Russia and the Ottoman Empire) and the United States of America. It marked the end of the European colonisers' 'scramble for Africa' by regularising trade and formalising European territories in Africa.

33 Anghie, A. (2005) *Imperialism, Sovereignty and the Making of International Law*, Cambridge: Cambridge University, 95.

34 Tan, C.G.S. (2012) 'On law and orientalism', *Journal of Comparative Law*, 7(2): 5–17, at 6.

35 McBride (n 3) 32.

36 Whereas non-European British subjects could be tried by an adjudicator of any race.

Crucially, closely following the discriminatory codified laws allowed the coloniser to portray themselves as following the rule of law – if only in the formalist sense. This provided impetus for introducing codified laws across the British colonies, and networks of laws and law makers spread across the British Empire. For instance, the Indian Penal Code (IPC) (1860) went on to influence the development of colonial legal regimes in distant parts of the Empire, including Malaya (now Malaysia), Singapore, Egypt, Somalia and the Sudan, and further afield to Cyprus and Nigeria.[37] In fact, during the colonial period all criminal codes in common law countries in Africa could trace their ancestry to the IPC, the St Lucia Criminal Code of 1889 or the Queensland Criminal Code of 1899.[38] Further, direct connections were forged through peculiar legal arrangements necessitated by colonial exigencies; for instance, from the late 19th century, appeals from the Consular Court in Zanzibar (in modern Tanzania) and later Mombasa (in modern Kenya) in Africa were designated to be heard at the Bombay High Court (in modern Mumbai) in India.[39]

This leads us to our next question: since colonial legal systems by their very nature are based on the absence of freedom of the colonised and actively enforce inequality between the coloniser and the colonised, can they ever be said to maintain the rule of law?

The rule of law in the colony

Despite its claim to the universal, as we have seen in the previous section, the rule of law as we understand it today has a very particular origin, historical context and mode of travel across the globe. Originating in Europe, its introduction – in concept, if not in practice – to non-European states was part and parcel of the colonial project, whether we speak of Asia, Africa, the Americas or Australia. Within the British Empire, this claim to the equality of individuals, whether they were from the colonising race or the colonised ones, and the promise that the law offered equal protection to all was not just a tenet of the rule of law, but was also an important part of Britain's self-perception of its commitment to the rule of law in the colonies. This so-called commitment was placed in direct opposition to the rule of the 'oriental despot' that the coloniser (cl)aimed to replace.

[37] Mawani, R. and Hussin, I. (2014) 'The travels of law: Indian Ocean itineraries', *Law and History Review*, 32(4): 733–47, at 741; and McBride (n 3) 11.

[38] Morris, H.F. (1970) 'How Nigeria got its Criminal Code', *Journal of African Law*, 14(3): 137–54, at 137.

[39] Metcalf, T.R. (2007) *Imperial Connections: India in the Indian Ocean Arena, 1860–1920*, Berkeley: University of California Press, 23–5.

Though some attempts were made to honour the principle of equality under the rule of law doctrine, these were limited. For instance, in the late 18th century in the case of *Campbell v Hall*, almost echoing modern substantive – especially rights-based – ideas of the rule of law, Lord Mansfield noted: 'An Englishman in Ireland, Minorca, the Isle of Man, or the Plantations, has no privilege distinct from the natives while he continues there.'[40] Despite these claims, the rule of law was largely a formalist enterprise in the colonies. As we shall see later on, even at the time it was made, Lord Mansfield's statement did not ring true as slavery was still being widely practised across the British Empire. The end of slavery coincided with new forms of racial distinctions and violence being instated across the Empire. Yet, while turning a blind eye to these deep racial and colonial inequalities, 'the English prided themselves on possessing a rule of law surpassing in its perfection that of other peoples'.[41]

At the time of the *Campbell* judgment, and a century before Dicey's interventions, debates already raged in Britain on whether the content of the rule of law extended to wider civil rights such as freedom of the press, conscience, religion, association and assembly.[42] These debates, however, remained restricted to Britain alone, and in the colonies only the narrowest version of the rule of law as formal legality was ever realised. For when it came to making laws for the colonies, 'British politicians, administrators, and jurists struggled with the effort to balance flexibility and a discretionary authority, putatively required by colonialism, with the stability and predictability associated with a rule of law regime'.[43] For instance, most colonised people were denied the right to a jury trial and, far from being independent, judges were appointed 'at pleasure' and were expected to be loyal to the colonial state, with their office being subject to executive removal. This latter objective led to the Privy Council advising that Joseph Beaumont be removed as the Chief Justice of British Guiana in South America in 1868 on the grounds that he lacked 'judicial temper' and tended to embarrass the colonial government by criticising their practices against indentured labourers in the colony.[44]

As critics have shown, rather than being an emancipatory ideal, in the colonial context the rule of law concept was 'a key coercive instrument

---

[40] *Campbell v Hall* (1774) 1 Cowp 204.

[41] Metcalf (2007) 17.

[42] McLaren, J. (2015) 'Chasing the chimera: the rule of law in the British Empire and the comparative turn in legal history', *Law Context: A Socio-Legal Journal* 33(1): 21–36, at 24–5.

[43] Hussain, N. (2019) *The Jurisprudence of Emergency: Colonialism and the Rule of Law*, Ann Arbor: University of Michigan Press, 42.

[44] McLaren (n 42) 30.

in the dispossession and subjugation' of the colonised people.[45] It was 'a handmaiden for economic expansion, an instrument of social control and propaganda that accompanied the violence of British rule'.[46] The concept veiled the exploitative reality of wealth extraction from the colonies while legitimising everyday inequalities and racial violence that were inherent to the colonial structure of law. Thus, the doctrine of rule of law was part and parcel of an oppressive colonial regime that continued to maintain colonial and racial difference, and privileged the rights of the coloniser above all else.

The rule of law and the rule of colonial difference

Partha Chatterjee has posited that the 'rule of colonial difference'[47] underlies all colonial legal systems. In other words, despite the supposed liberal ideology of the coloniser and their promises of equality, liberty and the 'gift' of law, the colonial systems could only operate through a preservation of the superiority of the ruling group. Thus, the hierarchy between the coloniser and the colonised was intrinsic to the system.

We find that the application of law in the colonies was dependant on the so-called dichotomy between the 'civilised' and the 'savage' and all the categories in between. These distinctions were based on ideas of permanent physical and biological difference in terms of either race or of cultural differentialism, with the white Anglo-Saxon man placed at the apex of both the racial and cultural hierarchies,[48] with biological racism and cultural differentialism acting as 'racism's two registers' and constantly slipping into one another.[49] Those who were considered racially 'inferior' were also considered to be culturally 'backward', with each category serving to reinforce the other. This involved the linking of hitherto value-neutral physical attributes or cultural practices and assigning to them value-laden interpretations, either positive (as in the case of the ruling races) or negative (as in the case of colonised races).[50] Thus, 'race' was a sociopolitical rather than a biological or cultural category, and the demarcation between races was constantly being redrawn.

---

45 Dunstall, G. and Godfrey, B. (2005) 'Crime and empire: introduction', in B. Godfrey and G. Dunstall (eds) *Crime and Empire 1840–1940: Criminal Justice in Local and Global Context*, Cullompton: Willan Publishing, 1–7, at 2.

46 McBride (n 3) 5.

47 Chatterjee (n 21) 18.

48 Hall, C. (2007) *Civilising Subjects: Metropole and Colony in the English Imagination 1830–1867*, Cambridge: Polity Press, 17.

49 Hall, S. (2018) 'The multicultural question', in D. Morley (ed) *Stuart Hall: Essential Essays*, Vol 2, Durham, NC: Duke University Press, 95–133, at 110.

50 Tabili, L. (1994) 'The construction of racial difference in twentieth-century Britain: the Special Restriction (Coloured Alien Seaman) Order, 1925', *Journal of British Studies*, 33(1): 54–98, at 59.

The perceived racial hierarchies played a crucial role of law in legitimising colonialism. Colonialism itself was projected as being for the 'good' of the colonised people, who could only hope to achieve civilisation through European intervention.[51] A stark example of this idea of racial difference can be seen in Lord Sumner's Privy Council judgment:

> The estimation of the rights of aboriginal tribes is always inherently difficult. Some tribes are so low in the scale of social organization that their usages and conceptions of rights and duties are not to be reconciled with the institutions or the legal ideas of civilized society. ... On the other hand, there are indigenous peoples whose legal conceptions, though differently developed, are hardly less precise than our own. When once they have been studied and understood they are no less enforceable than rights arising under English law. Between the two there is a wide tract of much ethnological interest.[52]

Race, thus, played an important role in determining the types of rights that were made available to the colonised populations. As a result, during the 19th century, white settler colonies came to enjoy some of the freedoms that were supposed to be ideologically linked to the rule of law, while the same freedoms continued to be denied to non-white colonial populations. In fact, based on where they were assumed to be on the 'scale of civilisation', some groups were regularly placed entirely outside the ambit of the rule of law altogether, but were still subject to law's coercion. For instance, the aboriginal people belonging to what were described as 'savage tribes' in Australia were seen to be inherently outside the law, as were those who were deemed to be 'hereditary criminals' and thus categorised within the colonially constituted 'criminal tribes' in India. In a blatant disregard for the rule of law doctrine, these communities were collectively punished for any crime committed by an individual of the group.[53]

As we shall see in the next section, the supposed racial and cultural superiority of the British became one of the key legitimising ideologies behind the British Empire. It allowed the coloniser to lay claim to following the rule of law doctrine, while justifying the colonial state's unequal legal treatment based on race.

[51] Fitzpatrick, P. (1992) *The Mythology of Modern Law*, London: Routledge, 110.

[52] *Re Southern Rhodesia* (1919) AC 211 (PC) 233, 234.

[53] Dunstall and Godfrey (n 45) 3; Singha, R. (2000) *A Despotism of Law: Crime and Justice in Early Colonial India*, New Delhi: Oxford University Press, 27–8.

The rule of law and racial discrimination in the colony

Nowhere were the limits of the rule of law clearer than when the concept met the everyday racial inequalities that sustained the Empire. At their most stark, these racial inequalities took the form of slavery that dehumanised the African origin population and remained legal until 1834.[54] For instance, the Slave Code passed in Barbados in 1668 explicitly noted that the slave population 'are of Barbarous, Wild, and Savage Natures, and such as renders them wholly unqualified to be governed by the Laws, Customs, and Practices of our Nation'.[55] This justified the creation of a dual legal system, in which 'slave crimes' were to be tried in slave courts without the benefit of juries. This and other similar slave codes in Barbados became the model for slave laws passed later in Jamaica, the Leeward Islands and even some American states.[56] Such laws not only created 'status crimes', that is, crimes that could only be committed by enslaved people, such as being a runaway, abusing a planter/free person and possession of weapons, but also created a dual system of punishment in which only enslaved people faced brutal punishments that sought to attack their bodily integrity, including flogging, branding, dismemberment and other bodily mutilations.[57] As a result, 'the dominant experience of [colonial] legalities' from the enslaved peoples' point of view 'was of terror and violence'.[58]

Not only did the colonial state turn a blind eye to everyday forms or racial violence in the colony, despite its claims to upholding the rule of law, it also often directly legally endorsed racial discrimination against the non-white populations. Elizabeth Kolsky argues in her study of colonial India that: 'The notion of a rule of law as a system of principles designed to govern and protect equal subjects – a notion introduced to India by Britons themselves – was blatantly contradicted by the institutionalization of racial distinctions in the statutory law and the overt partiality of white police, judges and juries.'[59] In fact, so aware were the ruling race of the partiality of the European judges and juries that one of the biggest legal controversies in colonial India arose out of the Ilbert Bill 1883, which proposed allowing Indian magistrates to preside over cases involving European British defendants. After sustained protest by the white population, the Bill was finally passed in 1884 after

[54] The slave trade across the British Empire was abolished through the Slave Trade Act 1807, but slavery itself was only abolished later through the Slavery Abolition Act 1833.

[55] An Act for the Governing of Negroes 1668 (Barbados).

[56] Morgan, K. (2007) *Slavery and the British Empire: From Africa to America*, Oxford: Oxford University Press, 113.

[57] Paton, D. (2001) 'Punishment, crime, and the bodies of slaves in eighteenth-century Jamaica', *Journal of Social History*, 34(4): 923–54, at 939.

[58] Ibid, 924.

[59] Kolsky (n 29) 12.

securing the compromise of ensuring that they could only be tried by European British majority juries. Of course, similar provisions were not made for the Indian population.

Similarly, in South Africa, the rule of law developed in the country 'primarily along the racial frontiers' and was used to determine what sort of rights the African and Asian population in the country might enjoy.[60] For instance, under the Urban Affairs Act 1923 increasingly arbitrary and despotic powers were exercised by local municipalities to remove Africans from urban municipal areas, including a regulation that empowered the local superintendent not only to remove people from an area, but also to order their huts to be destroyed if they did not comply within 24 hours. And yet, this regulation was found to be neither *ultra vires* nor unreasonable.[61] With regard to the Asian population, various laws sought to deny them licences to trade in South Africa. While couched in economic terms, that is, to protect white traders from being undercut by Asian traders who supplied the same goods for cheaper prices, the laws in fact reflected the racial unease of the ruling elite. They worried that the proximity of white housewives to Asian traders in the absence of their husbands might lead to inappropriate contact, that Asian traders extending credit facilities to poor whites might erode racial hierarchies and, similarly, white women working in Asian shops might lose their sense of 'racial superiority'.[62] As a result, we find that, though the colonial South African state continued to lay claim to ideas of the rule of law, racial difference was built into the very edifice of the law itself. This racial segregation was strengthened after South African independence and eventually took the form of Apartheid.

Direct racial discrimination was also apparent when the colonial state meted out punishment for crimes. The most severe punishments were saved for violence committed by non-whites against the white population. If the perpetrator was white, punishment for white-on-white violence was a lot more rigorous than the punishment for acts of violence committed by white men against the non-white population. In large part, the latter kind of violence was normalised through – and was an intrinsic part of – the colonial capitalist structure, which allowed 'masters' to have the 'right of correction' to brutally beat, flog, mutilate or confine their workers as and when they saw fit.[63] Even after the official end of slavery,[64] racial violence against the

[60] Channock, M. (2001) *The Making of South African Legal Culture 1902–1936: Fear, Favour and Prejudice*, Cambridge: Cambridge University Press.

[61] *Tutu and Others v Municipality of Kimberley*, 1918–23 GWLD 64; Channock (n 60) 485.

[62] Channock (n 60) 487–97.

[63] For instance, see Paton (n 57); and Kolsky (n 29) 55.

[64] The modern popular discourse in Britain on slavery in the British Empire overwhelmingly focuses on the British contribution to the abolition of slavery rather than centuries of British participation in the practice.

indigenous population was a 'constant and constituent element' of British colonialism and yet 'white violence remains one of the empire's most closely guarded secrets'.[65] White violence was invisibilised by its omnipresence and was embedded in the framework of colonial difference upon which the very structure of colonial law was built.

Further, the issue of equal punishment for the same crime for people of different races had always been contentious, and arguments against it focused both on the supposed mental and civilisational differences between the races and their physical or biological differences. For example, in the 19th century, Legislative Member Herbert Maddock argued for shorter jail sentences to be awarded to Englishmen in India: 'It would be even absurd to sentence an Englishman and an Indian to the same term of confinement in a jail. Such a confinement is of itself a very slight evil to the native and the heat of a crowded building surrounded by high walls is not at all injurious to his health.'[66]

Racial discrimination under the law was further entrenched through indirect means by restricting the access of the non-white populations to both legal education and legal professions. For instance, in Tanganyika, in the absence of any local legal training being available, the colonial government required a British law degree to practise law in the territory, while at the same time following a policy of preventing Africans from receiving scholarships to study in Britain.[67] Similar policies were followed by the British elsewhere in Africa, thus effectively excluding the non-white population from entering the legal profession in large parts of the continent. This discrimination helped to stifle local resistance against colonial law and governance.[68] As a result, except for Ghana and Nigeria, at the time of independence in the mid-20th century, most African countries had very few lawyers and even fewer Black lawyers.

Thus, we find that in the colony, the state paid lip service to its commitment to the rule of law while always possessing and frequently displaying a commitment to violence, which was seen as essential to protecting the coloniser from the 'savage', 'primitive' and 'barbaric' colonised population. If the rule of law failed – and its precarious establishment in the colony meant that it failed routinely – the rule and its suitability were

65 Kolsky (n 29) 1–2. For an account of 20th-century white violence in Kenya, see Elkins C. (2005) *Britain's Gulag: The Brutal End of Empire in Kenya*, London: Pimlico.

66 Maddock's minute of 4 September 1844, quoted in Kolsky (n 29) 80.

67 Joireman, S.F. (2001) 'Inherited legal systems and effective rule of law: Africa and the colonial legacy', *Journal of Modern African Studies*, 39(4): 571–96, at 580.

68 Ojwang, J.B. and Slatter, D.R. (1990) 'The legal profession in Kenya', *Journal of African Law*, 34(1): 9–26, at 11. See also the contributions to Dias, C.J. et al (eds) (1981) *Lawyers in the Third World: Comparative and Developmental Perspectives*, London: Holmes & Meier.

never questioned; instead, the failure was blamed on the corruption of local officials both white and non-white, or the backwardness and criminality of the native population. Both this 'corruption' and 'backwardness' were then posited as reasons for colonial rule to continue until the civilisation was 'advanced' enough to accept the mantle of the rule of law by itself. The rule of law emerged, then, as the 'stated goal, means, and justification for British colonialism'.[69]

Anti-colonial movements and the repurposing of the rule of law ideal

The rule of law discourse in the British Empire encountered an unexpected twist in the 20th century. As the struggle against colonialism intensified in Asia and Africa, British officials' lack of commitment to the rule of law in the colonies came to be branded by the anti-colonialists as 'un-British' and condemned as the 'lawless law of British rule'.[70] On the one hand, the idea of the rule of law was denounced as simply being a veil to cover the colonial and capitalist exploitation of the colonies, but on the other hand, colonised people actively chose to use the concept as a means of legal and political 'protection, resistance, adaptation and collaboration'.[71]

Even a scholar such as E.P. Thompson, a Marxist historian who was critical of law as a device that mediated and reinforced existing class relations,[72] valorised the idea of the rule of law and described the British contribution to it as a 'a cultural achievement of universal significance'.[73] In fact, Thompson, like others, justified the 'goodness' inherent in the rule of law by arguing that Indian freedom fighters including M.K. Gandhi and Jawaharlal Nehru had used the idea of the rule of law in their quest for Indian independence.[74] However, it is important to remember that when colonised people couched their own demands for greater rights in the conceptual language of the rule of law, they did so as a strategic move to gain legitimacy and visibility for their causes rather than because of any 'strong intellectual or emotional commitment to the Rule of Law in the British sense'.[75]

At the same time, the anti-colonialists' choice to use the rule of law rhetoric in their own movements, even if this was a choice made for strategic reasons, points to the endurance of some of the ideals associated with the rule of

[69] McBride (n 3) 23.

[70] Weiner (n 17) 232–3.

[71] Dunstall and Godfrey (n 45) 2.

[72] Thompson, E.P. (2013) *Whigs and Hunters: The Origin of the Black Act*, first published 1975, London: Breviary Stuff Publications, 205.

[73] Ibid, 207.

[74] Ibid, 208.

[75] McLaren (n 42) 35.

law concept. Despite the protest of formalists such as Raz, as we saw at the start of this chapter, for most supporters of the rule of law, the concept has come to stand as a shorthand for justice, equality and democracy, which were precisely the objectives that the anti-colonial struggles sought to achieve. Therefore, it can be argued that in this new pursuit of the rule of law, the anti-colonialists sought to distance themselves from the procedural idea of the rule of law that was favoured by the colonial state and replace it with a more substantive understanding of the rule of law, which was undergirded by truly equal rights for all races.

The rule of law and the rule of empire: an inherent incompatibility

If we move away from the European colonisers' view of the precolonial state, we must accept that the precolonial forms of society on other continents were not *terra nullius*. These societies in Asia, Africa, Australia and the Americas were governed by rules and laws that may not have been recognisable to European sensibilities, but nevertheless were used locally. If we take this as our starting point, we must also accept that the structure of colonial law could only come into being after the violent and illegal removal of the precolonial order. Thus, in the colonial setting, the discourse on the rule of law, with varying degrees of success, always sought to hide its illegitimate origin. This leads us to the inexorable fact that the rule of law and the rule of empire are inherently incompatible, and that the latter can only be achieved by, at worst, annihilating the former or, at best by upholding the weakest procedural notion of the rule of law and using it as a fig leaf.

A few key reasons point towards the inevitable failure of substantive notions of the rule of law in the colonies. First, the concept of the rule of law could not overcome its origins. Its cultural underpinnings meant that imposing it on other societies which did not share the same historical or cultural development could itself constitute a form of 'arbitrary domination'.[76] Despite its universal claims, the rule of law could not transcend its European social origins and, thus, took oppressive forms in 'the lands of others'.[77]

Second, the rule of law concept remained incompatible with the continuing need of colonial law to oppress and exploit the colonised population. As Nasser Hussain notes, in the colony the tension between 'illimitable sovereignty', which the coloniser required in order to rule over

[76] Lino (n 14) 743.

[77] Evans, J. (2005) 'Colonialism and the rule of law: the case of South Australia', in B. Godfrey and G. Dunstall (eds) *Crime and Empire 1840–1940: Criminal Justice in Local and Global Context*, Cullompton: Willan Publishing, 57–75, at 62–7.

an alien population, and the rule of law, which the coloniser claimed to possess, was at its most stark.[78] Due to its very nature, the colonial state needed to possess autocratic powers: 'Government was usually by decree or proclamation, while a battery of laws and reserve powers were directed at the maintenance and preservation of the colonial order.'[79] This left little room for a substantive rule of law regime to flourish.

Third, racial discrimination within the colony further weakened the commitment to the rule of law. As Bonny Ibawoh notes: 'A uniform rule of law would have profoundly threatened the power dynamic that distinguished colonizer from the colonized, and abrogated the very foundations of the imperial project.'[80] Indeed, as we saw in the previous section, despite the rhetorical stance of legal equality, legal practice and conventions awarded distinct privileges to the white population and frequently tolerated, and even excused, white violence against the non-white population.

And lastly, within the colonies, even formalist notions of the rule of law were regularly undermined by the frequent suspension of civil law through the invocation of autocratic martial law under which the colonised peoples' already limited freedoms were further restricted. Across the Empire, the British frequently resorted to martial law from the 19th century onwards,[81] especially in response to popular movements such as the Demerara slave rebellion of 1823 (in modern Guyana), the Indian Uprising of 1857 and the Mau Mau Uprising in Kenya in the mid-20th century. As R.W. Kostal notes in the context of the Morant Bay Uprising in Jamaica in 1865, events such as these and British responses to them 'exposed the tectonic stresses created by the nation's embrace both of the will to power and the rule of law'.[82]

While it is in the colonial context that the duplicitous nature of the rule of law becomes most evident, what we can learn from this setting about how law interacts with and relates to violence, race, oppression and power has global application, whether in states that have an imperial legacy or postcolonial states that continue to bear the structural imprints of colonial law.[83]

---

78 Hussain (n 43) 9.

79 Killingray, D. (1986) 'The maintenance of law and order in British colonial Africa', *African Affairs*, 85(340): 411–37, at 433.

80 Ibhawoh, B. (2013) *Imperial Justice: Africans in Empire's Court*, Oxford: Oxford University Press, 9.

81 For a list, see Hussain (n 43) 108; Kostal, R.W. (2005) *A Jurisprudence of Power: Victorian Empire and the Rule of Law*, Oxford: Oxford University Press, 8.

82 Kostal (n 81) 20.

83 Anghie, A. (2019) 'Foreword', in Hussain, N., *The Jurisprudence of Emergency: Colonialism and The Rule of Law*, Ann Arbor: University of Michigan Press, xiii.

Conclusion

Colonial law remains deeply intertwined with the history and development of British law and politics. But this relationship was not just one-way. While undoubtedly the various colonial legal systems were moulded by British ideals and desires, the British legal system too, and especially its constitutional arrangements, was constantly shaped by the development of colonial law. As Hussain notes: 'The colonies here become the site for both the manifestations of contradictions embedded in the British constitution and the alternative locale for elaborating on these questions of power and restraint.'[84] An analysis of the ways in which the rule of law doctrine was deployed in the British colonies, and the way in which it not only interacted with existing inequalities, but also helped to constitute and legitimise new regimes of inequalities reveals the ideological origins of the doctrine and its inextricable connection to modern liberalism and capitalism. Whether the law was deployed to treat enslaved people of African origin as less than human and the property of their masters, or to restrict Asian people from trading in South Africa or to overlook the daily violence perpetrated by the white population against workers across the British Empire, the claim to the rule of law sought to present the existing deeply unequal law as being 'sanitised of self-interest',[85] and therefore to hide the fact that it primarily worked to protect the privileges and the property of the ruling race. Once we understand the fact that the antecedents of the rule of law doctrine lie in a particular type of liberalism that is closely associated with capitalism, and the protection of property rights,[86] it also makes visible the use of the doctrine to mask class difference and oppression back at home.[87] In Britain, the elite attempted to use the claim to the rule of law as a means of maintaining the existing social order and, among other things, to resist the redistribution of property and the expansion of suffrage to women and working-class men.[88]

Today, the promotion of the rule of law has devolved into a multibillion-pound industry where international developmental aid is tied to rule of law commitments, and the so-called beneficiaries of such projects still largely comprise former colonies in the Global South.[89] Our study of the ways in which the rule of law doctrine was, and continues to be, used as a tool to

[84] Hussain (n 83) 24.

[85] McBride (n 3) 15.

[86] Tamanaha (n 4) 541.

[87] Thompson (n 72) 202–3.

[88] Tamanaha (n 4) 517–18.

[89] For a discussion of the promotion of rule of law and claims of 'neo-imperialism' in Africa today, see Humphreys, S. (2012) 'Laboratories of statehood: legal intervention in colonial Africa and today', *Modern Law Review* 75(4): 475–510.

legitimise British colonialism serves as a warning: we must guard against the use of the rule of law doctrine by the elite in the Global North to impose neoimperialist structures in new guises on the Global South.

Further reading

Evans, J. (2005) 'Colonialism and the rule of law: the case of South Australia', in B. Godfrey and G. Dunstall (eds), *Crime and Empire 1840–1940: Criminal Justice in Local and Global Context*, Cullompton: Willan Publishing, 57–75.

Hussain, N. (2019) 'Introduction: the historical and theoretical background' in *The Jurisprudence of Emergency: Colonialism and The Rule of Law*, Ann Arbor: University of Michigan Press, 1–33.

Ibhawoh, B. (2013) 'Africa and the umpires of empire', in *Imperial Justice: Africans in Empire's Court*, Oxford: Oxford University Press, 1–24.

Kolsky, E. (2010) 'Introduction', in *Colonial Justice in British India: White Violence and the Rule of Law*, Cambridge: Cambridge University Press, 1–26.

McLaren, J. (2015) 'Chasing the chimera: the rule of law in the British Empire and the comparative turn in legal history', *Law Context: A Socio-Legal Journal*, 33(1): 21–36.

2

Parliamentary Supremacy and the People

Donal K. Coffey

The theory of parliamentary supremacy, or parliamentary sovereignty, remains the bedrock of the UK constitution. This theory, which received its classical definition in the late 19th century, has been subject to a number of different critiques and the subject of a number of debates. The basic claim of parliamentary supremacy is relatively simple: under the UK constitution, there is no legal limit on what the Crown in Parliament can enact. This chapter aims to consider the development, and criticism, of this theory by looking at two primary directions: (1) arguments within Parliament about its powers; and (2) arguments outside Parliament about its powers. At first glance, this may seem a strange way to consider the development of the theory, as we are not focusing solely on the judicial development of the doctrine at common law. We approach it in this fashion, however, because of the unique claims that parliamentary supremacy makes about its pre-eminence in the legal system, which we will consider in more detail below. It also helps us to see the commonalities between debates within and outside Parliament. The key commonality this discloses is the way in which the UK constitution has struggled, and continues to struggle, with the role of democracy itself. This chapter argues that the current articulation of constitutional debate in areas surrounding parliamentary supremacy in relation to ideas such as its interaction with the rule of law and constitutional statutes is best explained by the difficulty British theory has with the role of popular sovereignty within the confines of the traditional British parliamentary system. In order for us to track this debate, we must begin with the definition of parliamentary supremacy as put forward by the Vinerian Professor of English Laws at the University of Oxford, Albert Venn Dicey, who in 1885 wrote the single most influential textbook on British constitutional law, *Introduction to the Study of the Law of the Constitution.*

Introduction to the Study of the Law of the Constitution

Dicey was not the first person to put forward a theory of parliamentary supremacy; he drew on a long tradition of this idea, but his formulation of the idea remains the most influential. The basic idea is relatively straightforward – there is no legal limit on what the Crown in Parliament enacts as law. Dicey advanced three propositions in relation to this rule:

1. There is no law that Parliament cannot change.
2. There is no distinction between ordinary legislation and fundamental legislation.
3. No body exists that can treat an Act of Parliament as void.[1]

To this may be added another linked idea, called 'implied repeal', which states that where there is a conflict between two Acts of Parliament, the statute that was enacted later in time prevails, even if it does not explicitly state that it repeals the prior act.[2]

Dicey proved this theory in a number of ways, but it is important to note here that the third limb mentioned earlier is really a statement of institutional primacy – it is a claim made about the importance of Parliament relative to other bodies under the UK's constitution. Dicey stated this idea in a number of different ways in his monograph, but the idea is relatively simple: 'There is no power which, under the English constitution, can come into rivalry with the legislative sovereignty of Parliament.'[3] At the time that Dicey was writing, the question about the interaction between Parliament and other constitutional bodies had been settled – the claims of the monarchy to have pre-eminence in the British constitution had died out with the Stuarts and the Glorious Revolution, while the attempt by the courts to intervene in the operation of the Commons in the case of *Stockdale v Hansard* had been stymied by the simple expedient of locking up the court officials who had come to enforce the judgment.[4]

---

1 A.V. Dicey, *Introduction to the Study of the Law of the Constitution* (8th edn), London: Macmillan & Co, 1920, 84–7.

2 See, for example, ibid, 42–5.

3 Ibid, 52–6.

4 *Stockdale v Hansard* (1839) 112 ER 1112; the case concerned whether immunity from defamation that stemmed from parliamentary privilege extended beyond Parliament, and whether each House of Parliament had exclusive jurisdiction to assert the extent of its privilege. *Case of the Sheriff of Middlesex* (1840) 11 Ad & E 273 where the Court of Queen's Bench upheld the imprisonment of the executors of the *Stockdale* decision as a result of contempt of Parliament.

The claim that Dicey made in his monograph was that there were no legal limits on the powers of Parliament. He did not claim that there were no practical limits on this power. In fact, he argued that there were two practical limits: that people might stop obeying a law, and the limits imposed by socialisation (that is, what legislators believed was feasible based on what people like them thought).

The limitation on Dicey's theory of legal power was to be mediated through the actions of representative government:

> Speaking roughly, the permanent wishes of the representative portion of Parliament can hardly in the long run differ from the wishes of the English people, or at any rate of the electors; that which the majority of the House of Commons command, the majority of the English people usually desire.[5]

Therefore, in considering the operation of parliamentary supremacy, it is important to understand that representative government in the UK when Dicey was writing is not what we would automatically think of when we think about elections today. The period of 'one person, one vote' was more than 30 years in the future. While the UK was becoming more democratic, it was doing so through a hodgepodge of different rules that tied votes to a series of increasingly obscure hoops that the courts could scarcely understand.

It is difficult to overstate how complicated and convoluted the franchise was in the 19th century, although a flavour may perhaps be seen in *Bradley v Baylis*,[6] issued shortly before Dicey's first edition. In that case, Lord Jessel MR was confronted with a franchise based in part on the definition of 'dwelling-house' in which he was forced to concede of the relevant section: 'What that means nobody can say.'[7] There also remained the practice of plural voting, as an elector could qualify in a number of different constituencies by virtue of their property qualifications.

Not only was the franchise itself quite different from what we are now familiar with, but so too were the constituencies. There were university constituencies, for example, for graduates of Oxford, Cambridge, and other universities. There were the remnants of the multi-member constituencies, including the City of London which returned two Members of Parliament (MPs).

Most significantly, Dicey's formulation of 'the electors' above does not directly address the fact that the female franchise was systematically rejected until the Representation of the People Act 1918. Under that Act, the

[5] Dicey (n 1) 34.

[6] (1881) 8 QBD 195.

[7] Ibid, 216.

female franchise was subject to an age bar of 30 years and also a rateable value qualification.[8] Dicey himself was not ambivalent about this process, strenuously arguing against the extension of the female franchise and universal suffrage in the 8th edition of his textbook, arguing that the anti-suffragist claim 'conforms to the nature of things',[9] that is, that it would be unnatural to give women the franchise.

This context demonstrates the nature of the political restrictions that Dicey was prepared to countenance to the legal sovereignty of Parliament; the limitations were to be based on the wishes of the electors, and the electorate should be substantially what was set out in the Representation of the People Act 1884. What we see in the 20th century, however, is a series of questions being asked about the nature of parliamentary supremacy which is intimately tied to the role of the people in a democratic polity. While Parliament could claim unlimited legal supremacy, did the integration of the people into the British constitutional structure undermine or alter any of the claims relating to parliamentary supremacy? When we examine parliamentary supremacy in this light, we can see a continuity across a number of different constitutional flashpoints in relation to parliamentary supremacy. In many of these cases, the attempt to limit the exercise of parliamentary supremacy is to be found not in the courts, but rather articulated and debated through the political process. What we see as a recurring theme is the attempt to define a conventional rule governing the circumstances in which the legally unlimited power possessed by the Crown in Parliament should be exercised. The reason advocated in favour of this convention is that a democratic mandate had not been secured from the British people in favour of a particular course of action, and was typically to be found in an intraparliamentary confrontation.

The Political Constitution I: 1911 and Home Rule

The link between parliamentary democracy and parliamentary sovereignty in something like the current relationship was only achieved in the decade and a half surrounding Dicey's death, beginning with the removal of the veto of the Lords by the Parliament Act 1911 and the subsequent extensions of the franchise in 1918 and finally enacting full female suffrage by the Equal Franchise Act 1928. Even with these changes, the exact link between democracy and Parliament had not been settled. The Preamble

8 Section 4(1) of the Representation of the People Act 1918. The University franchise, which provided for special constituencies such as the Combined English Universities of which Bristol was a part, was subject to different rules, but retained an age requirement.

9 Dicey (n 1) lxvi.

to the Parliament Act 1911 famously stated the future aspiration, that where 'it is intended to substitute for the House of Lords as it at present exists a Second Chamber constituted on a popular instead of a hereditary basis', while the 1918 Representation of the People Act provided under section 20(2) for the preparation of a scheme for 100 MPs to be elected to the Commons by means of proportional representation. This scheme was ultimately never enacted, but it is notable that when a proposal to change the method of election to Parliament was mooted in 2011, the question was to be determined by a referendum rather than statute, reflecting a convention about the circumstances in which a referendum is appropriate in British constitutional life, which is established further below. The debate surrounding the passage of the Parliament Act 1911, however, disclosed a particular constitutional view of the House of Lords on the part of the Conservative Party – that there were limits on what the House of Commons could legitimately claim to enact without having first secured the imprimatur of the people (this was referred to as the 'referendal' view).

The theory of parliamentary supremacy places unlimited legal power in the hands of Parliament, and claims for it pre-eminence over all of the other branches of the state. This, however, put into play the operation of Parliament itself. It is important to note that in the 19th century the House of Lords had a veto over bills that were passed by the House of Commons. This veto was less important when the same party had a majority in the Commons as in the Lords; as the Lords was a hereditary House with an inbuilt Conservative majority, this applied in the case of one major party. Where the balance of powers between the Houses was tested was when the same party did not have a majority in both Houses, and this came to a head in the first decade of the 20th century. In this case, the House of Lords claimed a particular power where a mandate had not been secured at a prior election – the power to reject a government bill until the wishes of the electorate had been ascertained via the democratic process. The fundamental conflict as articulated at the time was between a legally unlimited Parliament and the claimed source of legitimacy of that Parliament. In 1910 it was not fully democratic, but the basic tension that was exposed in this period remains and echoes the same tension that has been evidenced in the 21st century.

In 1910 the question could be phrased as follows: did the House of Lords have to pass all forms of legislation that were initiated in the Commons or were there limits on what the Commons could do without having received the assent of the British people? It is important to understand what the second position entails, as it would constitute a conventional rule on the exercise of the legally unlimited power of Parliament. Constitutional conventions, under the British system of constitutional governance, are rules that constrain the exercise of legal power. As an example, there are numerous powers that are formally vested in the Crown, but the exercise of these powers is on the advice of responsible ministers. In a similar way, if there was a rule that governed the exercise of power in Parliament, this could also form a convention of the UK constitution.

In the 1910s, one issue at play was whether or not to grant Home Rule, a form of devolution, to Ireland. In 1910, in an attempt to reach a political consensus in relation to the powers of the House of Lords, Austen Chamberlain wrote: 'What we have been considering [in the Conference] is not *what changes* in our system of Government should be made but *how* such changes should be effected. This is a wholly different, though perhaps a not unrelated question, for what we desire is not a guarantee against all change but security against changes in the machinery of Government *which the people do not approve*.'[10] The traditional view as outlined above was that as Parliament possessed an unlimited legal power to alter British law, and there was no entrenched British law, Parliament could amend the British system of government simply by passing a new law.

Opponents of this view argued that this could not be achieved without the consent of the people, and millions of people, including Dicey, signed the British Covenant, which stated:

> Being earnestly convinced that the claim of the Government to carry the Home Rule Bill into law, without submitting it to the judgment of the Nation, is contrary to the spirit of our Constitution, we do hereby solemnly declare that, if the Bill is so passed, we shall hold ourselves justified in taking or supporting any action that may be effective to prevent it being put into operation, and more particularly to prevent the armed forces of the Crown being used to deprive the people of Ulster of their rights as Citizens of the United Kingdom.[11]

Here we can see the attempt to articulate a conventional rule: that passage of Irish Home Rule without 'submitting it to the judgment of the Nation, is contrary to the spirit of our Constitution'. Advocates proposed a referendum on the question of Irish Home Rule, and crucially this referendum was to be based on a franchise of the entire population of the UK (not simply that of Ireland). The Acts of Union which had established the United Kingdom of Great Britain and Ireland proclaimed, under Article 1, that the Kingdoms

[10] Chamberlain to F.E. Smith (21 October 1910), in Austin Chamberlain, *Politics from Inside: An Epistolary Chronicle 1906–1914*, New Haven: Yale, 1937, 285.

[11] L.S. Amery, *My Political Life: Volume One England before the Storm 1896–1914*, London: Hutchinson, 1953, 407. This was different from the Ulster Covenant, which was open for signature contemporaneously.

'shall … and for ever after, be united into one Kingdom'. Despite this seemingly permanent Union, the doctrine of parliamentary supremacy meant that the Acts of Union were not constitutionally protected above ordinary laws, and that they would be impliedly repealed by the operation of later statutes. This meant that, in strict legal theory, the Act of Union 1801 could be undone relatively simply, despite its text. The claim made by opponents of Irish Home Rule was therefore that, absent the clear assent of the British people, it was constitutionally improper to alter the constitution to include Home Rule.

In the end, the question was overtaken by the First World War. Home Rule was provided for by the Government of Ireland Act 1914, but was subject to a suspensory Act which prevented it from coming into operation. During the First World War, the Easter Rising occurred in Ireland in 1916, and the Irish War of Independence culminated in the Irish Free State becoming a Dominion in 1922. In the meantime, the Government of Ireland Act 1920 had provided for Home Rule for six counties which now make up Northern Ireland. The crisis of the 1910s and 1920s might seem to indicate that the legally unlimited power of Parliament was undiminished; after all, Parliament had eventually amended the Act of Union 1801 and ended the Union that was meant to exist for ever. However, if we consider merely the question of Irish Home Rule rather than Irish independence, the answer is considerably more complicated – proponents of the view that the Home Rule could not be introduced without the imprimatur of the people could point to the fact that Home Rule had not been introduced in the form proposed to claim that the referendal view had not been definitely rejected. Opponents of the referendal view could point to the existence of a new Dominion, one not countenanced by the Act of Union 1801, as evidence that there was within the Empire a polity which demonstrated the continued efficacy of parliamentary supremacy.[12] The next significant development in relation to the theory of parliamentary supremacy was to occur within the Empire, but in a different dominion – Australia. When we turn to Australia, we see the beginnings of a debate about whether it was appropriate for the judiciary to identify limits on the idea of parliamentary supremacy.

The 'manner and form' theory

The judicial questioning of the implications of Dicey's formulation first occurred not in the UK, but in the British Empire. There were two primary

12 Modern advocates of this referendal view include theorists such as Vernon Bogdanor; see V. Bogdanor, 'Europe and the Sovereignty of the People' (2016) 87(3) *Political Quarterly* 348: '[The referendum] is the people's veto'.

reasons for this. First, the British Empire was itself underpinned by the doctrine of parliamentary supremacy – Westminster retained the legal ability to legislate with regard to the different parts of the British Empire. Second, through the 19th and into the 20th centuries, the relationship between the UK and various parts of the Empire became gradually less invasive, so that these parts were essentially internally self-governing – the parts were known as the Dominions. These different countries, such as Canada, Australia and South Africa, were given constitutions that conferred wide legislative powers, and when questions arose as to how exactly to interpret these constitutions, the questions were addressed against the backdrop of Dicey's theory.

The most significant jurisdiction for the development of the theory of parliamentary supremacy in the early 20th century was Australia, involving a debate about what is called the 'manner and form' objection to Dicey's theory. The name comes from the Colonial Laws Validity Act 1865, which provided that every colonial legislature had power to amend the constitution, powers and procedure of that legislature provided that it was passed in conformity with 'such Manner and Form' as was in place. As an objection to Dicey's theory, it questioned whether or not the composition of the body that made up Parliament could be changed, or whether the ways in which laws made by that Parliament could be changed. It did not, therefore, claim that there was a limit on what Parliament could legislate in relation to; instead, it asked the question of what Parliament is and how Parliament passes legislation.

The background to the *Trethowan* case[13] arose as a result of the imminent arrival of a Labour government in New South Wales under Jack Lang. The Nationalist Government introduced section 7(a) into the constitution of New South Wales to provide that any attempt to abolish the Upper House, called the Legislative Council, and where the Nationalist Party would retain numerical superiority, would require a referendum. The proximate Australian example for this was the State of Queensland, which had abolished its Upper House in 1922. In December 1930, Lang succeeded in convincing the Legislative Council to sign its own abolition, assuring the members that there would be a referendum, but then attempted to renege on this assurance by presenting the Bill for the signature of the Governor as if it were an ordinary Bill. An injunction was issued to prevent the signing of the Bill.

13 *Attorney-General for the State of New South Wales v Trethowan* [1931] 44 CLR 394. The case has been the subject of a two-volume series by Ian Loveland: I. Loveland, *McCawley and Trethowan: The Chaos of Politics and the Integrity of Law*, Oxford: Hart Publishing, 2021.

The question that arose was whether or not the legislature retained 'full power' to amend any laws whatsoever to do with the constitution of the legislature, or whether it had to follow the procedure laid down in section 7(a). The answer given by the High Court of Australia was the latter, endorsing the idea that while the amendment could be made, the procedure had to follow the 'manner and form' laid out – an amendment without a referendum was not legally valid. There were two views of the majority of the High Court: (1) the legislature of New South Wales, for the purposes of abolishing the Upper House, was both Houses, the People of New South Wales voting through plebiscite, and the Governor;[14] and (2) the manner in which legislation could be passed in relation to section 7(a) no longer allowed the legislature itself to abolish the Upper House.[15]

This case clearly dealt with the powers of a limited state legislature in Australia, but the argument was pressed in relation to Westminster by Ivor Jennings, who argued that there was no reason that the same argument could not in principle apply to Westminster itself.[16] In fact, the factual matrix – a conflict between the Lower and Upper Houses, a question of the necessity of a referendum, and a threat to appoint peers to the Upper House to construct a new majority – was essentially the same that surrounded the passage of the Parliament Act in the UK. And, when one thinks of it, didn't the Parliament Act itself provide for a new method of enacting legislation, a method without the assent of the Lords, so hadn't the Parliament Act itself changed the composition of Parliament within the UK constitution? Dicey himself had been forced to confront the question of the composition of Westminster after the passage of the Parliament Act 1911 in the 8th edition of his textbook and, in this instance, he seems to have conceded the point.[17] Nonetheless, critics of the Parliament Act, including Sir William Wade, argued that as the power conferred under the Parliament Act was by virtue of statute, any legislation passed on foot of the new procedure was delegated legislation (delegated by the Crown in Parliament). The next significant development in the British constitution in relation to parliamentary sovereignty occurred again outside the courts – this time, it concerned the passage of the Parliament Act 1949.

[14] See *Attorney-General for the State of New South Wales v Trethowan* (n 13), Rich J, at 419–21.

[15] See Starke J, at 424–35.

[16] W. Ivor Jennings, *The Law and the Constitution* (3rd edn), London: University of London Press, 1943, 143–4.

[17] D.K. Coffey, 'Constitutional Law and Empire in Interwar Britain: Universities, Liberty, Nationality and Parliamentary Supremacy' (2020) 71(2) *Northern Ireland Legal Quarterly* 193, at 204–8.

The Political Constitution II: one convention is rejected, is another adopted?

The question of the link between Parliament and the people surfaced again in the passage of the Parliament Act 1949. This Act was introduced in order to ensure that nationalisation was possible in the tail end of the Parliament elected in 1945; it therefore shortened the time period in which the Lords could delay the passage of legislation. Under the original Parliament Act of 1911, the delaying power extended for two parliamentary years, which meant that the government's legislative programme was relatively difficult to stop in the early part of its tenure, but as it came closer to the end of its term, two years became a more significant barrier. In advance of the passage of the Act, a more wide-ranging debate on Lords' reform took place, and here the divide between the political parties became apparent, with Lord Salisbury noting that the 'Conservatives did not accept the view that the House of Commons inevitably represents public opinion'.[18] The divisions of the 1910s in relation to the role of the Lords in the UK's constitutional structure had resurfaced, and the claims of the Upper House to block initiatives of the Commons on the basis of public opinion were reasserted. The Labour Party stood on the proposition that the Lords could never claim to be more in tune with public opinion than the Commons, and therefore rejected the Conservative position. The Act was passed, but only by using the procedure established under the 1911 Act, so the formulation at the beginning of the 1949 Act is: 'Be it enacted by the King's most Excellent Majesty, by and with the advice and consent of the Commons.' In other words, the 1949 Act was passed on the authority of the Crown in the Commons, rather than the Crown in Parliament. The year 1949 also saw the passage of the Ireland Act, which provided in section 1(2) that under no circumstances would Northern Ireland cease to be part of the UK without the consent of the Parliament of Northern Ireland. This statement complicated the potential exercise of parliamentary supremacy in relation to Northern Ireland by inserting a requirement for consent from a body that was not Westminster, although that would have been presumed at the time to be subject to implied repeal.

After the passage of the Parliament Act 1949, the question of the relationship between the Lords and the Commons within Parliament had therefore been answered twice in favour of the Commons. The more vexed question within the political constitution, about whether there were circumstances under which a democratic mandate should be sought from

[18] C. Ballinger, *The House of Lords 1911–1921: A Century of Non-reform*, Oxford: Hart Publishing, 2014, 67.

the people outside of the normal electoral cycle, remained unanswered. In the 1970s, however, the question arose again as the UK joined the European Economic Community (EEC), which later became the European Union (EU). This entailed the guarantee within the British legal system that if there was a conflict between EEC law and UK law, the law of the EEC would be given full effect and the UK law would not. Joining the EEC was accomplished by a statute, the European Communities Act (ECA) 1972, but that exercise of parliamentary supremacy did not end the matter. When the Labour Party was returned to office in 1974, it committed to hold a referendum on membership. This was in part because the Labour Party did not agree among itself about the correct approach to be taken, but the referendum was justified repeatedly on the ground that the 1972 Act had fundamentally changed the relationship between the people and Parliament, as EEC law now had primacy, and therefore a referendum was appropriate.[19] Introducing the Bill in the Commons, the Lord President of the Privy Council[20] stated that there were three issues which made a referendum on membership of the EEC appropriate: 'Its fundamental implications for the future of this country, for the political relationship between the United Kingdom and the other member Governments of the Community and, most important of all, for the constitutional position of Parliament.' Here we start to see articulated a new potential convention on the exercise of parliamentary supremacy – that if the position of Parliament within the constitution, in this case parliamentary supremacy itself, is to be altered (here via membership of the EEC), then the wishes of the people must first be ascertained. This is less capacious than the views put forward in 1911 and 1947, as it does not relate to the internal mechanics of Parliament itself but, rather, to potential limitations on Parliament, however constituted. From a strictly legal point of view, the referendum was pointless – the basis of the UK's entry into the EEC was the ECA 1972 and the government may have simply chosen to ignore the result as a legal matter. At the level of a political convention, a convention expressly linked to a diminution of parliamentary supremacy, it was clear. Take Jennings' test for constitutional conventions in this context: (1) what are the precedents?; (2) did the actors believe they were bound by a rule?; and (3) is there a reason for the rule?[21] It is clear that each of the three criteria are met in this instance, particularly if it is borne in mind that Jennings states that 'a single precedent with a good reason may be enough to establish the rule'.[22]

[19] HC Deb 10 April 1975, col 1418.

[20] The presiding officer of the Privy Council.

[21] Jennings (n 16) 131.

[22] Ibid.

The 1970s also saw a number of referendums take place within the UK which were dealt with in the different nations – Northern Ireland had a vote on whether to leave the UK in 1973, while Scotland and Wales held votes on whether they should have national assemblies in 1979. None of these referendums led to a change in the status quo – the Northern Ireland referendum was boycotted by the nationalist and republican communities, while the Scottish vote for an assembly fell below the threshold required. The Northern Ireland Parliament had been suspended in 1972, but the formula adopted in Northern Ireland is significant, because now a fundamental decision about whether to exercise parliamentary supremacy in an area by repealing the Act of Union was made subject to a referendum at a level below that of the UK. Similarly, holding a referendum in Wales and Scotland in 1979 impliedly acknowledged that the authority to provide for an internal governance structure for these regions was to be found in the population of those regions, and not in the first instance in Westminster. The principles established by holding these referendums, which were not themselves legally binding, provides more evidence for the establishment of conventional rules governing the exercise of parliamentary supremacy when it concerns the internal governance of the UK – there were times when that power should be exercised on the authority of bodies that were legally unknown to the UK constitution.

The process of judicialisation

The forums in which parliamentary supremacy had been most robustly debated and tried in the domestic UK context before the 1980s had not been the courts, but in Parliament itself and in academia. The 1980s heralded a new period of interest in the potential legal limits that might be brought to bear in relation to parliamentary supremacy. The first was related to the constitutional changes introduced in the 1970s by membership of the EEC. The second was a theoretical argument, most commonly associated with T.R.S. Allan, which drew on an understanding of the core tension between democracy and parliamentary sovereignty, and attempted to articulate a legal limit that might be enforced by the courts.

Allan noted that the UK's political system was based on the background principle of the rule of law, and that this idea was not a neutral one, as it carried with it a series of presumptions in favour of its ideological underpinnings. The core idea was that the rule of law itself operated to blunt some of the wilder claims of parliamentary supremacy, requiring a commitment to political values underpinning the constitutional system. What do these values entail? According to Allan, they include commitments to constitutional democracy, freedom from arbitrary government, limited discretion, unambiguous rules of criminal law, the principles of natural justice, and the protection of traditional liberties. These principles inform the approach judges bring to bear in interpreting statutory provisions.[23]

As we have seen, membership of the EEC rested on the idea of a continuing restriction on parliamentary supremacy. This was based on a piece of legislation, the ECA 1972, which was further endorsed by the British public in a referendum. In 1988 Parliament attempted to revoke a provision of European law under the Merchant Shipping Act 1988. Under the Diceyan idea of parliamentary supremacy, the response of the courts should have been relatively straightforward – the 1972 Act did not possess a status as higher law and therefore the later Act took precedence. In *Factortame (No. 2)*,[24] the Appellate Committee of the House of Lords took the opposite view, accepting that the 1972 Act was intended to remain in force, and take precedence over subsequent legislation, until it was expressly repealed or overridden. This was justified on the basis of the terms of the 1972 Act itself, although as we have seen that logic had not been applied in relation to other basic constitutional texts such as the Act of Union 1801.

This left a glaring juridical hole in how the courts were interpreting statutes: some of them were being accorded a higher status than others, as they were not subject to the normal rule of implied repeal. The theoretical means to bridge this gap was provided in *Thoburn v Sunderland City Council*[25] – there was a group of 'constitutional statutes' which were not subject to the doctrine of implied repeal, and this included the ECA 1972. In the course of introducing this novel idea, Lord Justice Laws stated as follows:

> The common law has in recent years allowed, or rather created, exceptions to the doctrine of implied repeal: a doctrine which was always the common law's own creature. There are now classes or types of legislative provision which cannot be repealed by mere implication. These instances are given, and can only be given, by our own courts, to which the scope and nature of Parliamentary sovereignty are ultimately confided.[26]

This statement roots the doctrine of parliamentary supremacy and, by extension, implied repeal in the common law. If common law is the basis of parliamentary supremacy, then it follows that the judiciary can develop,

---

[23] T.R.S. Allan, 'Legislative Supremacy and the Rule of Law: Democracy and Constitutionalism' (1985) 44(1) *Cambridge Law Journal* 111.

[24] [1990] UKHL 7.

[25] [2002] EWHC 195.

[26] Ibid, para 60. On constitutional statutes generally, see F. Ahmed and A. Perry, 'Constitutional Statutes' (2017) 37(2) *Oxford Journal of Legal Studies* 461; J. McGarry and S. Spence, 'Constitutional Statutes: Roots and Recognition' (2020) 41(3) *Statute Law Review* 378.

extend and amend it through case law. This was arguably required as a matter of law in order to make the operation of the ECA 1972 cohere with what was an obvious departure from traditional legal doctrine. In doing so, however, it had to overlook the role that convention had played in shaping the operation of parliamentary supremacy, and cut directly across the reason articulated for the 1975 EU referendum – that a change in the constitutional position of Parliament involving a diminution of Parliament's powers required legitimacy to be conferred through a referendum. This was perhaps foreseeable, as the political constitution is by its very nature not cognisable by the courts, but it did mean a considerable alteration in the balance of powers in the UK's constitution.

The matter became more pointed in the subsequent case of *Jackson v Attorney-General.*[27] The case concerned the Hunting Act 2004, which was passed under the 1949 Parliament Act procedure. An argument had been advanced that legislation passed under this method was, in fact, delegated legislation, and was therefore subject to judicial control. Ultimately, the argument failed, but in the course of their opinions, the Appellate Committee of the House of Lords made a number of claims about theoretical limits on parliamentary supremacy. Lord Hope of Craighead stated, echoing Allan: 'The rule of law enforced by the courts is the ultimate controlling factor on which our constitution is based.'[28] Lord Steyn went considerably further on the basis that parliamentary supremacy was created by judges as part of the common law, albeit in an obiter comment that was not part of his ruling:

> In exceptional circumstances involving an attempt to abolish judicial review or the ordinary role of the courts, the Appellate Committee of the House of Lords or a new Supreme Court may have to consider whether this is a constitutional fundamental which even a sovereign Parliament acting at the behest of a complaisant House of Commons cannot abolish.[29]

Jackson confirmed the manner and form objection held in British law.[30] The judgments also indicated at various points that there were statutes which were

[27] [2005] UKHL 56.

[28] Ibid, para 107.

[29] Ibid, para 102.

[30] The most sophisticated modern articulation of this theory is M. Gordon, *Parliamentary Sovereignty in the UK Constitution: Process, Politics and Democracy*, Oxford: Hart Publishing, 2015. The view has been the subject of a lively debate in the *Public Law* journal: see J. Goldsworthy, 'The "Manner and Form" Theory of Parliamentary Sovereignty' (2021) *Public Law* 586; and M. Gordon, 'The Manner and Form Theory of Parliamentary Sovereignty: A Response to Jeffrey Goldsworthy' (2021) *Public Law 603*. Goldsworthy's

accorded a particular status in British constitutional law, although there was no unanimity on the point.[31] Nonetheless, the question of constitutional statutes was accepted by the Supreme Court in subsequent decisions such as the *HS2* case, where the list was elaborated to include the Magna Carta, the Petition of Right 1628, the Bill of Rights and the Scottish Claim of Rights Act 1689, the Act of Settlement 1701, the Act of Union 1707, the ECA 1972, the Human Rights Act 1998 and the Constitutional Reform Act 2005.[32]

These developments placed the judiciary in an interesting position, where they had claimed variously, albeit in obiter, that: (1) the basis of the UK's constitutional structure was the rule of law as developed by the courts; (2) the traditional basis of the British constitution – parliamentary supremacy – was capable of reinterpretation;[33] and (3) there existed a series of statutes of extraordinary constitutional significance which were not subject to the normal rules of implied repeal. These claims could not be justified on the basis of the traditional understanding of parliamentary supremacy.

The simplest, and most plausible, explanation for the change had been the expanded use of instruments of direct democracy in the UK's constitutional structure. As we have seen, the referendum relating to the EEC in the 1970s was justified on the basis that the people had to approve a change in the constitutional relationship between Parliament and the people. Similar successful plebiscites in the 1990s provided for the devolved governments, which introduced a territorial element to the UK's constitution. These devolution statutes provided for devolved legislatures in Scotland, Wales and Northern Ireland after votes adopting these arrangements were approved in the territories concerned.

It may be helpful here to pause and reflect on the Northern Ireland settlement as an example. The Northern Ireland Assembly set up under the 1998 Act was different from that set up under the Government of Ireland Act 1920, in that it had been approved by a majority of the people of Northern Ireland in a referendum.[34] The provisions of this new settlement therefore enjoyed a different authority, as it had been approved by the people of Northern Ireland as a whole, something which the earlier, abandoned settlement had never managed to achieve. Moreover, the Good Friday/Belfast Agreement provided that a choice relating to the future of Northern Ireland

---

views are more fully set out in J. Goldsworthy, *Parliamentary Sovereignty: Contemporary Debates*, Cambridge: Cambridge University Press, 2010.

31 Compare *Jackson* (n 27) 102, 106, 107, 159.

32 *R (on the Application of the HS2 Action Alliance Ltd) v Secretary of State for Transport* [2014] UKSC 3 at para 207.

33 See Lord Steyn (n 27).

34 A parallel referendum approving it was held in Ireland.

was to be made by the people of Northern Ireland alone. Finally, it provided that the British government would incorporate the European Convention on Human Rights into Northern Ireland law, and would include direct access to the courts. This final element was translated into a full UK-wide incorporation in the Human Rights Act 1998.

Crucially, the basis of the settlement was the popular acceptance of the existing arrangements, which was to be determined through popular sovereignty and not mediated through parliamentary institutions. It was provisions like this, and the analogous provisions of the Scotland Act 1998 and the ECA 1972, which undermined the traditional role of parliamentary supremacy by inserting the 'people' or 'peoples' (constituted differently according to the question asked) into the UK's constitution. This creates a difficulty for the courts, because each of these referendums is technically only advisory, but the changes that the judiciary have sought to introduce are best understood as attempts to articulate doctrinal safeguards around these referendal innovations. Viewed in this light, the innovations are shifts in the terrain from Parliament to the courts, which are called upon to interpret the weight to be given to these statutes, and can be justified on the basis that the provisions in question are expressions of popular sovereignty.

This explanation provides a clear rationale for the cases surrounding the Brexit process. *R (Miller) v Secretary of State for Exiting the European Union*[35] (commonly known as *Miller (No. 1)*) is best understood as a situation where the effects of a constitutional statute cannot be repealed by virtue of an act of the executive, and *R (Miller) v The Prime Minister*[36] (commonly known as *Miller (No. 2)*) provides that the democratic nature of the British state cannot be overridden by the executive, vindicating both parliamentary and popular sovereignty. In both instances, the courts are attempting to vindicate the deeper constitutional rule of democratic governance in the UK. Of course, in these instances, it might be argued that the vote to leave the EU should have been the determining factor, but that vote itself did not indicate with sufficient clarity the end result in advance. This meant that the parliamentary democratic process had to take place subsequent to, rather than prior to, the vote in question, and therefore the judiciary were minded to ensure that no 'shortcuts' to this parliamentary process would be tolerated, something which was not threatened, for example, in relation to the devolution statutes.

The elaboration of this underlying principle, however, would necessitate some revision of the various limbs of doctrine outlined earlier. The list of statutes which are 'constitutional' would necessarily be shorter. The devolution settlements would fall within this theory, as arguably would

---

35 [2017] UKSC 5.

36 [2019] UKSC 41. See particularly at para 55.

the Human Rights Act 1998 (at least insofar as it related to the devolution settlements), but other statutes would not. This would include the Constitutional Reform Act 2005, which can make two primary claims to changes – it established the Supreme Court and enshrined the value of the rule of law as a constitutional value. In relation to the former, the 2005 Act could hardly be said to have primacy over the Parliament Acts, and in relation to the rule of law, if its efficacy rests on statute, then it may be amended or repealed by statute. If this analysis is followed, it would require a modification in the lists of constitutional statutes currently identified by the courts, but the tendency of the courts to not enforce their own lists of constitutional statutes, indicates their difficulties with articulating a compelling and coherent normative basis for the doctrine.

A recent case heard by the High Court in Northern Ireland helps to expose some of the difficulties of the current iteration of constitutional rules – *Re Allister and In the Matter of the Protocol NI*.[37] The case concerned the introduction of the Northern Ireland Protocol as part of the Brexit process, which effectively erected a customs barrier down the Irish Sea. The applicants argued that this violated the Act of Union 1801. As the Act of Union was a constitutional statute, it was therefore argued that the doctrine of implied repeal did not apply, and therefore the legislation giving effect to the Northern Ireland Protocol was invalid as it did not specifically repeal the Act of Union.

The High Court adopted the conventional view of parliamentary supremacy – the later Act repealed the earlier one, and therefore there was no legal impediment to what Parliament had achieved. A second claim was that when the UK left the EU but Northern Ireland remained within the EU customs orbit, this violated the principle of consent which was part of the Belfast/Good Friday Agreement and was given the force of law by the Northern Ireland Act. This was also rejected, on the basis that the provisions in relation to consent related specifically to the question of whether or not Northern Ireland would remain part of the UK, rather than any internal arrangements within the UK.

Viewed from the articulated position in relation to constitutional statutes, these are problematic results. The Acts of Union are the constitutional core of the UK itself – if anything deserves to be called a constitutional statute, surely they do? Viewed from the point of view articulated in this chapter, however, the problem goes away. The Acts of Union do not have any greater direct democratic legitimacy that is conferred by a referendum, so the normal rules on implied repeal apply to them. The Northern Ireland

[37] The subsequent decision of the UK Supreme Court upheld these elements of the judgment; see [2023] UKSC 5, paras 66 and 84.

Act would benefit from heightened scrutiny, but only insofar as it concerned the principles accepted by the population at the plebiscite, and these had nothing to say about differences in customs borders.

Conclusion

Parliamentary supremacy was an institutional description of the primacy of the legislature within the UK's constitutional framework. The idea has been under consistent consideration, roughly every 30 years, since the UK began to move towards a parliamentary tradition based on the idea of universal adult franchise. Once this movement began, the possibility of a conventional check on the dominance of the Commons within the UK's constitutional structure on the basis of direct democracy gained traction. This was ultimately unsuccessful within the confines of Parliament, but the requirement of a direct democratic mandate outside of a general election was the grounds for the plebiscite on membership of the EEC in the 1970s. This spurred a new line of judicial innovation, which tried to chart a course that gave enhanced protection to this constitutional innovation. The difficulty that the judiciary have faced was that, from a strictly legal point of view, referendums are merely advisory within the UK. However, here the argument has been advanced that the innovations are in fact best explained by reference to this constitutional touchstone. The exact contours of what this means in the 21st century are uncertain, but if the use of plebiscites persists, or indeed accelerates, the maintenance of the Diceyan view of parliamentary supremacy will be unsustainable.

Further reading

Ahmed, F. and Perry, A., 'The Quasi-entrenchment of Constitutional Statutes' (2014) 73(3) *Cambridge Law Journal* 514.

Gordon, M., *Parliamentary Sovereignty in the UK Constitution: Process, Politics and Democracy* (Oxford: Hart Publishing, 2015).

Heuston, R.F.V., *Essays in Constitutional Law* (London: Stevens and Sons, 1961).

Lino, D., 'Albert Venn Dicey and the Constitutional Theory of Empire' (2016) 36(4) *Oxford Journal of Legal Studies* 751.

Young, A., *Parliamentary Sovereignty and the Human Rights Act* (Oxford: Hart Publishing, 2009).

3

Strong Executive, Weak Parliament?

Paul F. Scott

Introduction

The executive is often neglected in the treatment of the British constitution.[1] Partly because its work leaves a written record that is simultaneously more partial, more complex and more likely confidential than those of its counterparts, it is often bypassed in discussions of the appropriate balance of power between the traditional three branches of the state. Even when arguments about the appropriate extent of the executive's authority are made, they are frequently framed in terms of its relationship to those other branches. The executive is therefore for the most part addressed only indirectly.[2] Direct consideration focuses upon a linked set of questions regarding when the executive requires legal authority for its acts and where it might find such authority: statute, the increasingly-contested prerogative[3] and the still enigmatic 'third source'.[4] This chapter

1 The fullest treatment is found in T. Daintith and A. Page, *The Executive in the Constitution: Structure, Autonomy, and Internal Control*, Oxford: Oxford University Press, 1999. The most significant recent consideration of the executive in the UK constitution is found in T. Poole, 'The Executive in Public Law', in J. Jowell and C. O'Cinneide (eds) *The Changing Constitution* (9th edn), Oxford: Oxford University Press, 2019, pp 188–208.

2 A point made frequently in the literature. See, for example, Poole (n 1), quoting Daintith and Page (n 1): the executive 'tends only to be glimpsed in legal texts, usually seen "in some sense, as the reflection of some other organ's concerns and functions"'.

3 Following the decisions of the Supreme Court in *R (Miller) v Secretary of State for Exiting the European Union* [2017] UKSC 5 and *R (Miller) v The Prime Minister and Cherry v Advocate General for Scotland* [2019] UKSC 41.

4 On which see, for example, B.V. Harris, 'The "Third Source" of Authority for Government Action Revisited' (2007) 123 *Law Quarterly Review* 224; and A. Perry, 'The Crown's Administrative Powers' (2015) 131 *Law Quarterly Review* 652.

seeks to excavate the assumptions underlying the standard treatments of executive power within the constitution, starting with how it is that we define the executive, and to reaffirm its relationship to Parliament. This exercise permits a consideration of the executive which is attentive to the many forms it takes in modern times: though the Crown sits at the centre of the executive, and though lines of accountability run back to the Crown from the outer reaches of the modern administrative state, the executive has long ceased to be coextensive with it. This broader framing of the executive is then used to contest certain narratives – both latent and explicit – which have emerged in modern constitutional discourse. These narratives work to bolster the standing of the executive within the constitution, at times by bypassing the legislature out of which the executive is formed and to which it is accountable. They have even, occasionally, been used to attempt to openly subordinate that legislature to the executive.

The argument of the chapter is therefore twofold. First, the executive should be understood in a broader sense, going beyond the core political executive to encompass the wider administrative state which in domestic constitutional theory attracts too little attention. Arguments for a strong executive which ignore that portion of it that is not only empowered but in fact also created by statute are misleading. They encode certain political and legal presuppositions into the question of whether the executive should be, or is, strong. Most strikingly, such arguments have in recent years appeared to assign to the executive a legitimacy of its own, independent of that given to it by Parliament, but nevertheless benefiting from the distorting effect of an electoral system which often translates a minority of votes into the appearance of majority support. That legitimacy has at points been used to justify acting not merely without Parliament but also against it. Second, though there are myriad benefits to a strong executive – when the executive is understood in this sense – a strong executive need not and should not imply a diminished or even supine legislature. Rather, a strong executive of the sort that we should desire is possible only in the presence of a strong legislature, for it is from the legislature that the executive derives not only (the majority of) its legal power to act but also its legitimacy to do so. In the UK the executive, by virtue of the first-past-the-post system used in general elections, often enjoys a majority in the House of Commons which is disproportionate to the degree of support it attracted in the preceding general election. If, even in the context of that disproportionality and other systemic advantages the executive enjoys, the executive does not possess the strength that some desire it to have, perhaps the fault does not lie in the constitutional order. Perhaps it lies instead in the society the constitution governs and the divergences – in values, perhaps, or in material conditions – within it.

What is the executive?

In UK constitutional discourse, at least, the term 'executive' is deployed rather loosely. For the most part it is used to mean the government of the day, encompassing the various strata of ministerial and non-ministerial actors who make up the so-called 'payroll vote' because, as a matter of convention, crystallised in the Ministerial Code, they owe the government their vote. These range from parliamentary private secretaries, who are not part of the government and not paid, but are nevertheless bound by collective responsibility, through parliamentary under secretaries of state, ministers of state, secretaries of state and to, finally, the prime minister, first among equals by virtue (usually) of his or her position as leader of the governing party. Though government is carried out through a variety of departments – not always under that name – the key legal entity is in fact the secretary of state,[5] with the responsibilities of each department reflecting those of the secretaries of state rather than vice versa.[6] In the UK it is this executive that – by convention – exercises the majority of the powers still possessed by the Crown, and when Parliament grants new powers, it does so either to ministers of the Crown or to bodies for which those ministers are more or less directly responsible. Devolved equivalents exist in Scotland, Wales and – though it has often not been in place – Northern Ireland.

This core political executive, however central, is only part of the story. It is supported by a vast body of civil servants – approaching half a million in total.[7] In addition to the various government departments, there exist all manner of bodies that operate with a greater or lesser degree of autonomy: executive agencies, which are 'part of a department and are staffed by civil servants'; non-minsterial departments, which are 'central government departments staffed by civil servants' and are run by a board appointed by a sponsoring minister; and non-departmental public bodies, which 'have a role in the processes of national government, but are not government departments or part of one, and operate to a greater or lesser

---

5 'Secretary of state' means, by virtue of the Interpretation Act 1978, 'one of His Majesty's Principal Secretaries of State'. See, most fully, R. Brazier, *Ministers of the Crown*, Oxford: Oxford University Press, 1997.

6 Changes to the machinery of government therefore involve the making of transfer of function orders under the Ministers of the Crown Act 1975, where – inter alia – legislation makes reference not to 'the secretary of state', but to a specific secretary of state or where not all of those whose roles are implicated in the change are secretaries of state.

7 Cabinet Office, 'Statistical Bulletin - Civil Service Statistics: 2020', 26 August 2020, London: Cabinet Office.

extent at arm's length from ministers'.[8] Though the specific legal form of these bodies varies – even between bodies of the same category – each has two things in common. One is that they are all counted as part of the central government by the Office of National Statistics. A second is that bodies of each type are connected to Parliament via a chain of accountability that runs through one or another minister. What is crucial, however, is that though there is always ministerial accountability, the degree of such accountability varies significantly. The principle which guides the choice of body entrusted with any particular function is that its categorisation should be 'determined by the degree of freedom that body needs from ministerial control to perform its functions'.[9] There is for that reason a constant – if deliberate, and often no doubt productive – tension between the independence of each body and its accountability to Parliament, and before that to the government of the day.

In the modern UK, therefore, the core executive stands at the heart of a much bigger entity, one we might call the administrative state. This term does not sit easily in UK discourse, being used mostly in the US,[10] where the fundamental constitutionality of that administrative state has been disputed.[11] We should include under that heading not only those bodies engaged in the provision of public goods in fields such as welfare or education, but also those which regulate aspects of private enterprise, whether focused on particular sectors or operating across the wider economy. The use of the term is worth insisting upon, for references to administrative law are potentially misleading, in that the phrase refers to a set of general grounds, largely the product of the common law, on which the acts of these bodies might be challenged. Referring to administrative law contributes to the pervasive sense – as will be discussed further later on – that the state is only ever to be restrained and never empowered. To talk instead of the administrative state is to draw attention not only to the vast range of tasks the state undertakes far beyond what is or is not done by the core executive, and the tremendous variety of organisational and legal forms through

---

8 Cabinet Office, 'The cabinet manual: a guide to laws, conventions and rules on the operation of government' (2001) s 3.52, London: Cabinet Office. For further detail, see Cabinet Office, 'Classification of public bodies: guidance for departments' (2016), London: Cabinet Office.

9 Cabinet Office (2016) (n 8) 3.

10 The term was popularised, if not invented, by D. Waldo, *The Administrative State: A Study of the Political Theory of American Public Administration*, New York: Ronald Press Company, 1948.

11 A classic statement of the view that it is not is found in G. Lawson, 'The Rise and Rise of the Administrative State' (1994) 107 *Harvard Law Review* 1231, which opens with the claim that: 'The post-New Deal administrative state is unconstitutional, and its validation by the legal system amounts to nothing less than a bloodless constitutional revolution.'

which it acts, but also, more fundamentally, to the fact that the state exists in order to act. It is a first step towards an argument for a strong executive that reflects, rather than seeking to suppress, the complexity of the modern executive. Moreover, the state, which secures a body of private rights that acts as the background to any action it does or does not take in the here and now, is implicated in the status quo even where its immediate stance is one of inaction.

Strong executives

Modern constitutionalism, often dominated by human rights thinking, reflects a series of broadly liberal presuppositions. The state is supposed to be largely neutral as between different conceptions of the good, creating a framework of 'right' within which citizens can pursue different conceptions of that good. It does – or should – do so for the most part by protecting the freedom of the individual, with freedom understood negatively (so that one is free to the extent that one is not interfered with) and threats to freedom understood to derive primarily, perhaps exclusively, from the state. This sort of liberal constitutionalism is therefore concerned with introducing and enforcing restraints upon the state in its various forms in order to leave the room that the individual requires to pursue his or her ends, or at least to try to. This means, first of all, limits – even if only 'soft' in nature – upon the legislature that protect a set of fundamental rights belonging to individuals against encroachment by the state. But it also calls for limits upon the executive, which in the UK include both the distinct restrictions transposed from the European Convention on Human Rights (ECHR) into domestic law by the Human Rights Act 1998 and those limitations implied by common law grounds of judicial review. The identification of the latter with 'administrative law' both crowds out other forms of administrative justice and makes the same mistake of identifying a part with the whole – looking to put limits on action without first considering the ability to act.

This 'constraint first' approach to executive power has been and might be challenged in a number of ways. One applies distinctively, though not uniquely, to the UK, and follows from the fact that the contemporary executive possesses relatively few inherent powers. Even at the height of Stuart absolutism, when monarchs sought to rule via exercise of prerogative powers and so with minimal recourse to Parliament, there was much the Crown, and the monarch who wore it, could not do alone. Most importantly, the Crown could not change the law of the land, and its ability to tax was strongly contested. The suite of powers it did possess was diminished significantly by the constitutional settlement of 1689–1701, and has been whittled down even further in subsequent centuries, as well as being made subject to a supervision by the courts that is often indistinguishable from that which they carry out on the use of statutory powers.[12] Where, then, the executive seeks to act, especially in those myriad domains that are a concern to the modern administrative state, the executive must first ask Parliament for the power to act. In other words, it must start with authorisation. This does not, though, mean prizing authorisation over constraint – positive over negative constitutionalism, if one prefers.[13] All authorisation brings with it constraint and to that extent the two things are coequal. The question then is what is the nature of the constraints that exist upon any particular power: are they purely substantive or are they also procedural? Do they require ongoing parliamentary approval for particular acts? How are they enforced? These constraints are in the modern constitution augmented by the cross-cutting constraints found in the Human Rights Act,[14] which apply to all bodies that are either public in nature or which are exercising public functions, whether or not they are creatures of statute.

The same point might be made as regards political rather than merely legal restraints. In any passably democratic constitution, the political system, in both its formal and informal aspects, works to constrain the use made of the powers of the state and its organs. Indeed, the classic account of the constitution offered by Dicey is very clear that the absence of legal limitations upon the competence of Parliament goes hand in hand with significant political limitations, which he claims to mean that, in practice, 'the will of the electors shall by regular and constitutional means always in the end assert itself as the predominant influence in the country'.[15] Here too, though, the point might be reversed, so that political pressure not to act (or political backlash for acting in certain ways) must be set against the political expectation that certain actions will be carried out and the electoral and other rewards – actual or anticipated – that flow from acting or promising to act in certain ways. Mass democracy is for that reason often incompatible with a political agenda that wishes the state to restrict its activities to a limited domain or to only protect, and never alter, existing private rights. Accounts that emphasise political backlash yet overlook political demand are just as partial as accounts of executive power which see the law restrain, but never see it first empower. The very existence of the modern administrative state is, it would seem, a function of the democratic demand that the state provide certain goods and regulate private enterprise in the public interest. This point about the influence of politics on law is vital too from the perspective

[12] *Council of Civil Service Unions v Minister for the Civil Service* [1985] AC 374.

[13] The terms used by Nick Barber: see N.W. Barber, *The Principles of Constitutionalism*, Oxford: Oxford University Press, 2018, chapter 1.

[14] Human Rights Act 1998, s 6.

[15] A.V. Dicey, *Introduction to the Study of the Law of the Constitution* (8th edn), Indianapolis: Liberty Fund, 1982 [1885], 27–8.

of the relationship between the executive and legislature, to which we will return later on.

This logical challenge to constraint-first accounts of the executive power is buttressed by a series of political challenges. Many such challenges accept at least some of the basic suppositions of liberal thought outlined earlier, but apply them with varying intensity to certain domains of policy. To generalise crudely, the political right generally emphasises the need for a strong executive within a number of particular areas of policy, the aggregation of which reflects a particular vision of the appropriate role of the state: national security, defence and so on. At the same time, this worldview endorses – and at times demands – strong limitations on the ability of the executive to interfere in domestic affairs, often rising to a generalised and very profound suspicion of the wider administrative state, which interferes (it is said) with rights of property and of contract, which are treated by some as having an existence that precedes and transcends the state. Such a view is right-liberal, clearly, but still recognisably liberal. From the left, liberal arguments for executive constraint similarly reflect a vision of the appropriate role of the state, but the vision in question is, of course, very different. Broadly, such arguments focus upon the domains of foreign policy, defence and internal security. Intervention is, however, prized in broadly economic domains: individual rights of contract are to be circumscribed by rules of general applicability, limits are to be placed upon the use of property, and industry is to be regulated. The basic point, then, is that the dispute is not always, or even usually, between those who think the executive should be strong and those who think it should not be. Rather, the dispute is about where the executive should be strong and, relatedly, what the executive we have in mind is when advancing or rejecting claims of this sort.

In other words, though these positions might appear politically symmetrical, they are not – in the UK at least – legally so. Where the right wishes the state to be strong, we are often operating in the domain of the core political executive: 'His Majesty's Government'. The left, however, has generally looked for strength not in this core executive, but in the wider administrative state, which, though ultimately accountable to that core executive, is in large part operationally independent of it. Moreover, the substance of the residual prerogative power lines up closely with the right-liberal worldview, such that the preservation of that prerogative, and its protection against (further) inroads from the judiciary, is in practice very often a right-wing position. That said, the modern administrative state is almost entirely founded upon statute. The effect, as we shall see, is that the political right does not have to rely on Parliament to the same extent, or as consistently, in order to achieve those goals that, even today often distinguish it most clearly from the political left. It is logical, therefore, for it to seek to empower the executive not only as regards the judiciary – limiting the range of grounds on which executive action might be condemned by the courts – but also in relation to the legislature. This point might be evidenced by the changing nature of arguments about the appropriate scope of judicial power within the British constitution, and in particular the claim that such power already has or might in the future exceed the bounds of appropriateness. In the past such arguments, made mostly from the left, focused upon the encroachment – actual or hypothetical – of the courts upon Parliament. More recently such arguments, now at least as common from the right, are focused just as frequently upon the approach of the courts to the executive in its own right. As will be discussed further later on, such arguments often entail, or at least go hand in hand with, the decentring of Parliament, and sometimes the outright subordination of Parliament to the executive. To a considerable extent, this is a tenable position only because the executive to this day possesses certain limited powers for the existence and use of which it does not rely on Parliament, and because the background distribution of private rights persists whether or not the executive acts.

Though coming at the question from different political angles, both of these positions nevertheless represent varieties of liberal-legalism. More interesting, therefore, are those modern arguments for a strong executive that cut across the left–right spectrum by rejecting the presuppositions shared by liberalism in both its left and right varieties: that the individual stands at the heart of politics and that the state, including the executive, is to be restrained from interfering with at least some of the liberties of the individual. Excessive constraints on the executive will render it incapable of providing those goods that the polity legitimately demands, but which require positive action by the state. Of relevance here is the sense that threats to individual freedom do not emerge solely, perhaps even primarily, from the state, but that such threats can be horizontal in nature, posed by other individuals and private parties, which the state must be empowered to obstruct or ameliorate. For many years, one prominent example of this approach has been 'republican' in nature, premised upon a distinct understanding of what it means for a person to be free.[16] More recently, a distinctive approach to these questions has been that which revolves around the concept of the 'common good'.[17]

While it is obvious that the 'common good' is a formulation that might be made (more or less convincingly) to encompass all manner of substantive ideological projects, it seems equally true that – in the UK at least – any such project will rely not only, or even primarily, upon the executive in order to implement it. Rather, the pursuit of the common good or something like

[16] See, most influentially, P. Pettit, *Republicanism: A Theory of Freedom and Government*, Oxford: Oxford University Press, 1997.

[17] A. Vermeule, *Common Good Constitutionalism*, Cambridge: Polity Press, 2022.

it will require the detailed engagement and ongoing authorisation of the legislature, which alone can permit the sorts of interferences with individual and corporate liberty that the pursuit of any substantive conception of the common good requires. All of which is to say simply that the oft-complacent liberalism which sees executive power as something to be minimised invariably allows for exceptions reflecting particular political ideologies, and is now itself subject to more fundamental challenge with increasing frequency. What is crucial, again, is that all of these approaches argue that, in at least some domains, the executive should have considerable power to act strongly and decisively, effectively prioritising the ability to act ahead of the desire to limit. Where they vary, it is submitted, is in the content of their substantive commitments and – following on from that – the extent to which the positive elements of their vision call for the involvement of the legislature in achieving that vision. The next section will outline the traditional picture of the relationship between Parliament and the executive in the UK before turning to consider the way in which that relationship is subtly reframed in the context of (some) modern arguments for a strong executive in the UK.

The executive and Parliament

The position of the contemporary executive in relation to Parliament is a function of the historic shifts in the relationship between the Crown and Parliament. In the first half of the 17th century, the Crown frequently sought to govern independently of Parliament. This culminated in an 11-year period of personal rule (1629–40) by King Charles I which was brought to an end only as a result of the need to secure funds for the prosecution of the so-called 'Bishops' Wars' that marked the beginning of the 'Wars of the Three Kingdoms': England, Scotland and Ireland. Where that Parliament lasted only a matter of weeks, its successor – the Long Parliament – lasted 20 years, encompassing both that latter war and the formation of a republican Commonwealth across the entirety of Great Britain and Ireland. The Long Parliament eventually came to an end only shortly before the restoration of the monarchy under Charles II. The new constitutional settlement associated with the 'Glorious' Revolution, however, emerged more directly in response to fears that a Roman Catholic dynasty was taking hold under Charles' brother James II. James was deposed, with his crown handed over to his daughter Mary and her husband William of Orange. The operative body of legislation – most importantly, the Bill of Rights 1689 – demonstrates clearly the triumph of Parliament over the Crown. The Crown in Parliament is entitled to determine succession to the throne, as it did once more in the Act of Settlement 1701. A range of prerogative powers that had been claimed by the Stuart monarchs were abolished, and so the ability of the Crown to act without Parliament was significantly constrained. In particular, 'levying money for or to the use of the Crown by pretence of prerogative, without grant of Parliament', the source of much of the constitutional dispute of the first half of the century, was declared illegal.[18] In the same vein, the Meeting of Parliament Act 1694 provided that a Parliament must 'be holden once in Three years at the least'. Governing without Parliament, which had long been difficult, was no longer a practical option.

Not only was the Crown now clearly subordinate to the Crown-in-Parliament in formal terms, but the powers of the Crown were also slowly but surely handed over to a government that was formed out of, and responsible to, Parliament. A few decades after 1689, the modern system of government began to emerge with the appointment of Robert Walpole, who would in time come to be recognised as the first Prime Minister. The last refusal of Royal Assent for a Bill was, famously, the Scottish Militia Bill of 1708. Though the monarch retained a role in government, that role diminished over time, being replaced by a system which was at times described as 'responsible government'. The monarch's role is now governed largely by the 'cardinal convention' whereby the Crown acts on ministerial advice, subject only (it seems) to the tripartite convention of Bagehot – the rights of the monarch to be consulted, to encourage and to warn – and specific conventions relating to the exercise of particular prerogative powers that underpin the political order, such as the appointment of a prime minister. The effect is that though the residual prerogative powers appertain to the Crown and though they are exercised mostly by or on the advice of the government – the political executive – of the day, that government's right to exercise them derives ultimately from Parliament. It was Parliament that won the Civil War, preserving the basic constitutional structure while transforming its normative foundations. The underlying democratic principle – which was weak originally, but became stronger over time – also explains the fact that the centre of gravity within Parliament has shifted so as to privilege the elected Commons over the House of Lords. With this growing democracy comes, as was noted earlier, a growing demand for the state to act, which is difficult to reconcile with the notion that the executive should be weak or that it be strong only in certain, limited areas.

In the contemporary constitution, therefore, the executive is formed out of Parliament and is accountable to it. The key organising principle of that relationship is the confidence principle. The government is the government because it commands the confidence of Parliament.[19] The relationship between the two is in many ways conventional. It is convention

[18] Article 4 of the Bill of Rights 1689.

[19] 'The government of the day holds office by virtue of its ability to command the confidence of the House of Commons': Cabinet Office, 2011 (n 8) para 2.

that the person most likely to command the confidence of the House of Commons – in practice, almost invariably the leader of the largest party – is appointed as prime minister. It is convention that dictates that ministers must be members of the House of Commons or the House of Lords, and that certain ministers must sit in the former rather than the latter. It is convention that dictates the government must resign when it loses the confidence of the Commons. In the meantime, however, in the period between appointment and dismissal, the question arises as to the status of the executive and its legitimacy. The traditional constitutional account views the executive as deriving its legitimacy from Parliament and (it is submitted) as having no independent source of legitimacy.

The executive's 'right to govern'

The abstract picture painted in the previous section in practice brushes up against the practice of electoral politics as it plays out in elections to the Westminster Parliament. Politics is dominated by the leaders of the parties, two of which have dominated for much of the last century. An individual voting in a given constituency is likely to be (at least) as influenced by the desire to have one person rather than another as prime minister as a desire to be represented by a particular constituency member of Parliament (MP), even though his or her vote is several steps removed from the appointment of that, or any, prime minister. Moreover, the first-past-the-post system used in such elections means that it is possible – and, as history shows, by no means unlikely – for a party to command a large majority of the Commons with a vote share significantly lower than 50 per cent. The effect is that not only do voters likely often feel that they are choosing a government and a prime minister – when as a matter of constitutional theory, they are doing no such thing – but that the electoral system also creates the appearance of an executive with far greater underlying support than it in fact enjoys.

Against that background, there have been attempts in recent years to weaken the link between the legitimacy of the government of the day and Parliament, or at least to add to the legitimacy, described in the previous section. The executive derives from its ability to command a majority in the Commons an additional form of legitimacy, conferred directly by the electorate in its effective choice of government. How this distinctive extra-parliamentary legitimacy is framed varies, and – as is typical for arguments regarding the executive – it is often argued for not directly, but by reference to apprehended encroachments by the other elements of the state and in particular courts. So, for example, we see it accepted by the Chair of the Independent Review of Administrative Law at the outset of that body's work in 2020 that there is 'the need to strike a balance between the right of citizens to challenge government through the courts and the elected government's right to govern'.[20] Note in particular the way in which the formulation 'elected government' flattens down considerably the process described in the previous section. But assertions of discrete executive legitimacy are only contingently deployed against judicial power. Once the underlying logic emerges and takes hold, there is no reason to limit its application to that context. One key implication of identifying a source of legitimacy outside Parliament is that Parliament itself – not only the House of Lords, the (largely) appointed chamber, but also the House of Commons, the elected one – might act incompatibly with the legitimate authority of the executive. Stephen Laws, for example, has argued that the government – following Brexit – 'should reassert the right of the government to exercise the functions of government, including the initiative in policymaking and legislation, so long as it retains the confidence of the House of Commons'.[21]

This proposition borders on the senseless where it is considered that what the executive does is legitimate only if, and to the extent that, it commands the support of the House of Commons: not only its confidence but also its support for particular acts or omissions. In other words, the general effect of assertions of the executive's 'right to govern' or similar is, it seems, to extend the binary logic of confidence – either the government has it or it does not – beyond the bare topic of whether the government should remain the government to encompass a range of functions that the government exercises. While it commands the confidence of the House of Commons, the government should be permitted to govern. It, and only it, should be permitted to exercise the functions of government. Two questions might be asked. One is the obvious question of what are those functions of government that it is unconstitutional – in the UK – for Parliament to seek to obstruct or usurp. Second, what is unconstitutional interference with the right of the government to govern? The broader the answers given to these questions, the closer we come to denying Parliament's status as an ongoing source of executive legitimacy, replacing it within the constitutional order with a body that serves only to grant confidence and – exceptionally – to withdraw it. Moreover, this 'right to govern' not only limits what Parliament might do within the domain constitutionally recognised to the executive, but would – it seems – also go so far as to justify the executive acting in order to obstruct

[20] Lord Faulks, quoted in Ministry of Justice, 'Government Launches Independent Panel to Look at Judicial Review' (31 July 2020), Ministry of Justice [online]. Available from: https://www.gov.uk/government/news/government-launches-independent-panel-to-look-at-judicial-review [Accessed 2 April 2023].

[21] Sir S. Laws, 'The future for constitutional reform: lessons from the process of leaving the EU' (2020), London: Policy Exchange. Available from: https://policyexchange.org.uk/wp-content/uploads/Constitutional-Reform-Some-lessons-from-the-UK%E2%80%99s-withdrawal-from-the-EU.pdf [Accessed 2 April 2023].

or undermine the work of Parliament, both in terms of its work in holding the executive to account and in compelling the executive to act in certain ways. Witness, for example, the squabbles over the control of the House of Commons order paper within the context of the Brexit process. Government business – by virtue of Standing Order No 14 – normally takes precedence within the House of Commons, but the House is self-governing and if a majority of MPs chose (as they did) to set aside that rule in order to allow for the passing of legislation that conflicted with the government's intentions, no unconstitutional act had taken place. If the government wished to head off such a drastic course of action, it was of course welcome to suggest some other course of action, one capable of commanding the support of a majority of members of the House of Commons.

Though that was a particularly contested example, it was just one of a number of examples of the way in which the executive has demonstrated a belief that its privileged position in the constitution is necessary rather than contingent, and that such privilege should therefore survive even the direct disagreement of the Commons on particular issues. The most striking instantiations of this phenomenon are those that see the government use (or threaten to use) the formal cover and powers of the Crown – a Crown which in its own right is subordinate to the Crown in Parliament – in order to overcome its own inability to command a majority in Parliament on some particular issue. Two examples were floated more or less seriously within the Brexit process. One involved advising the late Queen to deny Royal Assent to a Bill seeking to delay Brexit. Exploiting the ambiguity as to whether the Royal Assent process is subject to the 'cardinal convention' – the monarch does what the government advises – or a sort of conventional *lex specialis*, whereby consent is given to any bill that has passed both the Commons and the Lords,[22] this argument would in effect have conjured up a new veto point that would allow the executive to block the clearly expressed wishes of a majority in both Houses.

A second would have been even more striking, involving as it did the mechanism known as 'Queen's consent', according to which a bill that affects the prerogative or the interests of the Crown cannot be passed by Parliament if the Queen's consent has not been signalled.[23] Though it is clear from the historical record that the various palaces at times take a close

[22] See the discussion in R. Craig, 'Could the Government Advise the Queen to Refuse Royal Assent to a Backbench Bill?' *UK Constitutional Law Association Blog* [online] (22 January 2019), Available from: https://ukconstitutionallaw.org/2019/01/22/robert-craig-could-the-government-advise-the-queen-to-refuse-royal-assent-to-a-backbench-bill [Accessed 2 April 2023].

[23] R. Craig, 'Proponents of the New Bill to Stop No Deal Face a Significant Dilemma over Queen's Consent' *LSE Brexit Blog* [online] (2 September 2019), Available from: https://blogs.lse.ac.uk/rexit/2019/09/02/proponents-of-the-new-bill-to-stop-no-deal-face-a-significant-dilemma-over-queens-consent [Accessed 2 April 2023].

interest in the detail of bills proposed by the government, what is less clear is the role of the government in this process and whether – as was suggested – it might be able to advise that a bill requiring such consent not be given it.[24] In the event, the issue did not arise, but the belief that such veto points not only exist, but that their use is also constitutionally legitimate indicates the strength of the belief that the executive possesses a legitimacy separate from, and if necessary in opposition to, the Parliament out of which it is formed. Most remarkable of all was the use of the prerogative power of prorogation to shut down Parliament when it appeared liable to force the government to act against its policy on Brexit by seeking a further extension to the Article 50 process.[25] Lord Templeman once noted that a proposition advanced on behalf of the government in litigation before the House of Lords would, if accepted, 'reverse the result of the Civil War'.[26] That claim would seem as – if not more – true of attempts by the government to use the legal form of the Crown (which lost the Civil War) to stymie the efforts of Parliament (which won it) to assert its will when that will contrasts with that of the executive. Moreover, such manoeuvres risk weakening or even breaking the link that Dicey identified between political and legal sovereignty, so that at certain times and on certain issues, the 'predominant influence' in the country is something other than the will of the electors (a category which is much closer to being coextensive with the population now than was the case when Dicey was writing). Like the underlying notion of a 'right to govern', these manoeuvres should be rejected. They reflect a desire for the executive to be strong even in the absence of a clear and ongoing democratic mandate for its deeds, rather than an executive that is strong only where it can command the ongoing and specific support of the House of Commons which gives it legitimacy. They therefore sidestep the real difficulty: achieving strong government in the context of an electorate deeply divided along a variety of lines.

24 House of Commons Political and Constitutional Reform Committee, *The Impact of Queen's and Prince's Consent on the Legislative Process*, Eleventh Report of Session 2013–14, House of Commons, HC 784 (2014), London: The Stationery Office, para 35, which claims that '[w]hen the Queen or the Prince of Wales grant their Consent to Bills, they do so on the advice of the Government' and so, though the process might be characterised as a veto, 'it is a veto that could be operated by the Government, rather than the monarchy'. It may in fact be better understood as a form of pocket veto: rather than advising that consent be withheld, the executive might choose not to seek it in the first place.

25 This was held to be unlawful in *R (Miller) v The Prime Minister and Cherry v Advocate General for Scotland* (n 3).

26 *M v Home Office* [1994] 1 AC 377, at 395.

Strong Parliament, strong executive

None of this is to say, however, that the desire for a strong executive is misguided. As noted previously, most arguments about the appropriate extent of executive power call for the executive to be strong in some areas. Rather, they differ in where the executive should be strong and – in turn – from where its strength should derive. Those on the left, whose political priorities do not usually align with the powers to be found in the residue of the prerogative, have long been accustomed to the idea that to achieve their goals calls for an engagement with Parliament that cannot begin and end with votes of confidence and no confidence, but which must be ongoing. As we have seen previously, the legal powers the executive will need to act broadly and decisively outside of the small domains in which the state was historically empowered by prerogative come from Parliament. So too does the legitimacy to use these powers. Though a vote of confidence may make a certain configuration of parties the government, it does not follow that Parliament must act in any particular way towards that government while it remains so. Parliament is entitled to withhold assent to particular proposals for which such assent is needed, to obstruct courses of action with which it disagrees, and even to seek to take the initiative in acting where the executive seeks, as with Brexit, to use the passage of time to get its way by default. Any of these things will of course be unusual, not only because of the first-past-the-post system but also because any member of the House of Commons – out of which that executive is mostly formed – will be aware of the likely consequences of obstructing a proposal which his or her party supports, to say nothing of the electorate at large. Nevertheless, doing so in extremis is not only constitutional, but also the only way to ensure that Dicey's 'political sovereign' exercises the same sort of influence over the executive's deeds as it does over those of the legislature.

Though much has been written about the concepts of legal and political constitutionalism over the decades, the key observation which would seem to underlie the latter is that within a democracy, what will ultimately happen (or not) should be a function of the ability to win the political argument for it. Obstacles to some initiative or other should not, in the final analysis, be the constitution, or the law, but the fact that enough of one's fellow citizens disagree. This remains true only while the link between the political will and what is or is not done by the political branches of the state remains intact. An approach like that implied by the 'right to govern' narrative, which seeks to make the executive stronger by subordinating Parliament, and especially the elected chamber, to that executive is therefore misguided. These claims are strengthened when we consider the question of the strength of the executive in explicit relation to the broader administrative state, where there is no question of subordinating Parliament to the executive. The relevant agencies, their powers, their mandates and their structures exist – for the most part – only because of some active steps Parliament has taken. A degree of independence has been granted to them, so that the ability of the executive alone to interfere with or redirect their work is limited. The administrative state is a creature of the legislature and ultimately sits in the legislature's control and – at least as currently configured – is incompatible with an idea of a strong executive whose relation to Parliament is that of a zero-sum.

Conclusion

Executive power is making a comeback within constitutional thought, as part of a broader and as yet incomplete project of rebalancing – or seeking to rebalance – power between the different branches of the state. In the UK some of the concerns animating these attempts have been articulated under the heading of the executive's 'right to govern'. Though some such arguments are recognisable variants on well-known arguments about the appropriate role of courts within the constitutional order – albeit aimed more directly at the approach of the courts to executive rather than legislative power – these 'right to govern' claims are of interest in large part because of what they suggest about the relationship between Parliament and the executive within the UK: that the executive has a legitimacy separate from that which it acquires via Parliament, and which permits it to act not just independently of, but also against Parliament.

The framing of these claims at times encodes within them certain assumptions about what the executive is and where it might derive its powers. The executive in question, we understand, is the core executive, not the broader administrative state, which is often disregarded by considerations of the appropriate extent of executive power, at least in the UK. We see this, perhaps most clearly, in one of the most striking modern defences of the executive, by Timothy Endicott.[27] Endicott critiques what he calls the 'stubborn stain' theory of executive power, whereby 'the executive power of the Crown is a stubborn stain that we have only partly succeeded in washing out of the fabric of the constitution'.[28] But his defence of executive power is in large part a defence of prerogative power: there is no acknowledgement that the 'efficient and unified executive branch of government' which he (rightly) holds to be so vital might be efficient and unified in its exercise of statutory rather than prerogative powers. Moreover,

[27] T. Endicott, 'The stubborn stain theory of executive power', London: Policy Exchange, 2017. Available at: https://policyexchange.org.uk/wp-content/uploads/2017/09/The-Stubborn-Stain-Theory-of-Executive-Power.pdf [Accessed 2 April 2023].

[28] Ibid, 7.

for Endicott, as for others, 'the executive' seems to be first and foremost the core political executive – His Majesty's Government – rather than the sprawling administrative state of the modern UK. Here, unity is less easily achieved: the nature of the contemporary state means that different tentacles will have – by design – different interests and different priorities, and those interests and priorities might at times conflict with each other. Nevertheless, we have seen that the entirety of the administrative state can be traced – usually legally, but always constitutionally – back to the Crown.

Strengthening Parliament – even if only by resisting attempts to subordinate it to the executive – does not mean that the government will be left unable to act. The core political executive derives plenty of advantages from contemporary constitutional arrangements. There is much the government might want to do that can, because it has no legal effect, be done without any legal authority at all. Where legal power is required, the prerogative and the third source provide an ongoing ability to act in a number of ways without reference to Parliament. Both Parliament and the electorate – to the extent that the latter pays any attention to governance – are generally content with broad delegations of power to the executive, and the quality of scrutiny associated with secondary legislation is usually poor and often appalling.[29] If legislation is needed, the first-past-the-post system means that the government will usually be capable of attracting support for its proposals without relying on votes from outside the governing party. The ability of the House of Lords to counteract the government's plans is limited strongly by the various ways – legal and conventional – in which the primacy of the Commons is given effect and will be further diminished if the current approach to appointments to the Lords persists at length, such as to question the legitimacy of even the secondary role it performs in modern times. To demand that these advantages be compounded by an acceptance of a free-standing 'right to govern' risks exacerbating the already concerning minoritarian tendencies in contemporary British politics. Better, for our constitution and our politics, that the executive comes to terms with its own reliance on Parliament for its authority, abandoning the project of bringing it to heel. Doing so involves accepting the difficulty of achieving a strong executive in a democratic system where there is so little consensus on political issues, big or small, and in turn considering what steps might be necessary to attract such consensus.

[29] See Chapter 4 in this volume.

Further reading

Allen, J.G., 'The Office of the Crown' (2018) 77 *Cambridge Law Journal* 298.

Cohn, M., *A Theory of the Executive Branch: Tension and Legality*, Oxford: Oxford University Press, 2021.

Daintith, T. and Page, A., *The Executive in the Constitution: Structure, Autonomy, and Internal Control*, Oxford: Oxford University Press, 1999.

Poole, T., 'The Executive in Public Law', in J. Jowell and C. O'Cinneide (eds), *The Changing Constitution* (9th edn), Oxford: Oxford University Press, 2019, 188–208.

Sunkin, M. and Payne, S. (eds), *The Nature of the Crown: A Legal and Political Analysis*, Oxford: Oxford University Press, 1999.

4

Legislating for Seismic Events: An Examination of the Role of Delegated Legislation

Alexandra Sinclair[1]

Introduction

The oft-cited strengths of the UK's system of delegated legislation are its flexibility and responsiveness in the face of an ever-changing society and in moments of crisis. Broad emergency powers were used extensively by the UK Parliament in both World Wars, and in many other crises of the 20th century.[2] It is therefore not surprising that delegated legislation was again turned to during two seismic events affecting the British state in the 21st century: exiting the European Union (EU) and in response to COVID-19. Both events demonstrated that the UK's delegated legislation system needs reform. Delegated legislation is currently used for substantive policy making, far beyond its animating purpose of filling in the details that in practice cannot be dealt with in primary legislation. Delegated legislation's speed and flexibility have proved invaluable when a lot of law needs to

1 My biggest thank you goes to Joe Tomlinson, Public Law Project's former Research Director, who provided me with many hours of mentorship and guidance. I would also like to thank all those who have aided my understanding of delegated legislation, including Tom West, Ruth Fox, Joel Blackwell, Jeff King, Adam Tucker, Arabella Lang, Alison Pickup, Brigid Fowler, Ronan Cormacain and Katie Lines. Thanks also to Se-shauna Wheatle, Lizzie O'Loughlin, the Public Law Project and the Hansard Society.

2 J. King, 'The Province of Delegated Legislation', in E. Fisher, J. King and A. Young (eds) *The Foundations and Future of Public Law: Essays in Honour of Paul Craig*, Oxford: Oxford University Press, 2020, 149.

be made quickly, but its use has had significant drawbacks. Much Brexit and COVID-19 regulation was made with little public consultation or parliamentary oversight.

This chapter begins by examining what delegated legislation is and how it is made in the UK. It then tracks its place in the UK's constitution over the last 100 years and the various attempts to control its growth. The chapter identifies six key problems with the way in which delegated legislation is presently used in the UK, before turning to more recent uses of delegated legislation during the process of exiting the EU and responding to the COVID-19 crisis. It reaches the conclusion that legislating for those two events was a process driven by the executive, with little meaningful parliamentary oversight. Delegated legislation has an awkward role in the UK's constitutional structure, as executive law-making undermines the separation of powers and parliamentary sovereignty, and the present system of delegated law-making leaves little capacity for parliamentary scrutiny. Accordingly, existing oversight mechanisms need to be strengthened to avoid delegated legislation's current democratic deficit.

What is delegated legislation?

Delegated legislation (also known as secondary legislation or regulations) is law made by the executive, that is, by ministers and their government departments under powers given to it by the legislature in primary legislation.[3] The majority of delegated legislation in the UK takes the form of Statutory Instruments (SIs). Unlike primary legislation, delegated legislation cannot be amended in Parliament; it can only be approved or rejected in its entirety. However, delegated legislation that goes beyond the authority granted by the parent act is *ultra vires* and can be declared unlawful by the courts.[4] The Hansard Society's 2014 report on the use of delegated legislation, *The Devil is in the Detail*, differentiates between primary and secondary legislation. Primary legislation is for matters of 'principle and policy', whereas delegated legislation is for 'the regulation of administrative procedures and technical areas of operational detail'.[5]

For the last century delegated legislation has been the predominant way in which laws are made in the UK.[6] The laws that control environmental

---

[3] A. Tucker, 'Brexit and the Problem with Delegated Legislation', in O. Doyle, A. McHarg and J. Murkens (eds) *The Brexit Challenge for Ireland and the United Kingdom: Constitutions Under Pressure*, Cambridge: Cambridge University Press, 2021, 240.

[4] *R (Public Law Project) v Lord Chancellor* [2016] UKSC 39, para 23.

[5] R. Fox and J. Blackwell, *The Devil is in the Detail: Parliament and Delegated Legislation*, London: Hansard Society, 2014, 28.

[6] A. Tucker, 'The Parliamentary Scrutiny of Delegated Legislation', in A. Horne and G. Drewry (eds) *Parliament and the Law*, Oxford: Hart Publishing, 2018, 350.

and food safety standards, financial regulation for banks and entitlements to government benefits are all contained in SIs. In 1921 Cecil Carr, a renowned barrister of the period, in his lectures on delegated legislation, stated that the 'child dwarfed the parent', referring to how much more delegated legislation than primary legislation was made each year.[7] King has observed that 'the child has grown yet larger, while the parent has shrunk'.[8] At present, around 1,750 SIs are made each year, whereas only approximately 30 Acts of Parliament are passed.[9] There is no doubt that it is now the 'standard form of law-making' in the UK, which 'vastly' outweighs the amount of primary legislation.[10]

The majority of SIs are simply 'signed off made' by a minister and never laid before Parliament.[11] SIs that do receive scrutiny are laid before Parliament using either the negative or affirmative resolution procedure – the parent act dictates which is required. SIs made under the negative resolution procedure are as a general rule not debated and automatically enter into force 'unless a motion is passed in either House annulling the instrument'.[12] Delegated legislation that is subject to the affirmative resolution procedure must receive a debate and vote in both the House of Commons and the House of Lords, either in a Delegated Legislation Committee (DLC) or on the floor of the whole house.[13]

DLCs contain 18 members and are made up of a majority of parliamentarians from the government of the day.[14] Negative and affirmative instruments can also be made and brought into force immediately. An instrument will only remain in force if it receives an approval vote in each House within 28 or 40 days of being laid before Parliament (for affirmative instruments) or if it is not prayed against within 40 days of being laid before Parliament (for negative instruments).[15]

The place of delegated legislation in the UK's constitutional order

For as long as delegated legislation has been in use in the UK, there have been concerns over its constitutional role. Delegated legislation sits uneasily

---

7 C.T. Carr, *Delegated Legislation: Three Lectures*, Cambridge: Cambridge University Press, 1921, 2.

8 King (n 2) 146.

9 P. Loft, 'Acts and statutory instruments: the volume of UK legislation 1950 to 2019', House of Commons Library, Commons Briefing Papers (CBP-7438 2019).

10 Tucker (n 6) 350.

11 Fox and Blackwell (n 5) 74.

12 Ibid, 17 and 78.

13 Ibid, 79.

14 Ibid.

15 Ibid, 76.

with parliamentary sovereignty and the separation of powers doctrine because it is essentially 'legislation by the executive'.[16] It gives the executive in effect the final word on many policy matters, with only nominal oversight by or debate within Parliament.[17] This is problematic because, as Tucker notes, 'the executive lacks both the procedural and democratic virtues of Parliament, which are the foundation of the legitimacy of primary legislation'.[18]

As the British state became an industrialised and world power in the 19th century, this resulted in a period of 'imperceptible growth' of delegated legislation.[19] This growth accelerated in the first part of the 20th century, when delegated legislation was vital in assisting the war machine in the First World War and the state's subsequent recovery.[20] Delegated legislation was favoured because it allowed laws to be made quickly and responsively as the state regulated many more areas of daily life. However, the rapid growth in its use during the interwar period began to cause alarm.[21]

This prompted Cecil Carr's lectures on delegated legislation in 1921. Carr noted that 'if [delegated legislation] did not exist it would be necessary to invent it'.[22] Carr described delegated legislation as essential because there was insufficient parliamentary time to make all law via primary legislation. Delegated legislation allowed for flexibility in emergencies and for the drafting of law by those with subject-matter expertise within government departments.[23] Carr viewed its use as consistent with the UK's constitutional arrangements.[24]

In 1928 Lord Hewart wrote a famous objection to delegated legislation, entitled *The New Despotism*.[25] At the time Hewart was the Lord Chief Justice of England and Wales, and his book was a 'blistering attack' on the expanding administrative state.[26] What Hewart viewed as particularly objectionable were

16 Tucker (n 3) 241.

17 Ibid.

18 Ibid.

19 M.J. Taggart, 'From "Parliamentary Powers" to Privatization: The Chequered History of Delegated Legislation in the Twentieth Century' (2005) 55 *University of Toronto Law Journal* 575–627, at 586.

20 Ibid, 613. See also M. Loughlin, *Foundations of Public Law*, Oxford: Oxford University Press, 2010, 443.

21 C. Harlow and R. Rawlings, *Law and Administration* (4th edn), Cambridge: Cambridge University Press, 2022, 213.

22 Carr (n 7) 20.

23 Ibid.

24 Ibid.

25 G. Hewart, *The New Despotism*, London: Ernest Benn Ltd, 1929.

26 Taggart (n 19) 576.

the delegated powers to legislate given to government departments, placing them 'above the Sovereignty of Parliament and beyond the jurisdiction of the Courts'.[27] He described delegated legislation as executive law-making cloaked in a 'parliamentary form'.[28] It was 'despotic' because it escaped parliamentary oversight and because these laws could be written in order to avoid oversight from the courts, meaning neither the legislature nor the judiciary could act as a check on executive power.[29]

Lord Hewart's book prompted the convening in 1929 of the Committee on Ministers' Powers, or the Donoughmore Committee, named after its convenor Lord Donoughmore. Its terms of reference were 'to consider the powers exercised by … Ministers of the Crown by way of … delegated legislation … and to report what safeguards are desirable or necessary'.[30] The Committee concluded that delegated legislation was a 'necessity'.[31] In its report, it offered six reasons for the use of delegated legislation:[32]

1. pressures on parliamentary time;
2. the technicality of the subject matter;
3. dealing with unforeseen contingencies;
4. the need for flexibility;
5. opportunity for experimentation; and
6. the requirement for emergency powers.

The Committee disapproved of delegated legislation in cases where Parliament had 'abandoned its legislative functions'.[33] It acknowledged that delegated legislation could be abused by the executive and was at its most problematic when:[34]

- it created policy;
- skeleton legislation was used where the details were left to ministers;
- Henry VIII powers enabled ministers to rewrite, delete and amend primary legislation when this was the role of Parliament;

[27] Hewart (n 25) 14.

[28] Ibid.

[29] Taggart (n 19) 576.

[30] Committee on Ministers' Powers, 'Report of the Committee on Ministers' Powers' (Cmd 4060, 1932) 6.

[31] Ibid, 51.

[32] Ibid, 51–2; and King (n 2) 147.

[33] Ibid, 20–1; and A. Sinclair and J. Tomlinson, 'Plus ça change? Brexit and the flaws of the delegated legislation system', London: Public Law Project, 2020), 9, Available from: https://publiclawproject.org.uk/content/uploads/2020/10/201013-Plus-ca-change-Brexit-SIs.pdf [Accessed 2 April 2023].

[34] Committee on Ministers' Powers (n 30) 53–4; and Sinclair and Tomlinson (n 33) 9–10.

- delegated legislation ousted the court's supervisory jurisdiction; and
- provisions of primary legislation that delegated power to ministers were so wide that it was not known what was intended by Parliament.

The Committee's recommendations included improving the drafting of bills and using clearer language when delegating powers to ministers, greatly restricting the use of Henry VIII clauses and limiting their duration to 12 months, ensuring that the courts could exercise supervisory control over delegated legislation and improving parliamentary scrutiny of delegated legislation by requiring that all delegated legislation be laid before Parliament.[35] It recommended the creation of standing committees in the Commons and the Lords to review delegated legislation, although it did not suggest that standing committees should have the power to quash unlawful SI.[36]

While the findings of the Committee were positively received, little was done in practice to implement its recommendations and delegated legislation further 'proliferated' during the Second World War and the post-war period.[37] In 1944 a standing committee for the review of delegated legislation was established in the House of Commons and in 1946 the Statutory Instruments Act was passed.[38] In 1949 the constitutional scholar Stanley A. de Smith reviewed delegated legislation in the UK and noted that since the Donoughmore Committee, its use had only increased and was now a 'fact of modern political life'.[39]

Further attempts to review and tame the rise of delegated legislation occurred in the latter half of the 20th century, again with limited effects. In 1973 the Joint Committee on Statutory Instruments (JCSI) was established to review all instruments for drafting errors and whether they exceeded the power given by the parent act. The Delegated Powers and Regulatory Reform Committee (DPRRC) was established in 1992 to review wide delegated powers in bills to help remedy the 'considerable disquiet over the problem of wide and sometimes ill-defined order-making powers which give Ministers unlimited discretion'.[40] In 1996, in the wake of the increase in the number of SIs in the 1990s 'from 2,953 in 1991 to 4,150

35 Committee on Ministers' Powers (n 30) 53–4; and King (n 1) 150–2.

36 Committee on Ministers' Powers (n 30) 53–4.

37 Harlow and Rawlings (n 21) 213.

38 King (n 2) 152.

39 S.A. de Smith, 'Delegated Legislation in England' (1949) 2 *Western Political Quarterly* 514; see also Taggart (n 19) 595.

40 House of Lords Select Committee on the Committee Work of the House ('the Jellicoe Committee'), *Report*, Session 1991–92, HL Paper 35-I; and Fox and Blackwell (n 5) 48.

just a decade later',[41] the Secondary Legislation Scrutiny Committee (SLSC) was established in the House of Lords. Its role is to review negative and affirmative SIs on their merits, in addition to the scrutiny on legality grounds conducted by the JCSI. However, to this day its conclusions remain recommendatory.

The purpose of parliamentary scrutiny of delegated legislation, including parliamentary committees, is in part to 'legitimate the delegation of legislative power' to another branch of government by attempting to 'replicate the parliamentary processes used for primary legislation'.[42] In primary legislation those processes include prior consultation, parliamentary debate, and publication and transparency of the law.[43] However, the weak parliamentary scrutiny processes for delegated legislation, while an improvement on the position when the Donoughmore Committee was convened, are at present insufficient to act as a meaningful check on law-making by the executive. The Supreme Court in *R (Public Law Project) v Lord Chancellor* described delegated legislation as 'subject to much briefer, if any, examination by Parliament'.[44] The inadequacy of these procedures in replicating the scrutiny that primary legislation receives is why delegated legislation is seen by some as on a 'legitimacy precipice'.[45]

The current system allows for very limited public participation, delegated legislation cannot be amended and is very rarely voted down – giving the executive a 'relatively free political hand'.[46] And despite the traditional distinction between primary and secondary legislation, uses of delegated legislation continue 'venturing into the territory of major policy formation'.[47] As this chapter will examine, the twin events of exiting from the EU and responding to COVID-19 highlight delegated legislation's constitutional dysfunction. Not a single Brexit or COVID-19 SI was defeated in Parliament, despite many instruments being subject to heavy criticism during parliamentary debate. In this regard, the traditional separation between the roles of the legislature and the executive is breaking down because it is 'exceptionally convenient' for the executive to write laws using delegated legislation, as the law does not risk amendment or defeat.[48]

---

41 Fox and Blackwell (n 5) 48.

42 Taggart (n 19) 610.

43 Ibid.

44 *R (on the Application of Public Law Project) v Lord Chancellor* [2016] UKSC 39, [2016] AC 1531.

45 Tucker (n 6) 370.

46 Sinclair and Tomlinson (n 33) 13.

47 Taggart (n 19) 608.

48 King (n 2) 156.

Key critiques of delegated legislation in the UK

Most of the contemporary problems with delegated legislation remain 'exactly the same' as those first raised in the early 20th century.[49] Taggart observes that 'there have been no significant advances in our understanding of the reasons for, uses of, and problems arising from delegated legislation since the 1940s'.[50] The six critiques set out in the following text are not an exhaustive list, but are particularly evident in the use of delegated legislation during the exit from the EU and the response to the COVID-19 pandemic.

Used to make policy

While delegated legislation was traditionally for matters of 'operational detail',[51] it is now frequently used to change policy and is 'often the way in which decisions of fundamental national importance are made'.[52] As Hooper says, 'compromises to parliamentary sovereignty and representative democracy inherent in the scrutiny of delegated legislation would be tolerable if its subject-matter was purely technical or trivial'.[53] But in fact it is used to legislate for criminal offences and for controversial law reform, including legal aid eligibility and the notorious 'bedroom tax'.[54] Also, the Country Planning (Napier Barracks) Special Development Order 2021 was used to give planning permission for the Napier Barracks to remain as asylum accommodation until September 2026.[55]

The use of delegated legislation for changes to social and economic policy undermines democratic norms because substantive policy making is deserving of scrutiny and debate by elected officials, which it is unlikely to receive if it is placed in delegated legislation.[56] The SLSC concurs, noting that 'the critical problem about relegating significant policy change to

[49] Fox and Blackwell (n 5) 33.

[50] Taggart (n 19) 608.

[51] Fox and Blackwell (n 5) 28.

[52] Tucker (n 6) 351.

[53] H. Hooper, 'Delegated Legislation in an Unprincipled Constitution', in R. Johnson and Y.Y. Zhu (eds) *Sceptical Perspectives on the Changing Constitution of the United Kingdom*, London: Bloomsbury, 2023 (forthcoming), 7.

[54] Tucker (n 6) 351–2.

[55] Town and Country Planning (Napier Barracks) Special Development Order 2021, SI 2021/962.

[56] Select Committee on the Constitution, 'Delegated legislation and parliament: a response to the Strathclyde Review', 9th Report of Session 2015–16, House of Lords, HL Paper 116, London: The Stationery Office, 2.

secondary legislation is that parliamentary scrutiny of secondary legislation is *far* less robust than that afforded to primary legislation'.[57]

Henry VIII powers

Henry VIII clauses are another key feature of contemporary delegated legislation. Henry VIII clauses are empowering provisions that allow any delegated legislation made under them to amend or repeal statutes.[58] These clauses are particularly 'pernicious'[59] as 'they give the executive the authority to override the requirements of primary legislation and thereby directly violate the principle of parliamentary sovereignty'.[60] For this reason the Constitution Committee has called them a 'departure from constitutional principle' and the Donoughmore Committee suggested they be used only in 'exceptional circumstances'.[61]

The volume of Henry VIII clauses in recent times is stark and appears unnecessary. Only nine Henry VIII powers were ever used before 1932 and Lord Rippon protested the use of four in the 1987–88 parliamentary session.[62] By contrast, Lord Judge gave a speech highlighting over 100 such clauses in the 2009–10 parliamentary session and there were 96 Henry VIII powers in 16 Government Bills in the 2015–16 parliamentary session.[63]

Skeleton bills

Skeleton bills provide 'only the broadest outlines of policy travel' and leave 'the parts that will have direct impact on members of the public to secondary legislation' where, as explained, it is subject to much lower levels of scrutiny.[64] They undermine the separation of powers by being essentially a 'legislative blank cheque' to the executive.[65] They also undermine Parliament's role

---

57 Secondary Legislation Scrutiny Committee, 'Government by diktat: a call to return power to parliament', 20th Report of Session, 2021–22, House of Lords, HL Paper 105, London: House of Lords, para 18.

58 N. Barber and A. Young, 'The Rise of Prospective Henry VIII Clauses and Their Implications for Sovereignty' [2003] *Public Law* 112.

59 Sinclair and Tomlinson (n 33) 12.

60 Tucker (n 6) 359.

61 Select Committee on the Constitution, 'The legislative process: the delegation of powers', 16th Report of Session 2017-19, House of Lords, HL Paper, London: House of Lords, para 67 and Committee on Ministers' Powers (n 30) 6.

62 King (n 1) 155.

63 Lord Judge, 'Ceding Power to the Executive: The Resurrection of Henry VIII' (King's College London, 12 April 2014; and Hansard Society, 'Westminster Lens: Parliament and Delegated Legislation in the 2015–16 Session' (2017), London: Hansard Society, 4.

64 Secondary Legislation Scrutiny Committee (n 57) para 1.

65 Ibid, para 30.

in scrutiny because 'there is nothing to scrutinise'.[66] While skeleton bills have always been used by governments, the SLSC, the DPRRC and the Constitution Committee have noted a 'growing tendency for the government to introduce skeleton bills, in which broad delegated powers are sought in lieu of policy detail'.[67] They have described this as an 'exceptional shift in power from Parliament to the executive'.[68]

Invulnerability to defeat

One of the key elements of effective parliamentary scrutiny of primary legislation is that the legislation can be, and often is, amended as it proceeds through both Houses. Legislation that does not have the support of a majority of both Houses cannot be passed. By contrast, delegated legislation is unamendable and is rarely ever voted down in DLCs. Parliamentary sovereignty is undermined because in effect the executive can make law unchallenged. Only 17 SIs have been voted down in the last 65 years and the House of Commons has not rejected an SI since 1979.[69] Between 1950 and 2017, the rejection rate for SIs was 0.001 per cent.[70] This means that unlike primary legislation, there is virtually no risk of a policy placed in delegated legislation not becoming law. This perversely incentivises the placing of controversial laws in delegated legislation because the government can be assured they will pass in their current form.[71]

Lack of consultation

Most SIs do not have minimum consultation requirements and due to this, consultation is 'rare', and when it occurs, it is generally 'ad hoc'.[72] This lack of public participation in the formation of the instrument is compounded by the fact that DLCs are poorly publicised and convened with little notice.[73] Nothing has been done to formalise public participation in the process.[74]

---

[66] Lord Judge, 'Annual Bingham Lecture 2017: A Judge's View on the Rule of Law' (2017). London: Bingham Centre for the Rule of Law, 3 May.

[67] Secondary Legislation Scrutiny Committee (n 57) para 31.

[68] Ibid, para 35.

[69] Hansard Society (n 63) 5; Loft (n 9).

[70] King (n 2) 161.

[71] E.C. Page, *Governing by Numbers: Delegated Legislation and Everyday Policy Making*, Oxford: Hart Publishing, 2001, 186.

[72] Sinclair and Tomlinson (n 33) 28.

[73] Fox and Blackwell (n 5) 184. See also Page (n 70) 129 and 153–5.

[74] Ibid, 184.

Inadequate scrutiny

The majority of secondary legislation is not laid before Parliament and so definitionally is not scrutinised.[75] Furthermore, the majority of the legislation that is laid before Parliament is subject to the negative resolution procedure, which presumptively means it is never debated.[76] In the 2016–17 parliamentary session MPs debated 0.9 per cent of the 537 negative procedure SIs laid before Parliament.[77] Even SIs that are 'prayed against' are not automatically debated as the government controls the parliamentary timetable. In the 2015–16 parliamentary session only five of the 12 prayer motions tabled by the opposition were granted a debate, thereby undermining the effectiveness of Parliament's only means of scrutinising negative procedure instruments.[78]

The level of debate and scrutiny afforded to affirmative procedure instruments tends to be poor. MPs are not placed in DLCs based on their subject-matter expertise, which means they do not always understand the highly technical and complex instruments they are debating. Furthermore, the quality of the impact assessments and explanatory material which is supposed to aid MPs and Peers in their understanding can be highly variable, making it even more difficult for parliamentarians to fulfil their scrutiny role. Fox and Blackwell note that 'as long as the quality of [explanatory memoranda] are below what Parliament ought to expect, it almost ensures that individual MPs and peers are unlikely to take up issues of concern because much of the process is impenetrable'.[79]

SIs can be long and complex, but tend not to be subject to sufficient debate to allow proper scrutiny. The average length of debate of an SI in the 2015–16 parliamentary session was 26 minutes, but one SI was debated for only 22 seconds.[80] The Constitution Committee has noted that 'there is little incentive for members of either House, but particularly the House of Commons, to spend their precious time debating legislation that they cannot change'.[81] Further, DLCs are seen as low status among MPs and peers. This is markedly demonstrated by the Hansard Society's observation that MPs have been told that 'it was perfectly acceptable – indeed preferable – to get on with their constituency correspondence during a DLC meeting'.[82]

---

[75] Ibid, 5.

[76] Ibid, 6.

[77] R. Fox, J. Blackwell and B. Fowler, 'Taking back control for Brexit and beyond: delegated legislation, parliamentary scrutiny and the EU (withdrawal)' *Bill*, London: Hansard Society, 2017, 30.

[78] Ibid.

[79] Fox and Blackwell (n 5) 214.

[80] Ibid, 80.

[81] Select Committee on the Constitution (n 56) 2.

[82] Fox and Blackwell (n 5) 182.

Committees cannot amend SIs, and only in the very rarest of circumstances can they vote them down. Therefore, the very highest level of procedural scrutiny afforded to SIs – the affirmative resolution procedure – affords them much less scrutiny than primary legislation. This only highlights delegated legislation's democratic deficit.

Brexit delegated legislation

The critiques of delegated legislation described earlier have been a consistent feature of debates on the failings of delegated legislation.[83] The UK's decision in 2016 to leave the EU brought these problems into sharp relief. Delegated legislation was the only way in which to adapt EU law in readiness for Exit Day. A total of 622 Brexit SIs were made between the EU (Withdrawal) Act 2018 (EUWA) receiving Royal Assent on 26 June 2018 and the eventual Exit Day of 30 January 2020.[84] The examples that follow show that this was a process dominated by the executive, where Parliament's scrutiny role was inhibited.

The EU (Withdrawal) Act 2018

In the aftermath of the UK referendum on EU membership, the government decided that to ensure legal continuity, EU law, as it stood on Exit Day, would continue to apply in the UK as part of domestic law. From Exit Day onwards, EU law could be changed and departed from. The EUWA was passed to create a 'snapshot' of all EU law operating in the UK on Exit Day.[85] This was called 'retained EU law'. Section 8 of EUWA gave the power to ministers via delegated legislation to amend any retained EU law so that it could 'operate effectively' in the UK after Exit Day.[86] For example, EU regulations that were to become part of UK domestic law needed to be amended so that they no longer made reference to EU organisations of which the UK was no longer a member. For ministers to make regulations under section 8, there needed to be a 'failure of retained EU law to operate effectively, or any other deficiency in retained EU law arising from the Withdrawal of the United Kingdom from the EU'.[87] Section 8 was a Henry VIII power that enabled ministers to amend any piece of existing primary legislation.[88] Notably, the EUWA contained an enhanced scrutiny procedure that provided for

[83] Ibid.
[84] Sinclair and Tomlinson (n 33) 21.
[85] Ibid, 16.
[86] EU (Withdrawal) Act 2018, s 8.
[87] Ibid.
[88] Ibid, s 8(5).

the European Scrutiny Committee to review all negative procedure SIs and make recommendations for SIs to be upgraded to the affirmative resolution procedure.

During the passage of the EUWA, the government was keen to distinguish between the 'mechanical act'[89] of converting EU law into retained EU law, which it said could be conducted using delegated legislation made under section 8, and changes in substantive UK policy post-Brexit which was to be done by the UK's key Brexit Bills.[90] These were pieces of primary legislation that were to herald a sea change in UK immigration, agriculture, fisheries, environmental and trade policy. The government said that section 8 'was not to be a vehicle for policy changes but it will give the Government the necessary power to correct or remove the laws that would otherwise not function properly once we have left the EU'.[91]

Features of Brexit SIs

Parliamentary scrutiny was severely hampered by the large number of SIs that needed to be scrutinised in a short period of time. A total of 359 Brexit SIs were laid before Parliament in the four months leading up to the initial March 2019 exit date.[92] During this time, MPs and peers were expected to review and debate long and highly complex instruments. SIs laid during this period were much longer than the average in a parliamentary session.[93] For example, the Plant Health (EU Exit) Regulations were 212 pages long and contained 17 separate schedules, and the Product Safety and Metrology etc. (Amendment etc.) (EU Exit) Regulations 2019 were 619 pages long. The SLSC said the size of the Product Safety Regulations 'inhibited effective scrutiny'.[94] As Dr Joe Tomlinson and I have pointed out, 'many of the instruments, when read alone, are simply a string of amending provisions referring to the provisions of other legal texts'.[95] Given this, good-quality supporting material was vital

89 Select Committee on the Constitution, 'The "Great Repeal Bill" and delegated powers', 9th Report of Session 2016–17, House of Lords, Paper, London: House of Lords, para 16.

90 See the Foreword by Rt Hon David Davis MP, Secretary of State for Exiting the European Union, to Department for Exiting the European Union, 'Legislating for the United Kingdom's withdrawal from the European Union', London: The Stationery Office, 7.

91 Ibid.

92 I here define a Brexit SI as any instrument in which the Explanatory Note stated that it was being made to facilitate the UK's withdrawal from the EU.

93 King (n 2) 168.

94 Secondary Legislation Scrutiny Committee (Sub-Committee B), 'Proposed Negative Statutory Instruments under the European Union (Withdrawal) Act 2018 [...]', '17th report of session 2017–19', House of Lords, Paper, London: House of Lords, para 55.

95 Sinclair and Tomlinson (n 33) 24.

to assist parliamentarians in reviewing the Brexit regulations. Unfortunately, the supporting material provided was not up to the task.

The role of explanatory memoranda is to explain what an instrument does and its purpose. Impact assessments (IAs) evaluate legislative policies and their projected financial costs and benefits. In the 2017–19 Parliamentary Session, the SLSC reported that 15 per cent of all explanatory memoranda for affirmative instruments needed replacing to correct errors, when its benchmark for replacement is 5 per cent.[96] The SLSC has been highly critical of the quality of explanatory memoranda provided. For example, the memorandum accompanying the Law Enforcement and Security (Amendment) (EU Exit) Regulations 2019 was so inadequate that the committee had to rely on a BBC news article to understand the costs of the instrument to the UK criminal justice system.[97] The government failed to lay the required IAs for the Brexit SIs before Parliament and on one occasion provided a single IA for ten instruments with a collective financial impact of £140 million.[98]

Extremely lengthy Brexit SIs were debated for short amounts of time, further undermining parliamentary accountability. The Aviation Safety (Amendment etc.) (EU Exit) Regulations 2019 were 146 pages long and were debated for 21 minutes in the House of Commons.[99] The Product Safety and Metrology etc. (Amendment etc.) (EU Exit) Regulations 2019 were 619 pages long and were debated in the Commons for 52 minutes and the Lords for 51 minutes.[100] The Financial Services (Miscellaneous) (Amendment) (EU Exit) Regulations 2019 were 26 pages long and made 36 different amendments to laws that Lord Tunnicliffe described as having 'no themes or interrelationship' and were debated for 11 minutes in the House of Commons.[101] It is 'patently impossible' to fully debate such long and complex instruments in such short time periods.[102]

Parliamentarians were highly critical of many of the Brexit SIs they debated, but no Brexit SIs were defeated.[103] The REACH etc. (Amendment

---

[96] Secondary Legislation Scrutiny Committee, 'Work of the Committee in Session 2017–19: Correspondence: quality of information provided in support to secondary legislation', 60th reports of session 2017–19, House of Lords, paper, London: House of Lords, para 18.

[97] Secondary Legislation Scrutiny Committee, (Sub-Committee A), 'Proposed Negative Statutory Instruments under the European Union (Withdrawal) Act 2018 [...]', 17th Report of Session 2017–19, House of Lords, HL Paper, London: House of Lords, para 18.

[98] Sinclair and Tomlinson (n 33) 25.

[99] A. Sinclair and J. Tomlinson, 'How Abuse of Delegated Legislation Makes a Mockery of Law-Making' (2020) *Prospect Magazine*, 8 December.

[100] Sinclair and Tomlinson (n 33) 21.

[101] Ibid; and HL Deb 21 March 2019, vol 796, col 1576.

[102] Sinclair and Tomlinson (n 33) 21.

[103] While this chapter has relied on data from those EU exit SIs laid before Parliament between 26 June 2018 and 30 January 2020, no Brexit SIs laid after that date have been annulled.

etc.) (EU Exit) Regulations 2019 were 68 pages long and were first tabled by the government three days before the initial 31 March 2019 Exit Day.[104] In debate, the opposition described the many 'flaws' in the legislation and described the government's timing in laying the regulations before Parliament immediately before Exit Day as 'brinkmanship', which left them with no option but to approve them or otherwise to risk gaps in the law.[105] Prayer motions were lodged against 10 of the 350 negative procedure SIs made, but the government scheduled only one debate – on the Railways (Interoperability) (Amendment) (EU Exit) Regulations 2019.[106] For affirmative procedure instruments there were ten non-fatal motions debated out of 272 instruments and only two motions of regret passed. However, motions of regret have no practical effect.[107]

The process also suffered from a lack of consultation or public input. Only around 11 of the 622 instruments passed before 30 January 2020 had any formal consultation process and the Nutrition (Amendment) (EU Exit) Regulations 2019 consultation was only open for 11 days.[108] There were notable problems with many instruments. The Plant Protection Products (Miscellaneous Amendments) (EU Exit) Regulations 2019 removed a provision banning hormone-disrupting chemicals in pesticides.[109] The Department for Environment, Food and Rural Affairs described the removal of the provision as 'erroneous' and reinstated it, after receiving a letter from the environmental organisation ChemTrust.[110] The Jurisdiction and Judgments (Family) (Amendment etc.) (EU Exit) (No 2) Regulations 2019 were laid before Parliament after concerns from family law practitioners that the initial SI prevented the courts from being able to issue certain orders.[111] It is likely these errors could have been avoided if there had been prior consultation with affected groups.[112]

The government laid 30 instruments before Parliament using the made affirmative urgency procedure under the EUWA, seemingly because it had

---

104 HL Deb 26 March 2019, vol 796, col 1731.

105 Ibid.

106 Railways (Interoperability) (Amendment) (EU Exit) Regulations 2019, SI 2019/345.

107 These instruments were the REACH etc. (Amendment etc.) (EU Exit) Regulations 2019, SI 2019/758 and the Freedom of Establishment and Free Movement of Services (EU Exit) Regulations 2019, SI 2019/1401. See HL Deb 26 March 2019, vol 796, col 1755; and HL Deb 23 October 2019, vol 800, col 640.

108 Sinclair and Tomlinson (n 33) 26.

109 Plant Protection Products (Miscellaneous Amendments) (EU Exit) Regulations 2019, SI 2019/556.

110 Sinclair and Tomlinson (n 33) 26.

111 Civil Jurisdiction and Judgments (Civil and Family) (Amendment) (EU Exit) Regulations 2019, SI 2019/1338.

112 Sinclair and Tomlinson (n 33) 26.

run out of time to debate them in advance of Exit Day.[113] In a no-deal scenario, this could have meant that significant instruments covering a range of policy areas would have been in force before being debated.

COVID-19 statutory instruments (SIs)

The process of exiting the EU was to be an 'unprecedented' exercise of delegated law-making, and then the COVID-19 pandemic arrived.[114] As of 3 March 2022, the government had laid 582 COVID-19 SIs before Parliament since the first COVID-19 SI was laid on 28 January 2020.[115] The flexibility of delegated legislation in responding to the COVID-19 crisis showed one of the biggest benefits of the UK's system. Laws were written quickly to respond to a problem that was inconceivable a year before. However, Parliament was afforded little input into these momentous laws. A total of 417 of the 582 COVID-19 SIs were subject to the negative procedure, meaning they received no debate in Parliament. Many of these regulations made significant changes to a wide range of UK law. The Prosecution of Offences (Custody Time Limits) (Coronavirus) (Amendment) Regulations 2020 extended the maximum period a person could remain in prison on remand from 182 to 238 days and were not debated.[116]

The government produced IAs for virtually none of the 582 COVID-19 SIs, saying they were unnecessary due to their time-limited nature, but many were extended past their initial 12-month period in force. MPs and peers repeatedly pointed out that a lack of IAs inhibited scrutiny. Baroness Thornton asked why Parliament was "not seeing any impact assessments at all, on any of these statutory instruments. Surely that must be possible, and it is not respectful of Parliament and accountability that those have not been forthcoming".[117] Sir Christopher Chope MP enquired how the government could ask the House to support the regulations that provided the roadmap for leaving the 2021 lockdown "when there is not even an impact assessment for them".[118]

---

113 See, for example, the Explanatory Memorandum to the Rights, Equality and Citizenship Programme (Revocation) (EU Exit) Regulations 2019, SI 2019/1339, para 5.2.

114 Select Committee on the Constitution, 'European Union (Withdrawal) Bill: interim report', 3rd Report of Session 2017–19, House of Lords, paper, London: House of Lords, para 44.

115 Hansard Society, 'Coronavirus Statutory Instruments Dashboard, 2020–2022'. Available from: https://www.hansardsociety.org.uk/publications/data/coronavirus-statutory-instruments-dashboard [Accessed 5 January 2023].

116 Prosecution of Offences (Custody Time Limits) (Coronavirus) (Amendment) Regulations 2020, SI 2020/953).

117 HL Deb 18 September 2020, vol 805, col 1561.

118 HC Deb 25 March 2021, vol 691, col 1153.

The explanatory memoranda provided for COVID-19 SIs were also inadequate. The SLSC pointed out that between July and September 2021, 12.5 per cent of explanatory memoranda had to be withdrawn for errors, when, as stated earlier, the SLSC's benchmark for replacement is 5 per cent. Some memoranda proved inadequate to the task of explaining the rationale for the decisions made. For example, the SLSC noted that none of the explanatory notes accompanying the four-tier COVID-19 alert system SIs 'provided evidence of the reasons for selecting those areas for the tier to which they have been assigned'.[119]

There is no better example of the way that Parliament was sidelined than the government's use of the made affirmative urgency procedure. A total of 118 of the 582 SIs were brought into force by the government immediately and were only debated once the law was already in effect and regulating the public's conduct. Some of these regulations introduced unprecedented criminal fines and restrictions upon the public. These SIs significantly affected civil liberties and were deserving of debate *prior* to their application to the general public.

For example, the Health Protection (Coronavirus, Restrictions) (England) (Amendment) (No 3) Regulations 2020 came into force on 1 June 2020 and were debated on 15 June 2020. However, by the time parliamentarians debated these regulations they were redundant, as the government had already brought into force on 12 June a further relaxation of restrictions. The new 'No 4' regulations allowed for the reopening of non-essential retail businesses and for individuals living alone to form 'bubbles' with another household.[120] Some MPs in the debate on the No 3 regulations wished to debate the No 4 regulations that had superseded them. Justin Madders MP said:

> We are here today to consider the third iteration of the regulations, just as further relaxations come into force to allow non-essential shops to open for the first time. Those measures are probably the single largest relaxation since lockdown was introduced – but we are not here to debate those changes.[121]

Many measures were laid before the parliamentary recess and debated after recess, meaning they were in force for up to eight weeks before the debate. In a DLC debate on 21 September 2020, Alex Norris MP pointed out that

[119] Secondary Legislation Scrutiny Committee, 'Draft Definition of Qualifying Northern Ireland Goods (EU Exit) Regulations 2020 [...]', '31st report of session 2019–21', House of Lords, paper, London: House of Lords, para 41.

[120] Health Protection (Coronavirus, Restrictions) (England) (Amendment) (No 4) Regulations 2020.

[121] HC Deb 15 June 2020, vol 677, col 587.

there were 17 measures being debated that week, all of which were already in force.[122] It was understandable when the COVID-19 pandemic first began that the government needed to introduce laws as a matter of urgency, but throughout 2020, 2021 and even 2022, the government continued to lay all SIs made under the Public Health (Control of Disease) Act 1984 before Parliament this way, bringing them into force immediately and only allowing for debate on them in the subsequent weeks. Justin Madders was again apposite on this point:

> As we have said many times, we of course accept that the initial regulations had to be introduced hurriedly, in response to the rising number of infections, but the House has been up and running for many months now, and with Members on both sides of this House and in the other place raising concerns about why time is not being provided to ensure that future changes are debated and therefore have democratic consent before they are introduced, we see no good reason why the Government continue to act in the way they do.[123]

No COVID-19 SI was defeated. A particularly controversial SI imposed a 10 pm curfew on pubs and restaurants in October 2020.[124] This SI appeared to significantly harm hospitality and the government's Scientific Advisory Group had said the curfew would have a marginal effect on transmission. MPs who were against the measure stated in debates that they felt they could not vote against it because to do so would be to vote down the other necessary COVID-19 measures contained within the same instrument.[125] This highlights one of the intrinsic flaws of SIs, which is that they cannot be amended, but can only be approved or annulled in their entirety.

The lack of consultation in the preparation of COVID-19 SIs was also exclusionary and potentially harmful. The Department of Transport failed to consult with the disabled community before introducing a requirement of wearing a face covering when using public transport. The Adoption and Children (Coronavirus) (Amendment) Regulations 2020 made significant changes to adoption and foster care protocols for the duration of the pandemic. The Court of Appeal found the lack of consultation and particularly the failure to substantively consult with the Children's Commissioner, save for sending the Commissioner one email, meant that the instrument was unlawful.[126]

---

[122] HC Deb 21 September 2020, col 8.

[123] Ibid, col 7.

[124] Health Protection (Coronavirus, Restrictions) (No 2) (England) (Amendment) (No 5) Regulations 2020.

[125] HC Deb 13 October 2020,vol 682, col 203.

[126] *R (on the Application of Article 39) v Secretary of State for Education* [2020] EWCA Civ 1577.

Conclusion

The SLSC is correct to observe that the balance of power between Parliament and government has shifted away from Parliament.[127] Parliament was sidelined in the process of Brexit and COVID-19 law-making. Negative procedure SIs were prayed against in the House of Commons and the government did not schedule debates. Time and time again, the government chose to bring very significant laws into force, prior to parliamentary debate. Public consultation was severely lacking and resulted in one successful challenge in the courts. Not a single SI was defeated in Parliament despite the controversial nature of many of the measures.

The problems with delegated legislation highlighted here need to be addressed or they will almost certainly reappear the next time there is a need for rapid law-making. Delegated legislation is a modern-day necessity; due to the limitations on parliamentary time and the myriad things to which a modern administrative state must tend, it would be impossible for all law-making to be conducted via primary legislation. However, the UK's system of delegated legislation currently concentrates too much power in the executive, leaving little room for parliamentary oversight. Much delegated legislation is not placed before Parliament, and Parliament is not given the time, supporting material or procedures to effectively scrutinise that which is.

The Hansard Society has made recommendations for reform, including allowing conditional amendments of certain SIs, guaranteeing debate on negative procedure SIs that are prayed against and imposing penalties for poor-quality memoranda or failures to lay IAs before Parliament.[128] Sadly, there does not seem to be much appetite for reform, as the current system benefits the government of the day. The Constitution Committee has recognised this bind and notes that 'the Government can pass legislative proposals with greater ease and with less scrutiny where they are able to do so through secondary, rather than primary, legislation'.[129] The reality is that 'delegated powers are exceptionally convenient for a government'.[130] Unfortunately, as long as substantive policy continues to be enacted through delegated legislation, where effective scrutiny of it is limited, delegated legislation will continue to exist on its 'legitimacy precipice'.[131]

[127] Secondary Legislation Scrutiny Committee (n 57) para 15.

[128] For instance, see the proposals in Fox and Blackwell (n 4).

[129] Select Committee on the Constitution (n 56) 2.

[130] King (n 2) 156.

[131] Tucker (n 6) 370.

Further reading

Fox, R., Blackwell, J. and Fowler, B., *Taking Back Control for Brexit and beyond: Delegated Legislation, Parliamentary Scrutiny and the EU (Withdrawal) Bill*, London: Hansard Society, 2017.

King, J., 'The Province of Delegated Legislation' in L. Fisher, J. King and A. Young (eds) *The Foundations and Future of Public Law: Essays in Honour of Paul Craig*, Oxford: Oxford University Press, 2020, 145–72.

Lines, K., *18 Months of COVID-19 Legislation in England: A Rule of Law Analysis* (16 October 2021), London: Bingham Centre for the Rule of Law.

Secondary Legislation Scrutiny Committee, 'Government by diktat: a call to return power to parliament', 20th Report of Session 2021–22, House of Lords, paper 105, London: House of Lords.

Sinclair, A. and Tomlinson, J., 'Plus ça change? Brexit and the flaws of the delegated legislation system', London: Public Law Project, 2020.

Tucker, A., 'The Parliamentary Scrutiny of Delegated Legislation', in A. Horne and G. Drewry (eds) *Parliament and the Law*, Oxford: Hart Publishing, 2018.

5

Scotland, Devolution and Independence: A Union at its Limits?

Coree Brown Swan

Introduction

Devolution saw the significant transfer of power from the UK to the Scottish level – including competences over health, education, agriculture and the environment. These powers were used to deliver policies unique to Scotland – the abolition of university tuition fees and prescription drug charges, minimum pricing for alcohol and the reduction of the voting age. However, little attention was paid to how devolution might impact the governance of the UK as a whole or how, after devolution, governments would work together to address common challenges.

Devolution was, in the words of George Robertson, the former Labour Shadow Secretary of State for Scotland, designed "to kill nationalism stone dead",[1] satisfying the self-government ambitions of most Scots and undercutting the Scottish National Party (SNP), which had demanded, with little success, independence for Scotland. However, in the two decades since the first election to the Scottish Parliament, the issue has been anything but settled.

Devolution enjoys broad support among the electorate and recent years have seen the further transfer of powers – including elements of taxation, borrowing powers and further legislative competences. However, these efforts

[1] https://www.scotsman.com/news/scottish-news/scottish-parliament-20-why-devolution-failed-kill-nationalism-stone-dead-1418095; https://www.bbc.co.uk/news/uk-scotland-31129382

have not satisfied those who want further devolution or independence. In 2014, following successive victories by the SNP, Scottish voters were asked, in a referendum agreed by the UK government, 'Should Scotland become an independent country?'. The proposal was rejected, albeit by a narrower margin than expected, but the issue remains a live one. It also has implications beyond Scotland, leading to questions about the future of devolution in Wales and Northern Ireland – each with its own form of devolution and constitutional dynamics – the governance of England, and the very future of the Union.

The UK's 2016 vote to leave the European Union (EU) – and the protracted negotiations that followed the referendum – raised both the salience and the stakes of these questions. It fuelled demands for a second referendum on independence in Scotland, which had voted by a significant majority to remain. It also exposed the weaknesses in the UK's uncodified constitution – calling into question the status of the devolution settlements and laying bare the inadequacies of the UK's system of intergovernmental relations, through which different levels of government coordinate. These questions are likely to be central to Scottish political life in the coming years.

The first section of this chapter sets out key principles necessary for understanding debates on devolution, independence and union. The second presents the devolution settlement, elaborating on the primary constitutional structures, the distribution of powers and its evolution from 1999 to the present day, encompassing the independence debate. The third explores the constitutional chain reaction set off by the Scottish vote on independence and places Scottish devolution in a broader UK context. The final section examines the implications of the UK's vote to leave the EU for both the internal functioning of the UK and the Union's future.

Devolution, power and parliamentary sovereignty

Devolution was one of the UK's most significant constitutional reforms, seeing the transfer of power to Scotland, Wales and Northern Ireland.[2] However, it did not fundamentally change the structure of the UK as a state or alter the balance of power within it. 'But for devolution', Aileen McHarg argues, 'the UK remains a highly centralised state'.[3] As a result, there has been a tendency to *devolve and forget*, and a reluctance to reform or adapt the structures of the

[2] Devolution to Northern Ireland long predated devolution to Scotland and Wales, but has had long periods of suspension and direct rule. Devolution was restored in Northern Ireland with the Belfast/Good Friday Agreement, which was contemporaneous with the devolution agreements.

[3] McHarg, A. (2019) 'The future of the United Kingdom's territorial constitution: can the Union survive?', in A. López-Basaguren and L. San-Epifanio (eds) *Claims for Secession and Federalism*, London: Springer, 139–61.

UK state to better accommodate the preferences of the devolved nations or allow for cooperation on shared issues. Despite widespread acknowledgement of the deficiencies of the UK's current structures, the prospect for a broader reform appears unlikely and is probably more complex than further devolution to Scotland (and Wales) or even independence. There have, however, been more piecemeal reforms, in the form of metropolitan mayors[4] and the transfer of health and social care competences to cities and regions like Greater Manchester.[5] The 'levelling up' agenda pursued by the current Conservative government is also unlikely to involve fundamental reform.[6]

The constitutional settlement was one designed around a principle of central autonomy, which allowed considerable 'operational autonomy to peripheral governments and political organizations, so long as they do not challenge its autonomy over matters of "High Politics"'.[7] This principle is epitomised in section 28(7) of the Scotland Act's (1998) declaration that: 'This section does not affect the power of the Parliament of the United Kingdom to make laws for Scotland.' An identical statement is also found in the legislation underpinning Welsh and Northern Irish devolution.[8] And while the Act also includes the so-called Sewel Convention (discussed in detail later on), which states that the UK Parliament will not 'normally' legislate in devolved areas without the consent of devolved institutions, it retains its ability to do so, an assertion underpinned by the presumption of parliamentary sovereignty.[9]

We can also identify a conflict over understandings of sovereignty – the parliamentary sovereignty that underpins the UK's constitutional settlement, and the assumption of popular sovereignty which unifies Scottish nationalists.[10] The UK government's insistence on parliamentary sovereignty suggests that

---

4 Giovannini, A. (2021) 'The 2021 Metro Mayors elections: localism rebooted?', *Political Quarterly*, 92(3): 474–85.

5 Kenealy, D. (2016) 'A tale of one city: the Devo Manc deal and its implications for English devolution', *Political Quarterly*, 87(4): 572–81.

6 Tomaney, J. and Pike, A. (2020) 'Levelling up?', *Political Quarterly*, 91(1): 43–8; Jennings, W., McKay, L. and Stoker, G. (2021) 'The politics of levelling up', *Political Quarterly*, 92(2): 302–11.

7 Bulpitt, J. (1983) *Territory and Power in the United Kingdom: An Interpretation*, Manchester: Manchester University Press.

8 Government of Wales Act 1998, s 107(5); Government of Northern Ireland Act 1998, s 5(6).

9 Keating, M. (2021) *State and Nation in the United Kingdom: The Fractured Union*, Oxford: Oxford University Press.

10 For a more detailed discussion of sovereignty in a Scottish context, see Ichijo, A. (2009) 'Sovereignty and nationalism in the twenty-first century: the Scottish case', *Ethnopolitics*, 8(2): 155–72; Pittock, M. (2012) 'Scottish sovereignty and the Union of 1707: then and now', *National Identities*, 14(1): 11–21; MacCormick, N. (1995) 'Sovereignty: myth and reality', *Scottish Affairs*, 11(1): 1–13; Tierney, S. (2005) 'Reframing sovereignty? Sub-state national societies and contemporary challenges to the nation-state', *International &*

power lies exclusively with the centre, and devolution allows for policy variation and local accountability.[11] Others who envisage radical reform to accommodate demands for self-government throughout the UK imagine a more dispersed sovereignty or a post-sovereign understanding of the UK, with the Union based on consent and partnership. Despite the rejection of independence at the polls in 2014, tensions over sovereignty persist. The referendum appeared to be a recognition of Scotland's right to self-determination and an acknowledgement that the Union is underpinned by consent. But as political positions seem entrenched over the prospect of another referendum on independence, it is unclear what resolution might be achieved.

Brexit further exacerbates this tension over what Sandford and Gormley-Heenan describe as *Schrodinger's devolution*: 'Extensive devolved self-rule in practice (permissive autonomy) has co-existed with UK-level parliamentary sovereignty. Brexit will subject this co-existence to unprecedented stress.'[12] The repatriation of competences over domains like agriculture, consumer protection and the environment, from the EU to the UK and the devolved governments, will require significant degrees of cooperation, for which there is not a clear model.[13] Although efforts have been made to establish common frameworks that set out a common UK or British approach,[14] the stage appears set for contentious debates over the management of the internal market. The UK government must decide whether market considerations override the political costs of constraining the power of devolved governments.

The UK's processes of decentralisation and delivery of devolution were not accompanied by an infrastructure to facilitate information sharing, coordination, joint decision making and dispute resolution. Intergovernmental relations (IGR) in the UK remain ad hoc, informal and dominated by the centre. This contrasts with structures and processes in other decentralised and federal states.[15] Intergovernmental tensions have

Comparative Law Quarterly, 54(1): 161–83; McCrone, D. and Keating, M. (2021) 'Questions of sovereignty: redefining politics in Scotland?', *Political Quarterly*, 92(1): 14–22.

[11] Keating (2021).

[12] Sandford, M. and Gormley-Heenan, C. (2020) '"Taking back control", the UK's constitutional narrative and Schrodinger's devolution', *Parliamentary Affairs*, 73(1): 108–26.

[13] Page, A. (2017) 'Brexit, the repatriation of competences and the future of the Union', *Juridical Review: The Law Journal of the Scottish Universities*, 2017(1): 38–47.

[14] Due to the Northern Ireland Protocol, some frameworks will apply only to England, Scotland and Wales, as in certain issue areas Northern Ireland is treated as part of the European single market. This arrangement remains contentious.

[15] Bolleyer, N. (2006) 'Federal dynamics in Canada, the United States, and Switzerland: how substates' internal organization affects intergovernmental relations', *Publius: The Journal of Federalism*, 36(4): 471–502; Bolleyer, N. (2009) *Intergovernmental Cooperation: Rational Choices in Federal Systems and Beyond*, Oxford: Oxford University Press.

increased during the two decades of devolution, as the competences and confidence of the devolved governments have grown, party incongruence[16] has increased, and contentious constitutional issues like independence and Brexit have dominated the debate.

The UK's constitutional structure is often heralded by constitutional thinkers and politicians for its flexibility. Robert Hazell describes the UK as 'a union of four nations that works in practice but not in theory'.[17] In the absence of a single constitutional text, actors rely on political rather than legal answers to constitutional questions. This system has, to date, been able to introduce and accommodate asymmetric territorial arrangements and a range of political preferences. However, conflict in recent years over the prospect of a second independence referendum, Brexit and the future of the Union suggests that this flexibility may have reached its outer limits.

Understanding Scottish devolution

Scotland's journey to devolution was lengthy, beginning in the late 1960s when increasing (although still marginal) electoral support for the SNP prompted the Conservative and Labour Parties to consider how Scotland might be accommodated within the UK. The urgency of these efforts increased when, in October 1974, the SNP secured 11 seats in Scotland, and exerted greater influence on the then minority Labour government, which relied on smaller parties in key votes.[18]

In 1979, the issue of devolution was brought to a vote in Scotland and Wales, with referendums on a Scottish and a Welsh Assembly.[19] However, a consensus on devolution had yet to emerge. Many within Labour questioned whether the nationalist threat would be sustained, while the SNP, after much debate, took the view that the proposals for a Scottish Assembly, with limited competences, would hinder its independence ambitions. Labour backbenchers introduced a mechanism in which an additional threshold was imposed: a 50 per cent plus one vote majority would not be sufficient

[16] In the early years of devolution, Labour was in government in London, Cardiff and Edinburgh – Northern Ireland sits outside this party structure. Party congruence facilitated cooperation between levels of government. This party congruence helps explain the lack of investment in intergovernmental structures. At the time of writing, there are different parties in power in all four capitals.

[17] Hazell, R. (2006) 'The English question', *Publius: The Journal of Federalism*, 36(1): 37–56.

[18] Rose, R. and Shephard, M. (2016) 'The long and the short of the SNP breakthrough', in P. Cowley and D. Kavanagh (eds) *The British General Election of 2015*, Basingstoke: Palgrave Macmillan, 126–39.

[19] Denver, D., Pattie, C., Bochel, H. and Mitchell, J. (1998) 'The devolution referendums in Scotland', *Representation*, 35(4): 210–18.

to secure devolution; 40 per cent of the total voting population would be required. The vote passed the first hurdle, but not the second and, in a controversial move, the SNP joined the Conservatives in a vote of no confidence in the Labour government, leading to new elections.

As a result, Margaret Thatcher entered Number 10. Thatcher's hostility to devolution was well documented.[20] Thatcher abandoned the Conservative Party's commitment to devolution when she assumed leadership of the Party in 1976 and campaigned against devolution in 1979, describing Labour's proposed Assembly as a 'time-bomb under the unity of the United Kingdom'.[21] During the Conservative government (1979–97), Scottish civil society and opposition parties coalesced around devolution, with Labour and the Liberal Democrats convening the Campaign for a Scottish Assembly.[22] This culminated in the Claim of Right 1989, which asserted 'the sovereign right of the Scottish people to determine the form of Government best suited to their needs' and pledged to further the cause of a Scottish Parliament. In 1995, the Scottish Constitutional Convention published *Scotland's Parliament, Scotland's Right*, which was to provide the blueprint for the devolved legislature.[23] The position of the SNP also changed between the 1970s, in which the UK first voted on membership of what was then the European Community, and the late 1980s. The Party's vision of independence became more supportive of the EU as a supporting structure for an independent Scotland during this period.[24]

In 1997, the Labour manifesto included a commitment to votes on devolution for Scotland and Wales, and following the Labour victory, referendums were held. The proposal for what had become a Scottish Parliament was overwhelmingly endorsed, with 74 per cent of the electorate voting in favour (a secondary question on taxation powers was endorsed by 63.5 per cent of those who voted yes).

The devolution delivered by the UK Labour government in the 1990s was asymmetric, responding to bottom-up demands for further power.[25] The Scottish Parliament and the Welsh Assembly were endowed with different

---

[20] Stewart, D. (2009) *The Path to Devolution and Change: A Political History of Scotland under Margaret Thatcher*, London: I.B. Tauris.

[21] Thatcher, M. (1979) 'NO says the Leader of the Opposition', *Sunday Post,* 25 February.

[22] Mitchell, J. and Bennie, L.G. (2020) *Thatcherism and the Scottish Question*, Abingdon: Routledge, 90–104.

[23] Lynch, P. (1996) 'The Scottish Constitutional Convention 1992–5', *Scottish Affairs*, 15(1): 1–16.

[24] Dardanelli, P. (2013) *Between Two Unions: Europeanisation and Scottish Devolution*, Manchester: Manchester University Press.

[25] Harvey, M. (2020) 'Devolution', in M. Keating (ed) *The Oxford Handbook of Scottish Politics*, Oxford: Oxford University Press, pp 370–85.

powers, and the London Assembly and the post of mayor were also created as part of this devolutionary wave.[26] However, there was little political appetite for English devolution.[27] A referendum on devolution for North East England in 2004 was decisively defeated, and demand for more formal devolution to England is limited. Northern Ireland is set apart from Scotland and Wales, given the complex political history, although the Belfast/Good Friday Agreement coincided with the devolution debates. The Northern Ireland Act 1998 provided for a model of devolution with excepted, reserved and transferred matters.

The Scottish Parliament: a new kind of politics?

In 1999, the first Scottish Parliament was elected. Scottish Labour came first in the 1999 Holyrood election, forming a government in coalition with the Liberal Democrats. The SNP, a marginal force at the Westminster elections, became the second-largest party, illustrating the way in which devolution became a boon to the independence cause rather than an impediment.[28]

The Scottish Parliament is composed of 129 members (MSPs), who are elected through an additional member system. A total of 73 MSPs are elected in individual constituencies, while the remainder are elected on the regional list, and smaller parties have benefited from the list system.

Devolution was to represent an opportunity for 'new politics', a change from the more confrontational politics taking place at Westminster.[29] Institutional architects aspired to 'the development of a radically new legislative culture – one which championed consensualism over the "yah-boo" adversarialism associated with the House of Commons'.[30] This is symbolised by the institutional structures, including processes to allow for public petitions and members' bills, and the physical space, including the horseshoe chamber in which members sit together.

[26] Mitchell, J. (2013) *Devolution in the UK*, Manchester: Manchester University Press.

[27] Paun, A. (2018) 'Sovereignty, devolution and the English Constitution', in M. Kenny, I. McLean and A. Paun (eds) *Governing England*, London: British Academy, 45–67.

[28] Curtice, J. (2009) 'Devolution, the SNP and the electorate', in G. Hassan (ed) *The Modern SNP: From Protest to Power*, Edinburgh: Edinburgh University Press, 55–67.

[29] For a detailed discussion of the Scottish Parliament, see St Denny, E. (2020) 'The Scottish Parliament', in Keating (n 24: 481–99).

[30] Arter, D. (2004) 'The Scottish committees and the goal of a "New Politics": a verdict on the first four years of the devolved Scottish Parliament', *Journal of Contemporary European Studies*, 12(1): 71–91.

The Scottish Parliament was also to be more representative of the population.[31] However, the reality, as indicated by the proportion of historically underrepresented groups, is mixed. A total of 48 of the 129 MSPs (37.2 per cent) elected to the first Parliament were women, but progress from 1999 onwards was not linear.[32] The year 2021 saw a breakthrough in female representation, with women making up 45 per cent of the 129 MSPs. But here we see variation between the parties, with Labour, the SNP and the Greens – each of which has made a concerted effort to increase representation with innovations like all-women shortlists – outpacing the Conservatives, of whom only 26 per cent of elected MSPs were women.[33] Minority ethnic representation remains weak, with representation in government falling short of that in the broader population.[34] It was only in 2021 that the first women of minority ethnic background entered Parliament, alongside the first permanent wheelchair user. Further work is necessary to ensure sustained representation, as well as genuine engagement with the growing diversity of Scotland's population.[35]

The devolution settlement

The devolution settlement is underpinned legally by the Scotland Act 1998, which established the Scottish Parliament and the Scottish Executive (later government).[36] The judicial system predates devolution, and the

31 Shephard, M., McGarvey, N. and Cavanagh, M. (2001) 'New Scottish Parliament, new Scottish parliamentarians?', *Journal of Legislative Studies*, 7(2): 79–104.

32 Kenny, M. and Mackay, F. (2020) 'Women, gender, and politics in Scotland', in M. Keating (ed) *The Oxford Handbook of Scottish Politics*, Oxford: Oxford University Press, pp 59–77. See also Kenny, M. (2013) 'Political recruitment in post-devolution Scotland', in *Gender and Political Recruitment: Theorizing Institutional Change*, Basingstoke: Palgrave Macmillan, 63–84; Mackay, F., Myers, F. and Brown, A. (2003) 'Towards a new politics? Women and the constitutional change in Scotland', in *Women Making Constitutions*, Basingstoke: Palgrave Macmillan, 84–98.

33 Kenny, M. 2021. 'A record-breaking election, but what next?', *Centre on Constitutional Change*, 14 May. Available from: https://www.centreonconstitutionalchange.ac.uk/news-and-opinion/record-breaking-election-what-next [Accessed 23 December 2022].

34 Hill, E. and Meer, N. (2020) 'Ethnic minorities and political citizenship in Scotland', in M. Keating (ed) *The Oxford Handbook of Scottish Politics*, Oxford: Oxford University Press, pp 336–53.

35 For more on this, see Meer, N. (2020) 'Race equality policy making in a devolved context: assessing the opportunities and obstacles for a "Scottish approach"', *Journal of Social Policy*, 49(2): 233–50.

36 For an analysis of the Scotland Act as a constitutional document, see Winetrobe, B.K. (2011) 'Enacting Scotland's "written constitution": the Scotland Act 1998', *Parliamentary History*, 30(1): 85–100.

Table 5.1: Distribution of powers

Reserved	**Devolved**
Broadcasting	Agriculture, forestry and fisheries
Constitutional affairs, the Crown and parliaments	Education and training
	Environment
Currency	Health and social services
Defence	Housing
Drug control	Justice and policing
Fiscal, economic and monetary policy	Local government
Foreign affairs	Police and fire services
Economic policy	Sports and the arts
Immigration and nationality	Some aspects of tax and social security
Telecommunications	Tourism
	Transport

maintenance of Scotland's distinct legal system was provided for in the Act of Union of 1707.[37] This includes the High Court and the Court of Session. Devolution has been iterative, with the further transfer of powers in the Scotland Act 2012 and Scotland Act 2016. The Scotland Act 1998 set out the distribution of powers between Westminster and Holyrood, employing a reserved powers model, in which Westminster's powers are outlined, and everything not explicitly listed as reserved is open to legislation by the Scottish Parliament (summarised in Table 5.1). The reserved powers, set out in Schedule 5 to the Scotland Act 1998, include, among others, the monarchy, the constitution and the union, international affairs, economic and monetary policy, defence, immigration, social security, broadcasting, employment and equal opportunities. Devolved powers, at the time of writing, include health, education and training, local government, the legal system, agriculture, forestry and fishing, sports and the arts, and environmental protection.

In the Scotland Act 2012, the Scottish Parliament was granted additional fiscal powers – the variation of income tax, devolution of stamp duty and landfill tax, and borrowing powers.

The Scottish Parliament has a significant degree of control over its own internal functioning. Further control was extended in the Scotland Act 2016, in which the Scottish Parliament received control over Scottish elections (modification requires the assent of two-thirds of all MSPs). It has used

[37] White, R., Willock, I. and MacQueen, H. (2013) *The Scottish Legal System*, London: Bloomsbury.

these powers to extend the franchise to include 16- and 17-year-olds (who were first able to vote in the 2014 referendum).[38] The franchise was also extended to foreign nationals legally resident in Scotland, including those with refugee status.

Limitations to the legislative competence of the Scottish Parliament included restrictions on laws incompatible with the European Convention on Human Rights (ECHR) or EU law, modifications to the Act of Union, or related to reserved powers. Unlike Acts of the UK Parliament, which are protected by the principle of parliamentary sovereignty, devolved legislation can be referred to the courts if it infringes on a reserved policy area, or is incompatible with ECHR or (prior to Brexit) EU law. Bills are referred either by the UK or devolved law officers.[39] Referrals by the UK government include the incorporation of the United Nations Convention on the Rights of the Child and the adoption of the European Charter of Local Self-Government.[40] Both bills were passed unanimously at Holyrood in 2021, but were challenged by UK law officers on the grounds that they were beyond the remit of the Scottish Parliament, imposing obligations on the UK government. The courts have decided that each bill contains provisions that are outwith the competences of the devolved Parliament and have returned the legislation to Holyrood for revision.[41]

Conflict and cooperation: the Sewel Convention and intergovernmental relations

The focus of devolution's architects was on self-government, transferring the necessary powers to allow for significant autonomy, and quelling nationalist demands for independence. Little attention was paid to forums and mechanisms to allow for information sharing, negotiation and decision making between levels of government. And with Labour in power in London, Cardiff and Edinburgh, such formal mechanisms that exist in federal countries perhaps seemed unnecessary, with questions of policy negotiated among the Labour leadership rather than through

---

38 Huebner, C. and Eichhorn, J. (2020) 'Votes at 16 in Scotland: political experiences beyond the vote itself', in J. Eichhorn and J. Bergh (eds) *Lowering the Voting Age to 16*, Basingstoke: Palgrave Macmillan, 121–42; Eichhorn, J. (2018) 'Votes at 16: new insights from Scotland on enfranchisement', *Parliamentary Affairs*, 71(2): 365–91.

39 Commons Law Briefing 2016.

40 *Reference by the Attorney General and the Advocate General for Scotland – European Charter of Local Self-Government (Incorporation) (Scotland) Bill; Reference by the Attorney General and the Advocate General for Scotland – United Nations Convention on the Rights of the Child (Incorporation) (Scotland) Bill* [2021] UKSC 42.

41 *Reference by the Attorney General and Her Majesty's Advocate General for Scotland and Lord Advocate and Counsel General for Wales* [2021] UKSC 42.

intergovernmental forums.[42] While contentious issues were often discussed, the reliance on direct, bilateral and informal channels largely kept disputes from public view.

As a result, intergovernmental forums were often neglected. The Joint Ministerial Committee (JMC), which was designed to bring the governments of the UK together on a multilateral basis, was rarely convened in the early years of devolution, with politicians resorting to bilateral talks or meetings outside the formal JMC structure. The JMC (Europe) was the only committee to meet regularly, ahead of European Council meetings.[43] Between 2002 and 2007, the JMC (Plenary) did not meet. Efforts were made to institutionalise intergovernmental relations when the SNP entered government in 2007, with an uptick in plenary sessions. A Memorandum of Understanding was also agreed in March 2010 setting out a 'Protocol for Avoidance and Resolution of Disputes', but the devolved governments have voiced concerns that the UK government remains the arbiter of any disputes between the central and devolved governments. The highly asymmetric nature of intergovernmental relations in the UK has also inhibited coordination by the devolved governments, rendering 'a concerted approach between the devolved territories often difficult or unnecessary'.[44]

As devolution entered its second decade, critiques of the UK's system of intergovernmental relations – as a system to both facilitate cooperation and to manage conflict – were growing. There was a growing consensus among parliamentary committees, think tanks and academics[45] that the UK's system of intergovernmental relations was no longer fit for purpose. The system was to come under growing strain as the SNP made its bid for independence, and

---

[42] McEwen, N., Swenden, W. and Bolleyer, N. (2012) 'Intergovernmental relations in the UK: continuity in a time of change?', *British Journal of Politics and International Relations*, 14(2): 323–43.

[43] Ibid.

[44] Ibid.

[45] House of Commons Justice Committee (2009) "Devolution: A Decade On: Fifth Report of Session 2008-9, Volume 1, London: The Stationery Office. Available from: https://publications.parliament.uk/pa/cm200809/cmselect/cmjust/529/529i.pdf [Accessed 6 March 2023]; Bingham Centre for the Rule of Law (2015) 'A Constitutional Crossroads: Ways Forward for the United Kingdom', British Institute of International and Comparative Law. Available from: https://www.biicl.org/documents/595_a_constitutional_crossroads.pdf [Accessed 6 March 2023]; Select Committee on the Constitution (2015) 'Inter-governmental Relations in the United Kingdom: 11th Report of Session 2014–15', House of Lords, HL Paper 146, London: The Stationery Office. Available from: https://publications.parliament.uk/pa/ld201415/ldselect/ldconst/146/146.pdf [Accessed 6 March 2023]; Trench, A. ed. (2007) *Devolution and Power in the United Kingdom*, Manchester: Manchester University Press; McEwen, N., Petersohn, B. and Brown Swan, C. (2015) *Intergovernmental Relations and Parliamentary Scrutiny: A Comparative Overview*, Edinburgh: Centre on Constitutional Change.

the Brexit process saw a simultaneous breakdown in relationships between the UK and devolved governments, and a greater need for coordination.

While in principle, the Scottish Parliament was to be able to exercise its authority over areas set out in the devolution settlement, Westminster reserved the right to intervene, although by convention it would not do so unless truly necessary. In instances where there is a need to legislate in the areas of devolved competences, the UK government is to seek the consent of the devolved legislatures, a convention known as the Sewel Convention.[46] Under this convention, the UK government is expected to consult with devolved governments early on in the process, and once the bill is introduced, the devolved governments publish legislative consent memorandums (LCM) and seek the consent of their respective legislatures. It is then up to the UK government, in the face of opposition, whether to amend the bill or to proceed in the absence of this consent. The process has broadly been consensual, with the Institute for Government identifying 350 LCMs between 1999 and 2020, with consent denied in just 13 of these.[47] The Sewel Convention was placed on a statutory footing in the Scotland Act 2016 and the Wales Act 2017, which sought to 'recognise' the mechanism,[48] reassuring the devolved parliaments that they would have input into legislation within their areas of competence. However, the sovereignty of the UK Parliament remains untouched by the devolution settlement[49] and while there is a political incentive to seek consensus, there is no constitutional requirement to do so.

Scotland decides: the independence referendum

In 2007, the Scottish political scene was upended by the surprise victory of the SNP, which formed a minority government. In government, the party used its position to show what a nationalist government could achieve while also demonstrating the limitations or inadequacies of devolution. In 2011, the SNP formed a majority government, in a system designed, in part, to prevent such an occurrence.[50] This result, the SNP argued, gave the Scottish government a mandate to hold a referendum on independence.

---

46 For more on the Sewel Convention, see Evans, A. (2020) 'A tale as old as (devolved) time? Sewel, Stormont and the legislative consent convention', *Political Quarterly*, 91(1): 165–72.

47 Institute for Government (2020) 'Sewel Convention' [online] 16 January. Available from: https://www.instituteforgovernment.org.uk/explainers/sewel-convention [Accessed 24 December 2022].

48 Himsworth, C. (2016) 'Legislating for permanence and a statutory footing', *Edinburgh Law Review*, 20(3): 361–7.

49 Keating, M. (1998) 'Reforging the union: devolution and constitutional change in the United Kingdom', *Publius: The Journal of Federalism*, 28(1): 217–34.

50 Carman, C., Johns, R. and Mitchell, J. (2014) *More Scottish Than British: The 2011 Scottish Parliament Election*, Basingstoke: Palgrave Macmillan.

How it would do so was not immediately clear. Recall that 'the constitution' falls within reserved Westminster competences, and the UK government maintained that the Scottish Parliament lacked the legislative competence to hold a referendum. A political rather than a legal solution was found. In October 2012, David Cameron and Alex Salmond negotiated the *Edinburgh Agreement* to allow a referendum to take place.[51] Cameron's motivations in doing so were likely shaped by polling showing that only between a quarter to a third of people were in favour of independence, suggesting that the Unionist side would easily prevail.[52] The Edinburgh Agreement, which was signed by both governments, set out the terms for the 2014 vote. The referendum was to have a clear legal base, be legislated for by the Scottish Parliament, 'be conducted so as to command the confidence of parliaments, governments and people' and 'deliver a fair test and a decisive expression of the views of people in Scotland'.[53] The powers necessary to hold the vote were temporarily transferred through a Section 30 Order (a section of the Scotland Act 1998 that allowed Holyrood to legislate in a reserved sphere). This transfer of power was time-limited and needed to be exercised before the end of 2014.

The referendum rested on two assumptions, which were recognised by both sides of the independence debate: first, it was agreed that Scotland was a nation and, second, that as a nation, it had a right to decide its own political future. These assumptions underpinned the referendum campaign, which centred on competing knowledge claims across a range of policy areas, including EU membership, what currency an independent Scotland would use, and the economic prospects of an independent Scotland.[54] This set the Scottish experience apart from independence-seeking efforts elsewhere.[55]

---

51 Adam, E.C. (2014) 'Self-determination and the use of referendums: the case of Scotland', *International Journal of Politics, Culture, and Society*, 27(1): 47–66; Tierney, S. (2016) 'The Scottish independence referendum: a model of good practice in direct democracy?', in *The Scottish Independence Referendum: Constitutional and Political Implications*, Oxford: Oxford University Press, 53–74.

52 For a comparative analysis of the UK and Spanish decision making in response to referendum demands, see Cetrà, D. and Harvey, M. (2019) 'Explaining accommodation and resistance to demands for independence referendums in the UK and Spain', *Nations and Nationalism*, 25(2): 607–29.

53 Edinburgh Agreement 2012.

54 Brown Swan, C. (2020) 'The independence question', in M. Keating (ed) *The Oxford Handbook of Scottish Politics*, Oxford: Oxford University Press, pp 633–49; Dekavalla, M. (2016) 'Framing referendum campaigns: the 2014 Scottish independence referendum in the press', *Media, Culture & Society*, 38(6): 793–810; Douglas-Scott, S. (2019) 'Scotland, secession, and the European Union', 'Queen Mary School of Law Legal Studies Research Paper No. 301', 16 January. Available from: https://papers.ssrn.com/sol3/papers.cfm?abstract_id=3316715 [Accessed 24 December 2022].

55 Qvortrup, M. (2014) 'Referendums on independence, 1860–2011', *Political Quarterly*, 85(1): 57–64.

A negotiated, rather than opposed or merely tolerated, referendum allowed for a greater level of legitimacy. Both sides participated actively in the campaign, and the result was understood by participants to be fair and binding.

The 'Yes Scotland' campaign argued in favour of a 'utilitarian' approach to independence, with independence presented as the best means to advance a variety of policy aims, including improving Scotland's economic performance and welfare system, and reducing child poverty. The 'Better Together' campaign put forward counterclaims stressing the economic strength of the UK, its potential in the face of shared challenges, and the inherent economic uncertainty of independence.

Days before the vote and faced with polling that suggested that the 'Yes' vote might win out, Unionist leaders pledged a new iteration of the devolution settlement on the front page of the *Daily Record*. In 'The Vow', they pledged to 'deliver faster, safer and better change than separation'. This included an acknowledgement of the permanency of the Scottish Parliament, the maintenance of the Barnett Formula through which Scotland is funded, and the transfer of 'extensive new powers for the Parliament.[56] This effectively changed the terms of the 2014 vote, from independence versus the status quo to independence versus further devolution.[57]

After a hard-fought campaign, Scottish voters went to the polls on 18 September 2014 to vote on the following question: 'Should Scotland be an independent country?' The referendum was won by those in favour of Scotland remaining a part of the UK, but by a much narrower margin than the polls had suggested at the outset of the campaign, and by much less than Unionist political leaders would have preferred.

A constitutional chain reaction?

The 2014 vote set off what has been described as a 'constitutional chain reaction'[58] with far-reaching implications not just for Scotland but also for the other constituent nations of the UK, and the broader Union.

---

56 'The Vow', *Daily Record*, 15 September 2014.

57 Page, A. (2019) 'Scotland in the United Kingdom: an enduring settlement?', in A. López-Basaguren and L. San-Epifanio (eds) *Claims for Secession and Federalism*, Cham: Springer, 127–38.

58 Jeffery, C. 'Scotland's decision: a constitutional chain reaction', 19 September, Edinburgh: Centre on Constitutional Change. Available from: https://www.centreonconstitutionalchange.ac.uk/opinions/scotlands-decision-constitutional-chain-reaction [Accessed 24 December 2022].

The most powerful devolved parliament in the world?

The expansion of powers to the Scottish Parliament took the form of the cross-party Smith Commission, which on a tight timescale produced proposals for the transfer of additional powers to Scotland. The Commission was to secure 'a durable and responsive constitutional settlement for the governance of Scotland'.[59] In the resulting Scotland Act (2016), the Scottish Parliament gained control over its size and composition, electoral system and franchise, substantial control over income tax, management of the Crown Estate, as well as important social security benefits.

In addition to this transfer of competences, the Commission also acknowledged the permanency of the Scottish Parliament, fulfilling one of the commitments made in 'The Vow' of September 2014. This was realised with an amendment to the Scotland Act 1998, which stated:

1. The Scottish Parliament and the Scottish Government are a permanent part of the United Kingdom's constitutional arrangements.
2. The purpose of this section is, with due regard to the other provisions of this Act, to signify the commitment of the Parliament and Government of the United Kingdom to the Scottish Parliament and the Scottish Government.
3. In view of that commitment it is declared that the Scottish Parliament and the Scottish Government are not to be abolished except on the basis of a decision of the people of Scotland voting in a referendum.[60]

The Commission acknowledged 'the sovereign right of the people of Scotland to determine the form of government best suited to their needs'. The report also noted that 'nothing in this report prevents Scotland becoming an independent country in the future should the people of Scotland so choose'.[61] However, this was not legally entrenched, and efforts by Scottish MPs to amend the bill to include a right to hold another referendum were rejected in the House of Commons.[62] These powers have political effect, and one would struggle to imagine a scenario in which a UK government

[59] Smith Commission (2014) 'Report of the Smith Commission for further devolution of powers to the Scottish Parliament', Edinburgh: Smith Commission, p 12. Available from: https://webarchive.nationalarchives.gov.uk/ukgwa/20151202171059/http://www.smith-commission.scot/smith-commission-report [Accessed 6 March 2023].

[60] Scotland Act 2016, Part 2A: 'The permanence of the Scottish Parliament and the Scottish Government'.

[61] Smith Commission (2014).

[62] McHarg (n 3).

sought to abolish the Scottish Parliament. But the principle of parliamentary sovereignty remains in effect.[63]

Unionists hoped that the Smith Commission and resulting legislation would undercut the case for independence by realising the demand for further devolution. However, further devolution may reinforce a distinct sense of Scottish identity. In addition, the areas devolved are less clear-cut than those in the original settlement, and their implementation requires greater cooperation between the UK and Scottish governments, straining already weak structures of intergovernmental relations and increasing the opportunity for conflict between the two governments.[64]

The extension to the devolution settlement in the form of the Smith Commission failed to settle the constitutional debate in Scotland. In a historic victory, the SNP secured 56 out of 59 seats in the 2015 UK general election. The party was also returned to government at Holyrood, albeit a few seats short of majority, in 2016 and 2021.

'A balanced settlement?'

In his speech following the referendum result, David Cameron promised broader constitutional reforms. The extension of Scottish devolution should be, he argued, 'accompanied by a new and fair settlement that applies to all parts of our United Kingdom'.[65] In doing so, Cameron attempted to address the English question not through devolution, for which there is little political appetite, but through English Votes for English Laws (EVEL)[66] and City deals. Proposals for English Votes for English Laws attempted to remedy the so-called West Lothian Question,[67] which

---

[63] For a discussion of the issue of permanence and the Sewel Convention, see Elliott, M. (2014) 'A "permanent" Scottish Parliament and the sovereignty of the UK Parliament: four perspectives', *UK Constitutional Law Association Blog* [online], 24 November. Available from: https://ukconstitutionallaw.org/2014/11/28/mark-elliott-a-permanent-scottish-parliament-and-the-sovereignty-of-the-uk-parliament-four-perspectives/ [Accessed 24 December 2022].

[64] McEwen, N., Kenny, M., Sheldon, J. and Brown Swan, C. (2020) 'Intergovernmental relations in the UK: time for a radical overhaul?', *Political Quarterly*, 91(3): 632–40; Kenny, M. and McEwen, N. (2021) 'Intergovernmental relations and the crisis of the Union', *Political Insight*, 12(1): 12–15.

[65] Cameron, D. (2014) Speech on the referendum result. London, 19 September. Available from: https://www.gov.uk/government/news/scottish-independence-referendum-statement-by-the-prime-minister [Accessed 6 March 2023].

[66] Graham, C. (2016) 'Delivering EVEL: English Votes for English Laws', *European Public Law*, 22(4): 597–612.

[67] The 'West Lothian Question' emerged in the devolution debates of the 1970s, brought about by West Lothian Labour MP Tam Dalyell who raised the concern that in the event of devolution, Scottish, Welsh and Northern Irish MPs would be able to vote on

had bedevilled previous governments.[68] The unfortunately acronymed EVEL would see bills certified as pertaining only to England, in part or in full. Those bills would then be subject to a double majority, voted on by English MPs (or English and Welsh MPs if it fell within this jurisdiction) in Legislative Grand Committees and then by the House of Commons. The proposals came into force in 2015, but were repealed in 2021 on the basis that the process was overly complex and time-consuming.[69] Wales too saw an extension in its powers, bringing it more into line with the powers of the Scottish Parliament. The Wales Act 2017 replaced the conferred powers model, in which the powers of the then Welsh Assembly (now the Senedd) were explicitly set out, with a reserved powers model, similar to that of Scotland. The schedule of reserved powers includes the constitution, the legal jurisdiction of England and Wales, foreign affairs and defence, energy, transport, justice and social security.[70] This was viewed by many as a remedy for what then Secretary of State for Wales Alun Cairns described as "the constant squabbles over where powers lie".[71] However, the list of reserved powers is much more expansive than that of Scotland and Northern Ireland. This legislation also echoes the promises made to Scotland by declaring the permanence of the Senedd and recognising the Sewel Convention.[72] Finally, the Northern Ireland Assembly and Executive, which had experienced significant periods of suspension, was also to be restored.

The 2014 vote on Scottish independence therefore led to broader reflection on the Union, and the unsettled and unfinished nature of the devolution settlements. While the post-2014 period saw further devolution and attention to the relationships between the devolved and central governments, questions about consent and the nature of parliamentary sovereignty remained live ones, and would become more acute with the UK's vote to leave the EU and the subsequent negotiation process.

---

issues that pertained to England alone. This question re-emerged with devolution in 1999, when larger efforts (with little progress) were made to explore the governance of England.

[68] Gover, D. and Kenny, M. (2018) 'Answering the West Lothian Question? A critical assessment of "English Votes for English Laws" in the UK Parliament', *Parliamentary Affairs*, 71(4): 760–82.

[69] Evans, A. (2022) 'Parliamentary representation at Westminster and devolution: from the "in and out" to EVEL', *Public Law*, 1: 9–18.

[70] Schedule 7A to the Wales Act 2017.

[71] BBC (2016) 'Alun Cairns hails "new era" for devolution to Wales', *BBC News* [online], 13 September. Available from: https://www.bbc.co.uk/news/uk-wales-politics-37346880 [Accessed 16 February 2022].

[72] Rawlings, R.W. (2018) 'The strange reconstitution of Wales', *Public Law*, 2018: 62–83.

Brexit and Scotland

In 2016 the UK's Conservative government called a referendum on the UK's membership of the EU, and in June, the UK voted to leave. This vote was primarily motivated by concerns internal to the Conservative Party, in particular pressure by backbenchers and the electoral threat posed by the UK Independence Party (UKIP).[73] The potential territorial implications of the vote for both Scotland and Northern Ireland were not considered in any significant detail.[74] The salience of the European question was different in Scotland. In the run-up to the 2016 EU referendum, all parties in Holyrood campaigned to remain within the EU, and anti-EU parties had no presence within Holyrood. As a result, the referendum debate was refracted through the lens of independence – Unionist campaigners warned that the UK's departure from the EU would re-ignite the independence debate, while the SNP pledged that if Scotland was removed from the EU against the preferences of its people, the conditions for another referendum would be met.

The vote for Brexit and the subsequent agreement with the EU introduced new debates over power, sovereignty and the *will of the people*, not just in Scotland but also throughout the UK.[75] The referendum result varied throughout the UK, with a majority in England and Wales voting to leave, while a majority in Scotland and Northern Ireland voted to remain. In the SNP's view, the result was the 'material change in circumstances' necessary for another referendum, a claim rejected by the UK government. Polling

---

73 Smith, J. (2018) 'Gambling on Europe: David Cameron and the 2016 referendum', *British Politics*, 13(1): 1–16; Vasilopoulou, S. (2016) 'UK Euroscepticism and the Brexit referendum', *Political Quarterly*, 87(2): 219–27.

74 For further analysis of Brexit and devolution, see Sandford and Gormley-Heenan (n 12); Murphy, M.C. (2021) 'Northern Ireland and Brexit: where sovereignty and stability collide?', *Journal of Contemporary European Studies*, 29(3): 405–18; Murphy, M.C. and Evershed, J. (2022) 'Contesting sovereignty and borders: Northern Ireland, devolution and the Union', *Territory, Politics, Governance*, 10(5): 661–77; Kenny, M. and Sheldon, J. (2020) 'When planets collide: the British Conservative Party and the discordant goals of delivering Brexit and preserving the domestic union, 2016–2019', *Political Studies*, 69(4): 965–84.

75 McEwen, N. and Murphy, M.C. (2021) 'Brexit and the Union: territorial voice, exit and re-entry strategies in Scotland and Northern Ireland after EU exit', *International Political Science Review*, 43(3), 374–89; Daniels, L.A. and Kuo, A. (2021) 'Brexit and territorial preferences: evidence from Scotland and Northern Ireland', *Publius: The Journal of Federalism*, 51(2): 186–211; Casanas, Adam E. (2020) 'Brexit and the mechanisms for the resolution of conflicts in the context of devolution: do we need a new model?', *Edinburgh School of Law Research Paper* (2020/25); Keating, M. (2021) 'Taking back control? Brexit and the territorial constitution of the United Kingdom', *Journal of European Public Policy*, 29(4): 1–19.

suggested a brief Brexit bounce in support for independence followed by a stabilisation at 2014 levels.[76] But by 2020, following prolonged and contentious negotiations between the UK and the EU, a consistent 50/50 split in the population emerged in polling data. The SNP was also returned to government, this time in coalition with the Scottish Greens, in 2021.

In Scotland, calls by the SNP-led Scottish government for a softer Brexit or a custom solution for Scotland that would allow Scotland to maintain closer relationships were rejected by the UK government, and little fruitful collaboration over the withdrawal agreement took place. In Wales too, conflict erupted between the Welsh and UK governments over both withdrawal and the internal market, some of these debates ending in court.

Intergovernmental relations and Brexit negotiations

The Brexit process exacerbated tensions throughout the Union and called its future into question. Brexit had implications beyond Scotland, where partisans clamoured for another independence referendum, but also in Wales, where the Welsh government called for a softer Brexit and pollsters saw small but notable increases in support for Welsh independence. And in Northern Ireland, the possibility of a border between Northern Ireland and the Republic of Ireland or between Great Britain and Northern Ireland exacerbated tensions and risked undermining the peace process.[77]

The UK's system of intergovernmental relations had long been criticised, but the Brexit process further laid bare its inadequacies. Despite promises from the then Prime Minister Theresa May that the devolved governments should be "fully engaged in the process",[78] the devolved governments and parliaments struggled to make themselves heard at the centre. Theresa May's Lancaster House speech which set out the UK government's approach to Brexit was delivered without consultation. While the Joint Ministerial Committee (EU Negotiations) met regularly, devolved representatives complained they had little input in the process and that the Committee did not, ultimately, fulfil its remit to "seek to agree a UK approach to, and objectives for, Article 50 negotiations".[79]

---

[76] McHarg, A. and Mitchell, J. (2017) 'Brexit and Scotland', *British Journal of Politics and International Relations*, 19(3): 512–26.

[77] Murphy (n 74); Gormley-Heenan, C. and Aughey, A. (2017) 'Northern Ireland and Brexit: three effects on "the border in the mind"', *British Journal of Politics and International Relations*, 19(3): 497–511; Hayward, K. (2018) 'The pivotal position of the Irish border in the UK's withdrawal from the European Union', *Space and Polity*, 22(2): 238–54.

[78] May, T. (2019) 'I want an exit that will work for all of us', *The Times Scotland*, 19 January.

[79] Exiting the European Union Committee, 'Oral evidence: the UK's negotiating objectives for its withdrawal from the EU' (HC 1072, 2016–17, 7 March 2017, Q1296).

Contentious debates between the UK and devolved governments – over the withdrawal agreement, the repatriation of competences and internal market legislation – saw relations worsen further between the governments. There was horizontal coordination among the devolved governments, with the First Ministers of Scotland and Wales issuing joint statements calling on the UK government to involve the devolved governments in the negotiations and to remain within the customs union and the single market. The Scottish and Welsh law officers joined legal challenges to the UK government's Brexit legislation. Both the Scottish Parliament and the Senedd also withheld consent on the Withdrawal Bill.

The Brexit process presents a substantial challenge to the coordination between different levels of government. The UK's exit from the EU and the need to ensure the efficacy of the internal market will require common frameworks and coordination, as policy fields sit astride reserved and devolved competences. And the necessity of coordination is not restricted to economic management post-Brexit, but also includes the handling of public health crises, like the COVID-19 pandemic and climate change.

Brexit and devolution in the courts

Brexit, the UK Supreme Court acknowledged in its *Miller* judgment, represents a fundamental change to the UK's constitutional arrangements, with a significant impact on the devolution settlements and the competences of the devolved governments.[80] However, whether this took the form of a *power grab* by Westminster, as Nicola Sturgeon[81] and Carwyn Jones argued, or a significant expansion of the powers available to devolved governments is hotly contested.

Brexit was to see the repatriation of competences back to the UK. In her Lancaster House speech in January 2017, May declared that "[l]eaving the European Union will mean that our laws will be made in Westminster, Edinburgh, Cardiff and Belfast" and members of her administration spoke

[80] For analyses of *Miller* – *R (Miller) v Secretary of State for Exiting the EU* [2017] UKSC 5 – and devolution, see McHarg, A. (2018) 'Constitutional change and territorial consent: the *Miller* case and the Sewel Convention', in M. Elliott, J. Williams and A.L. Young (eds) *The UK Constitution After Miller: Brexit and Beyond*, Oxford: Hart Publishing, pp 155–80; Baroncelli, S. and Rosini, M. (2020) 'Brexit, sovereignty and devolution: the view of constitutional law', in Bongardt A, Talani L.S. and Torres F. (2020) *The Politics and Economics of Brexit*, Cheltenham: Edward Elgar, pp 56–87; Casanas, Adam E. (n 75); Elliott, M., Williams, J. and Young, A.L. eds (2018) *The UK Constitution after* Miller*: Brexit and Beyond*, Oxford: Hart Publishing.

[81] Scottish Government (2017) EU (Withdrawal Bill), 13 July. Available from: https://www.gov.scot/news/eu-withdrawal-bill/ [Accessed 24 December 2022].

of the potential for a powers bonanza.[82] In the case of reserved issues, like trade and immigration, the process was relatively straightforward – those powers would return to Westminster and the UK Parliament could repeal or amend legislation. The devolved competences, however, required additional consideration. Devolution was delivered in the context of EU membership and was very much embedded in an EU context. As a result, the process by which competences would return to the devolved governments was less clear, potentially requiring changes to the devolution settlement.[83] A direct transfer from Brussels to Belfast, Cardiff and Edinburgh could lead to policy divergence, risking the emergence of barriers to trade within the UK and threatening the UK internal market.

The UK government set out its plan in the form of the EU Withdrawal Bill, by which the European Communities Act 1972 would be repealed and the *acquis communautaire*[84] to be retained in domestic law would be repealed or modified according to the preferences of the UK and the devolved parliaments. The EU Withdrawal Bill was scrutinised by the Scottish Parliament, and consent was ultimately withheld, on the basis that powers which were not expressly reserved were in fact devolved and therefore should return to the Scottish Parliament.

The Scottish Parliament passed the UK Withdrawal from the European Union (Legal Continuity) (Scotland) Bill to guarantee the stability of the legal system, but the bill was viewed to be outside the legislative competence of the Scottish Parliament and was referred to the Supreme Court.[85] The Supreme Court ruled that while at the time of passing, the bill was within devolved competences, it was later superseded by the legislation of the UK Parliament through its EU Withdrawal Bill.

While in general, the prevailing norm in the UK is to settle disputes by political rather than legal means, the Brexit process was contested in the

[82] May, T. (2017) 'The government's negotiating objectives for exiting the EU, speech, Lancaster House, 17 January.

[83] Page, A. (2017) 'Brexit, the repatriation of competences and the future of the Union', *Juridical Review: The Law Journal of the Scottish Universities*, 2017(1): 38–47; Tierney, S. (2019) 'The territorial constitution and the Brexit process', *Current Legal Problems*, 72(1): 59–83; McEwen, N. (2020) 'Negotiating Brexit: power dynamics in British intergovernmental relations', *Regional Studies*, 55: 1–12.

[84] The *acquis communautaire* is the body of common rights and obligations that are binding on all EU member states. Applicants are required to accept the *acquis* before they join the EU.

[85] McCorkindale, C. and McHarg, A. (2021) 'Litigating Brexit', in O. Doyle, A. McHarg and J. Murkens (eds) *The Brexit Challenge for Ireland and the United Kingdom: Constitutions under Pressure*, Cambridge: Cambridge University Press, pp 260–91; McCorkindale, C. and McHarg, A. (2019) 'The Supreme Court and devolution: the Scottish Continuity Bill reference', *Juridical Review*, (2): 190–7.

courts, with *R (Miller) v Secretary of State for Exiting the European Union*[86] having implications for Brexit and for devolution. The *Miller* case was brought to challenge the government's power to invoke Article 50 – the process by which the UK would begin negotiations for its exit from the EU – without prior parliamentary authorisation.

Both the Lord Advocate for Scotland and the Counsel General for Wales were interveners in the case, arguing that the Sewel Convention was applicable to the withdrawal legislation and therefore consent of the devolved parliaments was needed. The UK government rejected this claim.[87] In its ruling, the Supreme Court described Sewel as a political rather than legal convention and declined to rule on it. The courts, the ruling concluded, 'are neither the parents nor the guardians of political conventions; they are merely observers'. While courts can 'recognise the operation of a political convention in the context of deciding a legal question', it is not their place to 'give legal rulings on its operation or scope, because those matters are determined within the political world'.[88]

The *Miller* ruling had implications for the Brexit process, but also called into question the status of the devolved governments within the Union more broadly. The judgment, and later the actions of the UK government, indicated that the devolved legislatures had little remit to block the actions of the UK government. This demonstrates that while the devolution settlement is very much entrenched in Scotland's political life, the supremacy of the UK government, underpinned by the principle of (UK) parliamentary sovereignty, remains untouched. This has, historically, not led to major conflicts, with research showing that out of over 400 legislative consent motions, only 20 had been denied by the devolved legislatures,[89] with compromises often reached between governments. However, political dynamics between the Scottish and UK governments remain contentious, with future conflicts likely.

Ultimately, in 2020, the European Union Withdrawal Agreement Act 2020 was passed without the consent of all three devolved legislatures. In addition, the UK Internal Market Act 2020 was passed without the consent of Holyrood and the Senedd. The Scottish government objected on the basis that the proposed Internal Market Bill breaches the devolution settlement, facilitates UK intervention in devolved areas, and allows for

[86] *R (Miller) v Secretary of State for Exiting the EU* [2017] UKSC 5, para 146.

[87] McHarg (n 80).

[88] *R (Miller) v Secretary of State for Exiting the European Union* [2017] UKSC 5, para 146.

[89] Paun, A., Sargeant, J., Nicolson, E. and Rycroft, L. (2022) 'Explainer: Sewel Convention', Institute of Government [online] Available from: https://www.instituteforgovernment.org.uk/explainers/sewel-convention [Accessed 1 April 2022].

breaches of international law.[90] The Welsh government also launched legal action against the Act.

The independence question post Brexit

The Brexit process re-ignited the independence debate, returning the independence question to the foreground of Scottish politics. In the intervening years, one might argue that the case for independence has been bolstered, given the strength of support for EU membership. However, the 2014 independence prospectus was predicated on the assumption that both Scotland and the rest of the UK would remain in the EU, and the EU umbrella would facilitate trade and movement between the two countries. In the absence of this supporting structure, the practicalities of independence become more complex.

The Scottish Parliament debated the prospect of a second referendum in 2017, but Nicola Sturgeon's efforts were rebuffed by then Prime Minister Theresa May, who suggested a vote would be unwise during the Brexit process. Her successor Boris Johnson also pledged to block another referendum, as did Prime Minister Liz Truss. The 2021 results of the Scottish parliamentary elections saw the SNP again returned to government and a pro-independence coalition was formed with the Scottish Greens.

However, the process by which a referendum might be held is less clear than it was in 2017.[91] While Northern Ireland has the right to secession, set out in the Northern Ireland Act of 1998, a formal process does not exist in Scotland, and there appears to be little political incentive to clarify this path. McHarg explains that: 'While lawful secession by Scotland clearly is possible under the UK constitution, there is accordingly deep uncertainty around when, for what reasons, and by whom an independence referendum may legitimately be called.'[92] In June 2022, the Scottish government published a draft bill on a referendum, and referred this matter to the UK Supreme Court to rule on whether the Scottish Parliament has the authority under the Scotland Act 1998 to pass a bill, and thus to hold a referendum. In Autumn 2022, the UK Supreme Court ruled that the proposed referendum bill, which makes provision for a consultative referendum on the question

---

90 Scottish Government (2020) *After Brexit: The UK Internal Market Act and Devolution*, Edinburgh: Scottish Government.

91 Clark, A. (2020) 'More than IndyRef2? The Referendums (Scotland) Act 2020', *Political Quarterly*, 91(2): 467–72; Casanas, Adam E. (2021) 'Alternative pathways to an independence referendum: some reflections based on the experience of Catalonia', *Edinburgh Law Review*, 25(1): 125–30

92 McHarg, A. (2018) 'Navigating without maps: constitutional silence and the management of the Brexit crisis', *International Journal of Constitutional Law*, 16(3): 952–68.

of 'Should Scotland be an independent country?' relates to reserved matters and is outside the legislative competence of the Scottish Parliament.[93] The SNP will now attempt to reframe any future UK general election as a de facto referendum on independence.

Reforming the Union?

This crisis of the Union was precipitated by the debates over Scottish independence, but stretches beyond Scotland. Pollsters have documented increases in support for both Welsh independence[94] and Irish reunification,[95] alongside the persistent demand for Scottish independence.[96] In response, there are proposals to reform or strengthen the Union by both countering arguments in favour of independence and reunification, and reforming the Union to better reflect the nations and regions of the UK.

The arguments for the Union in a post-Brexit economic and political landscape are broadly instrumental, borrowing from the successful arguments made in the 2014 independence referendum.[97] Proponents of the Union of all political stripes cite the economic strength of the UK and the Union as a guarantor of the social welfare of its inhabitants. The National Health Service (NHS) – both its foundation and its maintenance – and the defeat of fascism in the Second World War are invoked as a symbol of what the UK nations can achieve by working together.[98]

Despite widespread recognition of the challenges the Union faces, at the time of writing, a coherent programme for reform has not been identified. Proposals have originated outside of Whitehall and the current government, instead coming from the House of Lords, where the Constitutional Reform Group advances a bill that would reinvigorate the Act of Union,[99] from the Labour Party in opposition and from former Prime Minister Gordon

---

93 Reference by the Lord Advocate of devolution issues under paragraph 34 of Schedule 6 to the Scotland Act 1998 [2022] UKSC 31.

94 Nyatanga, D. (2020) 'Welsh independence: can Brexit awaken the sleeping dragon?', *LSE Brexit* [blog]. Available from: https://blogs.lse.ac.uk/brexit/2020/06/04/welsh-independence-can-brexit-awaken-the-sleeping-dragon/ [Accessed 6 March 2023].

95 Garry, J., O'Leary, B., McNicholl, K. and Pow, J. (2021) 'The future of Northern Ireland: border anxieties and support for Irish reunification under varieties of UKexit', *Regional Studies*, 55(9): 1517–27.

96 For an up-to-date poll of polls, see https://whatscotlandthinks.org, which captures independence referendum vote intention over time.

97 Cetrà, D. and Brown Swan, C. (2021) 'Speaking for "our precious Union": Unionist claims in the time of Brexit, 2016–20', *Territory, Politics, Governance*, 10(5): 1–15.

98 Ibid.

99 House of Lords (2021) Act of Union Bill.

Brown,[100] and from Wales, where the Welsh government has set out proposals for reform.[101] On the table are reforms to transform the House of Lords into a senate in which the nations and regions of the UK would be represented, giving the devolved nations a greater stake in decision making at the centre, and reforms to transform patterns of cooperation between the devolved governments. However, without government support, these reforms seem unlikely to materialise.

An acknowledgement of the weaknesses of the UK's current system of intergovernmental relations culminated in the Joint Review of Intergovernmental Relations. The review, published in 2022, set out a tiered system of intergovernmental relations, bringing together the prime minister with his or her Scottish, Welsh and Northern Irish counterparts annually, and regular interministerial working agreements.[102] The review also sets out a mechanism for decision making and dispute resolution, previously lacking from the UK's informal system of intergovernmental relations. This signals a much needed and long-overdue reform, but as Nicola McEwen notes, 'Machinery matters. Process and organisation matter', yet ultimately 'the proof will be in the practice'.[103]

Will these efforts gain traction? It is not clear whether, given the difficulty of achieving constitutional reform in the UK and the strength of constitutional preferences in Scotland, these efforts will be sufficient.

Conclusion

In over two decades, devolution has radically transformed Scotland and, by extension, the UK. The year 1999 saw the significant transfer of power to the newly elected Scottish Parliament, and two additional rounds of legislation saw these powers enhanced further. Devolution enjoys widespread public support, with a majority supportive of the devolved

[100] Brown, G. (2017) *My Life, Our Times*, New York: Random House.

[101] Welsh Government (2021) 'Reforming our union: shared governance in the UK', June 2021, Cardiff: Welsh Government. See also Bradbury, J. (2021) 'Welsh devolution and the Union: reform debates after Brexit', *Political Quarterly*, 92(1): 125–31 for analysis of Welsh government proposals.

[102] UK, Scottish and Welsh Governments and Northern Ireland Executive Government (2022) 'Review of intergovernmental relations', Policy Paper, London: Cabinet Office and the Department for Levelling Up, Housing and Communities. Available from: https://www.gov.uk/government/publications/the-review-of-intergovernmental-relations [Accessed 24 December 2022].

[103] McEwen, N. (2022) 'Worth the wait? Reforming intergovernmental relations', Centre on Constitutional Change [online], 14 January. Available from: https://www.centreonconstitutionalchange.ac.uk/news-and-opinion/worth-wait-reforming-intergovernmental-relations [Accessed 24 December 2022].

institutions and of the further transfer of powers.[104] Devolution provided a platform for the SNP, once a marginal actor in Scottish politics, to enter into government and pursue its policy of independence. While its 2014 bid was not successful, constitutional questions continue to define Scottish political life. And Brexit both re-ignited the Scottish independence debate and placed a spotlight on broader issues of the Union, devolution and the UK's constitutional settlement.

Both those in favour of independence and those in favour of the maintenance of the Union will face major questions in the years ahead. The status quo is no longer tenable, but it is not clear that the further transfer of powers from the centre to Holyrood will satisfy the demands of those seeking independence. Proponents of independence face significant challenges. The prospectus advanced in 2014 for an independent Scotland within the EU, trading freely with the rest of the UK and benefiting economically from its own fossil fuel resources, appears outdated in a post-Brexit world defined by climate emergency.

For advocates of the Union, it is increasingly clear that the status quo cannot hold. Demands on the territorial structure of the UK are acute and go far beyond Scotland. At a fundamental level, these debates speak to the understanding of power in the UK's constitutional arrangements. Is power to be fiercely guarded at Westminster or is it to be dispersed throughout the UK? Does sovereignty sit with Parliament or with the people? These questions underpin the debates over devolution and independence, and it is not wholly clear whether the UK can accommodate these differing understandings, raising the question of whether the UK constitution's famed flexibility has, at last, reached its limits.

Further reading

Brown Swan, C. (2020) 'The independence question', in M. Keating (ed) *Oxford Handbook of Scottish Politics*, Oxford: Oxford University Press.

McEwen, N. (2018) 'Brexit and Scotland: between two unions', *British Politics*, 13(1): 65–78.

McHarg, A., Mullen, T., Page, A. and Walker, N. (eds) (2016) *The Scottish Independence Referendum: Constitutional and Political Implications*, Oxford: Oxford University Press.

[104] Social Research and Scottish Government (2019) 'Scottish Social Attitudes 2019: attitudes to government and political engagement', Scottish Government, 29 September. Available from: https://www.gov.scot/publications/scottish-social-attitudes-2019-attitudes-government-political-engagement/ [Accessed 6 March 2023].

Sandford, M. and Gormley-Heenan, C. (2020) '"Taking back control", the UK's constitutional narrative and Schrodinger's devolution', *Parliamentary Affairs*, 73(1): 108–26.

St Denny, E. (2020) 'The Scottish Parliament', in M. Keating (ed) *Oxford Handbook of Scottish Politics*, Oxford: Oxford University Press, 481–99.

6

Diverse Voices in the Judiciary

Alysia Blackham

Judges hold significant power: they are responsible for resolving disputes,[1] applying (and making) law,[2] acting as 'a safeguard against arbitrary power'[3] including by scrutinising government acts and legislation,[4] upholding the rule of law and protecting individual rights.[5] We should therefore be cautious about who is vested with that power and responsibility; there is a clear need for diverse voices in the judiciary. Judicial diversity is key to judicial legitimacy and securing public confidence in the courts. As Baroness Hale argues, the four cornerstone virtues of judges in a democratic society should be: independence; incorruptibility; quality; and diversity.[6] However, existing initiatives to promote judicial diversity have struggled to achieve meaningful change, in particular at the senior levels of the judiciary. This is not an issue confined to the UK; advancing judicial

1 *Huddart, Parker & Co Pty Ltd v Moorehead* (1909) 8 CLR 330, 357 (Griffith CJ).

2 Dicey, A.V. (1959) *Introduction to the Study of the Law of the Constitution* (10th edn), London: Macmillan & Co, 60.

3 Moore, W.H. (1910) *The Constitution of the Commonwealth of Australia* (2nd edn), Melbourne: Maxwell, 322.

4 Allan, T.R.S. (1993) *Law, Liberty, and Justice: The Legal Foundations of British Constitutionalism*, Oxford: Oxford University Press, 282.

5 See *Entick v Carrington* (1765) 19 St Tr 1030, 1066 (Lord Camden CJ); *Somerset v Stewart* (1772) 20 St Tr 1, 82 (Lord Mansfield).

6 Hale, B. (2017) 'Judges, power and accountability: constitutional implications of judicial selection', at the Constitutional Law Summer School, Belfast, 11 August. Available from: https://www.supremecourt.uk/docs/speech-170811.pdf [Accessed 30 September 2022].

diversity remains a priority internationally,[7] though the UK is arguably falling behind other nations.[8]

This chapter considers what we might mean by judicial 'diversity', current progress towards diversity, and why judicial diversity is important. It argues that diverse voices will only be present in the judiciary with a fundamental rethink of judicial careers. In addition to (re)considering how we appoint judges, we also need to consider how judges are supported throughout their career (including in relation to flexibility, appraisals, training, career development and professional support), at the end of their tenure (in relation to the impact of retirement ages) and post-retirement (including in relation to judicial pensions). Through this holistic approach, it will be argued that there is substantial scope to include more diverse voices in the judiciary.

What do we mean by 'judicial diversity'?

But what do we mean by 'judicial diversity' or a 'diverse judiciary'? Diversity is more than just freedom from discrimination.[9] A diverse judiciary is one that includes people with a range of different characteristics, backgrounds and perspectives – one that 'reflect[s] the society it serves'.[10] Diversity goes beyond just gender – it also requires us to think about ethnicity,[11] sexuality, age, class and social background, disability, and diverse perspectives and experiences. As the Constitution Committee has argued: 'The arguments in favour of a diverse judiciary are even stronger if diversity is approached in its widest sense.'[12] The Courts and Tribunals Judiciary's *Judicial Diversity and Inclusion Strategy 2020–2025*, which puts forward objectives and ambitions to improve judicial diversity in England and Wales over a five-year period, therefore defines 'personal and professional diversity' as: 'Ethnicity, gender, disability, religion or belief, sexual orientation, caring responsibilities,

---

7 See, for example, Kang, A. et al (2020) 'Diverse and inclusive high courts: a global and intersectional perspective', *Politics, Groups, and Identities*, 8(4): 812–21.

8 Hale, B. (2013) 'Equality in the judiciary', Kuttan Memorial Lecture, 21 February. Available from: https://www.supremecourt.uk/docs/speech-130221.pdf [Accessed 30 September 2022], 4.

9 Select Committee on the Constitution (2012) 'Judicial appointments', 25th Report of Session 2012–13, House of Lords, HL Paper 272, London: The Stationery Office. Available from: www.publications.parliament.uk/pa/ld201012/ldselect/ldconst/272/27210.htm#a46 [Accessed 19 March 2015], para 68.

10 Gee, G. and Rackley, E. (2018) 'Introduction: diversity and the JAC's first ten years', in G. Gee and E. Rackley (eds) *Debating Judicial Appointments in an Age of Diversity*, Abingdon: Routledge, pp 1–21.

11 Judicial statistics use the term 'BAME' (an acronym for Black, Asian and Minority Ethnic) as a broad umbrella term to describe diverse ethnic groups. The term is problematic and confusing, but is used in this chapter as it continues to be used in judicial statistics.

12 Select Committee on the Constitution (n 9) para 69.

socio-economic background, marriage/civil partnership and gender identity; and also, professional diversity, such as individual career paths and jurisdictional backgrounds.'[13]

Why focus on judicial diversity?

Our need to focus on judicial diversity comes from a current lack of diversity. As the Constitution Committee has argued:

> The judge inhabiting a court room in England and Wales is stereotypically a white male from a narrow social background. Despite concerns raised over the last few decades, the proportion of women judges, black, Asian and minority ethnic (BAME) judges and others from under-represented groups has increased too slowly. ... The slow rate of change is not only a problem for those whose careers are affected; it is a problem for society as a whole.[14]

The causes of a lack of diversity in the judiciary are complex and deep-seated.[15] A lack of diversity reflects historic sociocultural factors, entrenched power relations, educational and social inequalities, barriers to judicial appointment and progression, and 'pipeline' issues relating to underrepresentation in the legal profession and at the bar.[16] It may also reflect discrimination, harassment and bullying in the judiciary and in the legal profession more broadly.[17]

Judicial diversity is important for many reasons. First, judicial diversity is important for those who go to court: judges and magistrates should be seen as reflecting and reflective of the general population. This is important for people to see the courts as accessible and legitimate, and to promote public confidence in the judiciary and the rule of law.[18] As the Constitution Committee has persuasively argued:

---

[13] Courts and Tribunals Judiciary (2020) 'Judicial diversity and inclusion strategy 2020–2025', London: Judicial Office. Available from: https://www.judiciary.uk/wp-content/uploads/2020/11/Judicial-Diversity-and-Inclsuion-Strategy-2020-2025.pdf [Accessed 22 June 2021], 10.

[14] Select Committee on the Constitution (n 9) para 68.

[15] Malleson, K. (2009) 'Diversity in the judiciary: the case for positive action', *Journal of Law and Society*, 36(3): 376–402.

[16] Ibid; Hale (n 8).

[17] Judiciary of England and Wales (2022) 'Judicial wellbeing survey 2021 – report and action plan', London: Judicial Office. Available from: https://www.judiciary.uk/wp-content/uploads/2022/07/14.51_Judicial_Wellbeing_Survey_2021_Repo.pdf [Accessed 30 September 2022].

[18] Melville, A. (2014) 'Evaluating judicial performance and addressing gender bias', *Onati Socio-Legal Series*, 4(5): 880–97, at 889; Malleson, K. (2003) 'Justifying gender equality on the bench: why difference won't do', *Feminist Legal Studies*, 11(1): 1–24, at 18-21, DOI:10.1023/A:1023231006909, at 18–21.

> Judges are independent of Parliament and the executive, but they should not stand apart from the society in which they adjudicate: the public must have confidence in the judges who make the decisions which affect their day to day lives. This is less likely to be the case 'if you have tribunal after tribunal with three members, all of whom are white men, particularly if that does not reflect the applicants coming through'. People appearing before a court must trust the judges to make decisions based on fairness: levels of trust will be greater if the judiciary itself is seen to have been fairly appointed. As Lady Justice Arden argued: 'People may well have more confidence that their concerns have been taken into account if the judiciary reflects more of a cross-section of society.'[19]

Kate Malleson has therefore argued that judicial diversity and equal participation is 'an inherent and essential feature of a democracy without which the judiciary will lose public confidence'.[20] Notions of equal opportunities and equality – now embedded in equality law and human rights law – also demand that judges be selected 'on their merits' and without discrimination.[21]

Second, judicial diversity may lead to different – and better – judicial decision making. Appointing judges from a diverse pool of candidates is likely to ensure that the best candidates are identified and appointed. A diverse judiciary may have different experiences, perspectives and opinions on legal issues; it is therefore likely to have a better understanding of society, and of those who appear before it, improving the quality of judicial decision making and legal development.[22] For example, the feminist judgments project shows how applying different perspectives to legal issues may lead to improved outcomes.[23] Diverse groups are more likely to overcome 'groupthink', challenging dominant ideas and cognitive biases, and thereby avoiding faulty decision making.[24]

---

19 Select Committee on the Constitution (n 9) para 73.

20 Malleson (n 18).

21 Advisory Panel on Judicial Diversity (2010) 'The report of the advisory panel on judicial diversity 2010', London: Judicial Office. Available from: https://www.judiciary.uk/wp-content/uploads/JCO/Documents/Reports/advisory-panel-judicial-diversity-2010.pdf [Accessed 9 November 2021], 15.

22 Select Committee on the Constitution (n 9) para 70.

23 Hunter, R.C., McGlynn, C. and Rackley, E. (2010) *Feminist Judgments: From Theory to Practice*, Oxford: Hart Publishing.

24 Kamalnath, A. (2017) 'Gender diversity as the antidote to groupthink on corporate boards', *Deakin Law Review*, 22(1): 85–106.

Nonetheless, diverse judges will not always make different decisions or adopt different decision-making approaches.[25] Empirical studies of male and female judges, for example, have not consistently found differences in decision making on the basis of gender.[26] This may be because women judges still have 'token status' and have had to adapt to masculine approaches to judging,[27] their views being homogenised by existing structures;[28] or because those who succeed in a male-dominated field tend to be atypical of other women; or because the nature of judging allows little room for the expression of difference.[29] Relying on the 'difference' argument to justify judicial diversity may also pigeonhole nontraditional judges into certain roles or areas of law, force them to overperform to justify their position,[30] or essentialise gender and other forms of diversity.[31] Malleson concludes, then, that 'difference-based arguments are too weak to stand as the principal foundation of gender equality on the bench'.[32] Judicial diversity is better justified by a focus on equality and legitimacy.[33]

Progress towards diversity

What progress have we made towards judicial diversity? There are two main ways in which we can measure progress. First, what measures have been put in place to promote judicial diversity? Second, are these measures working in practice – is the judiciary becoming more representative of the general population?

Initiatives and measures

Opening up appointments: key diversity initiatives in the UK have focused on expanding judicial recruitment, including by moving towards more transparent and accountable appointment processes. The Constitutional Reform Act 2005 (UK) Part 4 (CRA) – as amended by the Crime and

25 Melville (n 18) 884–8.

26 Malleson (n 18) 5–8; Melville (n 18) 884–5.

27 Malleson (n 18) 8–9.

28 Schultz, U. (2017) 'Do female judges judge differently? Empirical realities of a theoretical debate', in N. Sonneveld and M. Lindbekk (eds) *Women Judges in the Muslim World: A Comparative Study of Discourse and Practice*. Boston-Leiden: Brill, 23–50, DOI:10.1163/9789004342200.

29 Malleson (n 18) 8–9.

30 Ibid, 13–14; Melville (n 18) 885–6.

31 Malleson (n 18) 12–13; Melville (n 18) 890.

32 Malleson (n 18) 21.

33 Ibid, 15–21; Melville (n 18) 888–9.

Courts Act 2013 (UK) c 22 (hereinafter the '2013 Act') – 'opened up' judicial appointments in England and Wales, requiring job descriptions, public advertising and interviews for most judicial positions, bringing the process into line with established recruitment processes in professional appointments.[34]

The Judicial Appointments Commission (JAC), established by the CRA, is the independent body that recommends candidates for judicial appointments in England and Wales. In Scotland, a similar role is played by the Judicial Appointments Board for Scotland, and in Northern Ireland by the Northern Ireland Judicial Appointments Commission. The JAC oversees the recruitment of between 300 and 800 tribunal and judicial members each year.[35] It has members drawn from the judiciary, legal practice, and laypeople who are not legally trained. It has statutory duties to: select candidates solely on merit;[36] select only people of good character;[37] and 'have regard to the need to encourage diversity in the range of persons available for selection'.[38] Following an open recruitment process, the JAC makes recommendations for appointments to the Lord Chancellor and the Lord Chief Justice, who have the final say. Most recommendations are accepted, meaning the JAC has effectively become an appointing body rather than a recommending body.[39]

The process of appointing Supreme Court judges is different: Supreme Court judges are appointed by the monarch by letters patent[40] on the recommendation of the prime minister.[41] The prime minister may only recommend a person selected by a selection commission[42] convened by the Lord Chancellor.[43] The selection commission must select one candidate on merit.[44]

Steps to achieve diversity: section 137A of the CRA imposes a duty on the Lord Chancellor and the Lord Chief Justice to take such steps as they consider 'appropriate' to encourage judicial diversity. A number of initiatives have since been introduced. The *Judicial Diversity Committee* supports the Lord Chief Justice in encouraging judicial diversity and works to increase the number of applicants for judicial appointment from nontraditional backgrounds. The

---

34 Malleson (n 15) 379; Maute, J. (2007) 'English reforms to judicial selection: comparative lessons for American states?', *Fordham Urban Law Journal*, 34(1): 387–423.

35 Gee and Rackley (n 10) 5, Appendix 1.

36 CRA 2005, s 63.

37 Ibid, s 63.

38 Ibid, s 64.

39 Gee and Rackley (n 10) 6.

40 CRA 2005, s 23(2).

41 Ibid, s 26(2).

42 Ibid, s 26(3).

43 Ibid, s 26(5).

44 Ibid, s 27(5).

Committee undertakes outreach activities, including through a pool of 128 volunteer Diversity and Community Relations Judges (DCRJs). DCRJs are judges and tribunal members from across England and Wales[45] appointed following an expression of interest exercise and induction training.[46] DCRJs link the public with the judiciary, undertake educational activities, and encourage legal professionals from underrepresented groups to consider a judicial career. In 2019–20 these activities reached 30,000 school, college and university students, community members and legal professionals.[47]

The *Judicial Diversity Forum* (JDF) provides strategic direction for diversity initiatives, including in relation to addressing barriers to appointment, gathering data and evidence on diversity, and coordination of diversity activities. The JDF's members include the Chair of the JAC, the Lord Chancellor, the Lord Chief Justice, the Chair of the Bar Council, the President of the Law Society, the President of the Chartered Institute of Legal Executives and the Chair of the Legal Services Board.[48]

The judiciary also runs a *Judicial Work Shadowing Scheme*, enabling lawyers to shadow sitting judges and gain insights into judicial work; a *Judicial Mentoring Scheme* for lawyers from underrepresented groups; application seminars for those seeking appointment; and targeted support and education programmes. This outreach work is seen as essential for achieving judicial diversity. As Hazel Genn has argued: 'In terms of widening the pool, it is about outreach work; it is about myth busting; it is about improving confidence; and it is about educating people about our processes so that they know what they have to do.'[49]

Outcomes and progress

These initiatives typically assume that encouraging diverse lawyers to 'lean in' and seek judicial appointment will promote judicial diversity. This individualises responsibility for addressing systemic barriers to diversity; it adopts a deficiency model of equality, holding those of diverse backgrounds

---

45 Courts and Tribunals Judiciary (2021) 'Diversity and Community Relations Judges (DCRJs)'. Available from: https://www.judiciary.uk/about-the-judiciary/who-are-the-judiciary/judicial-roles/list-of-members-of-the-judiciary/diversity-and-community-relations-judges-list/ [Accessed 9 November 2021].

46 Judicial Diversity Taskforce (2013) 'Improving judicial diversity: progress towards delivery of the "Report of the advisory panel on judicial diversity 2010"', London: Judicial Office. Available from: https://assets.publishing.service.gov.uk/government/uploads/system/uploads/attachment_data/file/244013/judicial-diversity-taskforce-annual-report-2013.pdf [Accessed 8 November 2021] p 17.

47 Courts and Tribunals Judiciary (n 13).

48 Ibid.

49 Select Committee on the Constitution (n 9) para 78.

'accountable' for discrimination by focusing on internal (not external) change.[50] Understandably, this is unlikely to achieve meaningful change.[51]

So, given these limitations, what progress has been made?

The JAC: the Ministry of Justice has concluded that, where data are available, in comparison to pre-JAC years (1998–99 to 2005–6), there has been a clear increase in women and BAME candidates at both application and recommendation stages of JAC processes.[52] In 2019–20, for example, the JAC ran 37 selection exercises, with 8,258 applicants and 959 recommendations (across legal and nonlegal roles).[53] Across all legal selections, women represented 50 per cent of applicants, 45 per cent of those shortlisted and 45 per cent of those recommended for appointment; candidates identifying as BAME represented 25 per cent of applicants, 14 per cent of those shortlisted and 12 per cent of those recommended for appointment. Thus, success rates were lower for women and those identifying as BAME, but these differences were not statistically significant overall. However, these differences were statistically significant for specific selection exercises: for example, BAME candidates applying for Deputy High Court Judge positions had success rates 75 per cent lower, and BAME candidates applying for Recorder positions had success rates 59 per cent lower, compared to white candidates.[54] Women applicants were more likely to be successful in tribunal exercises compared to court exercises.[55]

Reliable statistics on disability, social mobility, sexual orientation and religion are now available for judicial appointments, if not for current judges. At the JAC, candidates with a disability had similar recommendation rates (from application) as nondisabled candidates, but candidates who attended a UK state school had lower recommendation rates than those who attended fee-paying schools (11 per cent versus 14 per cent), as did those who were the first generation in their family to attend university (10 per cent versus 14 per cent).[56] Gathering this data is an important first step in promoting diversity across a broader range of grounds.

---

[50] Jackson, L. (2017) 'Leaning out in higher education: a structural, postcolonial perspective', *Policy Futures in Education*, 15(3): 295–308, DOI:10.1177/1478210317708496.

[51] He, J.C., Kang, S.K. and Lacetera, N. (2021) 'Opt-out choice framing attenuates gender differences in the decision to compete in the laboratory and in the field', *Proceedings of the National Academy of Sciences*, 118(42): e2108337118, DOI:10.1073/pnas.2108337118.

[52] Ministry of Justice (2020) 'Diversity of the judiciary: legal professions, new appointments and current post-holders: 2020 statistics', London: Ministry of Justice. Available from: https://assets.publishing.service.gov.uk/government/uploads/system/uploads/attachment_data/file/918529/diversity-of-the-judiciary-2020-statistics-web.pdf [Accessed 21 June 2021], 10.

[53] Ibid, 22.

[54] Ibid, 14.

[55] Ibid, 3.

[56] Ibid, 37.

The judiciary: it was argued that an open appointment process would naturally lead to a 'trickle-up' effect, inevitably and efficiently changing the judiciary's composition to reflect the increasing diversity of the legal profession.[57] This assumes, though, that the legal profession is diverse, that practitioners from all backgrounds will want to seek judicial appointment ('lean in'), and that 'fairness' and appointment on 'merit' are sufficient to overcome systemic and entrenched disadvantage. Understandably, this 'trickle-up' effect has not worked as well or as quickly as was originally envisaged.

At 1 April 2020, women represented 32 per cent of all court judges and 47 per cent of tribunal judges, but only 26 per cent of judges in the High Court and above. Those identifying as BAME represented 8 per cent of all court judges, 12 per cent of tribunal judges (both increased by 2 percentage points since 2014), but only 4 per cent of judges in the High Court and above.[58] There has therefore been some progress towards diversity, at least at the lower levels of the judiciary, but current initiatives have struggled to achieve diversity at the higher levels of the judiciary. As Karon Monaghan argues: 'If an increase in the proportion of underrepresented groups in the senior judiciary is to be taken as the measure of the JAC's success, then there is not much to celebrate.'[59] The ongoing exclusion of women from senior judicial positions may be due to emphasis on 'old' (masculine) judicial qualities in promotion processes and a narrowing eligibility pool.[60]

Kate Malleson has therefore summarised progress as follows:

> The empirical evidence is now clear, both from the UK and from judiciaries around the world, that reforms to the structure or processes of the courts or the judicial appointments process have very little effect on judicial diversity. The only structural change which makes a significant difference to the composition of courts is the introduction of quotas, which are currently off the political agenda in the UK.
>
> Whether or not it continues to be acceptable for the quality of the UK Supreme Court to be undermined by the over-representation of white, male, privately educated barristers is ultimately a political question … it is looking likely that Lord Sumption will be proved right when he predicted in 2012 that it would be 50 years before gender

57 Malleson (n 15) 379.

58 Ministry of Justice (n 52) 3.

59 Monaghan, K. (2018) 'Reflection', in G. Gee and E. Rackley (eds) *Debating Judicial Appointments in an Age of Diversity*, Abingdon: Routledge, 198–204.

60 Hunter, R. (2015) 'Judicial diversity and the "new" judge', in H. Sommerlad, S. Harris-Short, S. Vaughan and R. Young (eds) *The Futures of Legal Education and the Legal Profession*, London: Bloomsbury, 79–96.

> equality in the judiciary is achieved. If anything, he may have been overly optimistic.[61]

This bleak assessment only considers progress on gender and BAME representation; other grounds and forms of diversity are harder to measure. While there are some data on other characteristics for judicial appointments, there are limited data on judges who are already in post. Thus, it is difficult to track diversity on grounds other than gender and ethnicity, or to adopt a holistic or wide approach to diversity. While we are making progress on judicial diversity, there is still a long way to go.

Achieving judicial diversity

Diverse voices will only be present in the judiciary with a fundamental rethink of judicial careers. In addition to (re)considering how we appoint judges, we also need to consider how judges are supported throughout their career (including in relation to flexibility, appraisals, training, career development and professional support), at the end of their tenure (in relation to the impact of retirement ages) and post-retirement (including in relation to judicial pensions).[62] Through this holistic and systemic[63] approach, it is argued here that there is substantial scope to include more diverse voices in the judiciary.

Appointments

While the JAC appears to be promoting more diverse judicial appointments, there is still substantial progress to be made, particularly for senior appointments where the JAC does not supervise the process.[64] Progress is slow: on our current trajectory, it may take 50–100 years to achieve a diverse judiciary.[65] Further, current measures are fundamentally limited by the pool from which the judiciary is appointed: 'Without some kind of positive discrimination,

[61] Malleson, K. (2021) 'The problem of judicial diversity', *Policy Exchange*, 24 January. Available from: https://policyexchange.org.uk/the-problem-of-judicial-diversity/ [Accessed 22 June 2021].

[62] Mack, K. and Roach Anleu, S. (2012) 'Entering the Australian judiciary: gender and court hierarchy', *Law & Policy*, 34(3): 313–47, DOI:10.1111/j.1467-9930.2012.00365.x.

[63] Gee and Rackley (n 10) 2.

[64] Bowcott, O. (2015) 'Lady Hale: Supreme Court should be ashamed if diversity does not improve', *The Guardian* [online], 7 November. Available from: http://www.theguardian.com/law/2015/nov/06/lady-hale-supreme-court-ashamed-diversity-improve [Accessed 7 April 2016].

[65] Lord Sumption (2012) 'Home truths about judicial diversity', Bar Council Law Reform Lecture, 15 November. Available from: https://www.supremecourt.uk/docs/speech-121115-lord-sumption.pdf [Accessed 22 June 2021], 14.

the judiciary is never going to be significantly more diverse than the pool from which it is drawn'[66] – that is, the legal profession. As Lord Sumption has argued: 'We are simply deluding ourselves if we try to pretend that selection from that pool on merit alone will produce a fully diverse, or even a reasonably diverse judiciary quickly. It will happen, but it will take a long time.'[67]

Increasing the use of positive action is therefore an important means of promoting judicial diversity. However, positive action to promote diversity in judicial appointments is politically contentious and controversial.[68] In its report, the Advisory Panel on Judicial Diversity explicitly rejected the idea of quotas or specific diversity targets for judicial appointments.[69] Quotas might undermine the position of individuals from underrepresented groups who had been 'appointed on the strength of their true personal ability' and discourage applications from individuals from well-represented groups, 'who might fear the system is stacked against them'.[70]

Instead of imposing formal quotas for underrepresented groups, the Advisory Panel on Judicial Diversity recommended that the JAC make 'use of the Equality Bill positive action provisions where the merits of candidates are essentially indistinguishable'.[71] Section 159 of the Equality Act 2010 relevantly provides that:

> if a person (P) reasonably thinks that –
>
> (a) persons who share a protected characteristic suffer a disadvantage connected to the characteristic, or
> (b) participation in an activity by persons who share a protected characteristic is disproportionately low …
>
> [this Act] does not prohibit P from treating a person (A) more favourably in connection with recruitment or promotion than another person (B) because A has the protected characteristic but B does not, with the aim of enabling or encouraging persons who share the protected characteristic to –
>
> (a) overcome or minimise that disadvantage, or
> (b) participate in that activity.

66 Ibid, 9.

67 Ibid, 14. And, for Lord Sumption, diversity should not be pursued at the expense of 'merit' or 'the quality of the bench' (at 22); this will be discussed later.

68 Malleson (n 15) 385.

69 Advisory Panel on Judicial Diversity (n 21) 7.

70 Ibid, 20.

71 Ibid, 9.

However, this only applies, if:

(a) A is as qualified as B to be recruited or promoted;
(b) P does not have a policy of treating persons who share the protected characteristic more favourably in connection with recruitment or promotion than persons who do not share it; and
(c) taking the action in question is a proportionate means of achieving the aim.

The JAC made it clear that section 159 of the Equality Act 2010 was unlikely to have any practical impact on its decisions:

> The JAC will always select on merit and has to date been able to distinguish between the relevant merits of different candidates based on a careful assessment of an applicant's entire profile and background. The JAC therefore does not anticipate that this provision of the Equality Act will be relevant in practice.[72]

The 2013 Act amended section 27 of the CRA to explicitly provide that section 159 of the Equality Act 2010 does not apply to Supreme Court appointments. Instead, section 27 of the CRA now provides that a UK Supreme Court selection commission is not prevented from preferring one candidate over another for the purposes of increasing diversity where two candidates are of 'equal merit'. This is a very limited positive action measure: it merely provides 'negative permission' to use a 'tipping point' provision.[73] While this has theoretical potential to increase diversity, it is unlikely to be used in practice; it would be exceptional for two candidates to be regarded as being of 'equal merit'.

An issue at the heart of positive action is therefore how we define 'merit'. For Lord Sumption (an opponent of positive action and quotas): 'Selection on merit alone is … fundamental to the perceived legitimacy of the judiciary.'[74] But the idea of 'merit' is not objective or unambiguous. Margaret Thornton

---

[72] Ministry of Justice (2011) 'Improving judicial diversity: progress towards delivery of the "Report of the advisory panel on judicial diversity 2010", London: Ministry of Justice. Available from: https://assets.publishing.service.gov.uk/government/uploads/system/uploads/attachment_data/file/217354/judicial-diversity-report-2010.pdf [Accessed 9 November 2021], 33.

[73] O'Brien, P. (2012) 'Three thoughts about the Crime and Courts Bill and judicial appointments', *UK Constitutional Law Association*, 2 July. Available from: https://ukconstitutionallaw.org/2012/07/02/patrick-obrien-three-thoughts-about-the-crime-and-courts-bill-and-judicial-appointments/ [Accessed 9 November 2021].

[74] Lord Sumption (n 63) 22.

argues that 'merit' is just a rhetorical and performative device, shaped by power and designed to maintain power.[75]

At a practical level, too, the 'best' candidate for a judicial role depends on how that role and its criteria are framed: the Constitution Committee has warned of a risk of equating being a good advocate with being a good judge.[76] Even Lord Sumption has argued that one of the reasons for a lack of judicial diversity is the recruitment of candidates on narrow and 'highly prescriptive job descriptions', designed to find judges who can 'hit the ground running' without training:

> there are virtually no facilities for the training of those appointed to full-time judicial positions before they take them up. This lack of training facilities is aggravated by the highly prescriptive job descriptions prepared by the Courts Service and the Ministry of Justice when a vacancy needs to be filled. They commonly insist on the appointment of people who can, as the hackneyed phrase goes, 'hit the ground running' instead of having time to grow into the job. There is strong resistance to the appointment of people who may need time to acclimatise themselves to their new role. This attitude may be understandable at a time of financial stringency. But its effect is to put pressure on the Commission [to] choose 'safe' candidates in preference to those with less experience but greater potential.[77]

Thus, our idea of 'merit' is just a construction: a broader view of what makes a good judge is key to having diverse voices in the judiciary. This may be difficult to achieve if judges themselves are tasked with managing judicial recruitment and appointments: there is a risk that judges will 'subconsciously recruit in their own image'[78] or 'seek self-replication in those they promote',[79] limiting diversity. As Lord Sumption notes:

> I do not believe that the judges were out to clone themselves then, any more than they are now. But it would be foolish to pretend that they were not occasionally influenced by unconscious stereotyping and by perceptions of ability moulded by their own personal experience.[80]

[75] Thornton, M. (2007) 'Otherness on the bench: how merit is gendered', *Sydney Law Review*, 29(3): 391–414.

[76] Select Committee on the Constitution (n 9) para 84.

[77] Lord Sumption (n 63) 8.

[78] Advisory Panel on Judicial Diversity (n 21) 42.

[79] Malleson (n 15) 389.

[80] Lord Sumption (n 63) 7.

Selection panels should therefore be as diverse as possible, and include both lay and legal voices.[81] More fundamentally, though, we need to challenge and disrupt prevailing ideas of 'merit', recognising that they, too, are constructed to exclude diverse voices. There is a 'deep-seated reluctance' to disrupt what (or who) makes a 'good judge'[82] and the JAC continues to apply a narrow idea of 'merit'.[83] For John Morison, this is a 'very specific, largely male, hierarchical, Bar-oriented, advocacy-centred, judge-conditioned understanding of merit' which has done little to advance diversity.[84]

'Re-engineering' the idea of merit requires re-examining and better understanding the role of the 'modern' judge in order to better reflect the evolving role of the courts as a public service.[85] Drawing on interview s and focus groups with around 60 practitioners and public servants in Northern Ireland, Morison argues that 'merit' is seen by legal professionals in a broader way than what is used in judicial appointments exercises.[86] For the 'modern' judge, 'merit' entails more than just technical legal knowledge and skilled advocacy; it demands empathy and judgement, skilled case management, listening and problem solving.[87] Indeed, a nontraditional background itself can be meritorious.[88]

Retention

Arguably, too, we have focused too much on judicial appointments: while diverse recruitment and appointments are fundamental to promoting judicial diversity, we then need to support and retain diverse candidates once they are appointed. In the '2016 UK Judicial Attitude Survey', 144 of 472 female judicial respondents (31 per cent) were considering leaving the judiciary early (that is, in the next five years, when they were not scheduled to retire).[89] Similarly, 30 of the 77 BAME judicial respondents (39 per cent) were considering leaving in the next five years. How, then, should we support

81 Select Committee on the Constitution (n 9) paras 87–8.

82 Gee and Rackley (n 10) 17.

83 Monaghan (n 59) 202–3.

84 Morison, J. (2018) 'Beyond merit: the new challenge for judicial appointments', in G. Gee and E. Rackley (eds) *Debating Judicial Appointments in an Age of Diversity*, Abingdon: Routledge, 223–39.

85 Ibid, 237–9.

86 Ibid, 227.

87 Ibid.

88 Ibid.

89 Thomas, C.A. (2017) '2016 UK Judicial Attitude Survey: Report of findings covering salaried judges in England and Wales courts and UK tribunals', London: Judicial Office. Available from: www.judiciary.uk/wp-content/uploads/2017/02/jas-2016-england-wales-court-uk-tribunals-7-february-2017.pdf [Accessed 22 December 2021], 78.

judicial retention, particularly for diverse voices? This requires a focus on working conditions, support and training.

Judicial training, appraisal and career progression may have important repercussions for judicial retention and diversity. Performance processes can emphasise summative (judgmental) or formative (developmental) goals.[90] Currently, though, both goals are pursued only to a limited extent for judges and tribunal members.

In its 2010 report, the Advisory Panel on Judicial Diversity recommended 'the consistent implementation of appraisal and mentoring throughout the judiciary' for skill and career development.[91] This sentiment was echoed by the Constitution Committee, which recommended the introduction of a formal appraisal system for the judiciary: 'without an effective appraisals system, the public cannot be assured that the judiciary is of the highest possible quality … the cost of an appraisals system pales into insignificance compared with the cost of having poor judges'.[92]

However, in the '2014 UK Judicial Attitude Survey', the majority of respondents (64 per cent) were dissatisfied with opportunities for personal development.[93] Formalised processes for promoting judicial development are rare.[94] This leaves judges with limited guidance and support, particularly where they are new to their role. Graham Gee et al note the growing acceptance of the potential value of performance assessment in the UK judiciary.[95] However, performance appraisal is still rarely used in the UK courts: Deputy District Judges are the only judges in the court system who are subject to a formal appraisal scheme.[96] Gee et al argue that the reason this system has not been extended to other judges relates to a lack of practical resources.[97]

The UK tribunal system also makes use of appraisal mechanisms for tribunal members: almost all tribunals have an appraisal scheme in place, or

[90] Boswell, W.R. and Boudreau, J.W. (2002) 'Separating the developmental and evaluative performance appraisal uses', *Journal of Business and Psychology*, 16(3): 391–412, DOI:10.1023/A:1012872907525, at 392.

[91] Advisory Panel on Judicial Diversity (n 21) 5.

[92] Select Committee on the Constitution (n 9) para 186.

[93] Thomas, C.A. (2015) '2014 UK Judicial Attitude Survey: Report of findings covering salaried judges in England and Wales courts and UK tribunals', London: Judicial Office, 35. Available from: https://www.judiciary.uk/wp-content/uploads/2015/02/jac-2014-results.pdf [Accessed 6 March 2023].

[94] Wallace, A., Roach Anleu, S. and Mack, K. (2015) 'Evaluating judicial performance for caseload allocation', *Monash University Law Review*, 41(2): 445–68, at 447.

[95] Gee, G., Hazell, R., Malleson, K. and O'Brien P. (2015) *The Politics of Judicial Independence in the UK's Changing Constitution*, Cambridge: Cambridge University Press, 154.

[96] Ibid.

[97] Ibid.

plans to implement one.[98] The schemes vary across the tribunals, though all have an agreed number of appraisals each year, use self-assessment or 360-degree feedback, and create some record of the review.[99] In employment tribunals, for instance, fee-paid (casual) members participate in the appraisal scheme, but salaried (permanent) and regional members are not covered.[100] Assessment in the scheme includes observation of a hearing, a self-assessment and the creation of a self-development plan that identifies any training or development needs.[101] New employment tribunal appointees participate in the appraisal scheme within 18 months of their appointment; other fee-paid members participate every three years.[102] This is a significant period of time to elapse between appraisals: according to the UK Chartered Institute of Personnel and Development, 87 per cent of UK employers use some form of *annual* performance appraisal.[103] Thus, while UK tribunals are progressively introducing some form of appraisal and development, this still lags significantly behind the general workforce. There is therefore scope for the significant improvement of development and performance systems.

In terms of *career progression*, there is no formal judicial career structure in the UK.[104] In the '2014 UK Judicial Attitude Survey', 63 per cent of judges said that opportunities for career progression in their current post were poor or non-existent.[105] Opportunities for progression were particularly limited for tribunal judges: of employment judges, 87 per cent said opportunities for career progression were non-existent or poor.[106] If judges are appointed for a period potentially in excess of 20 years, there needs to be some scope for individual challenge and development after appointment, be that through allocation of more challenging tasks or formal promotion to a higher court. If being a judge is seen as a career with promotion possibilities, the judiciary will be more likely to attract good candidates for appointment,[107] and might attract a more diverse pool of applicants.[108] Conversely, a lack of promotion and development opportunities may impede judicial retention and satisfaction. In

[98] Judicial College (2015) *Tribunals*, Autumn. Available from: https://www.judiciary.uk/wp-content/uploads/2013/07/tribunals-journal-autumn-2015.pdf [Accessed 9 November 2021], 3.

[99] Ibid.

[100] Ibid, 4.

[101] Ibid.

[102] Ibid, 5.

[103] Ibid, 2.

[104] Davidow, R.P. (1981a) 'Beyond merit selection: judicial careers through merit promotion', *Texas Tech Law Review*, 12: 851–910, at 859.

[105] Thomas (n 93) 22.

[106] Ibid, 23.

[107] Davidow, R.P. (1981) 'Law student attitudes towards judicial careers', *University of Cincinnati Law Review*, 50: 247–83, at 277.

[108] Ibid, 278.

the '2014 UK Judicial Attitude Survey', lack of promotion was a factor that would prompt early retirement for 24 per cent of respondents.[109] Promotion to a higher post would make 41 per cent of respondents more likely to remain in the judiciary until retirement age.[110] Similarly, the opportunity to take a sabbatical would make 29 per cent of respondents more likely to remain in the judiciary until retirement age, and greater leadership responsibilities would influence 20 per cent to remain.[111]

Flexible work

Workplace flexibility is important for both recruiting and retaining diverse judges. Flexible work can help judges to manage health issues[112] and caring responsibilities,[113] particularly into older age.[114] This is important to promote diversity on the basis of gender, caring responsibilities, disability and age.

At present, flexible working is fairly uncommon in judicial roles. In England and Wales, part-time work has been available for all salaried (permanent) judicial roles since 2005, so long as it had 'no material adverse impact on the business needs of the court/tribunal or the services to users'.[115] Further, judges had '[no] absolute right to sit part-time nor is the opportunity to sit part-time reserved for discrete sections of the judiciary, such as those with caring responsibilities'.[116] Now, though, part-time working is available to all salaried judicial office holders, unless such an arrangement is refused on the basis of an operational requirement or business need.[117] The minimum sitting requirement remains at least 50 per cent of a full-time equivalent post.[118, 119] The 2013 Act amended s 23 of the CRA to provide that the

[109] Thomas (n 93) 46.

[110] Ibid, 51.

[111] Ibid.

[112] Burnay, N. (2011) 'Ageing at work: between changing social policy patterns and reorganization of working times', *Population Review*, 50(2): 150–65, DOI:10.1353/prv.2011.0020, at 161.

[113] Maltby, T. (2009) 'The employability of older workers: what works?', in W. Loretto, S. Vickerstaff and P. White (eds) *The Future for Older Workers: New Perspectives*, Bristol: Policy Press, 161–84.

[114] Blackham, A. (2015) 'Rethinking working time to support older workers', *International Journal of Comparative Labour Law and Industrial Relations*, 31(2): 119–40.

[115] Ministry of Justice (2009) 'Judicial salaried part-time working: a practical guide, April. Available from: https://parlament.mt/media/100472/03516.pdf [Accessed 17 May 2023].

[116] Ibid, 8.

[117] Ministry of Justice (2020) 'Judicial salaried part-time working policy'. Available from: https://judicialappointments.gov.uk/wp-content/uploads/2020/11/Revised-Judicial-Salaried-Part-Time-Working-Policy-Final-002.pdf [Accessed 4 May 2023].

[118] Ministry of Justice (2009), 11.

[119] Ministry of Justice (2020), 7.

Supreme Court must be composed of a maximum number of 12 full-time equivalent judges, rather than a maximum number of 12 individual judges. This may enable part-time judicial appointments to the Supreme Court, potentially allowing for more diverse appointments.

In the '2016 Judicial Attitude Survey', respondents were asked how important opportunities for flexible working were to them: in the results for England and Wales judges and UK tribunals, 44 per cent of respondents thought flexible work was important.[120] Despite this, only 13 per cent rated opportunities for flexible working as good or excellent; 54 per cent said they were non-existent.[121] That said, flexible working was found to be most important to tribunal judges, and tribunal judges also had the best access to flexible working.[122]

An absence of flexible working in the higher judiciary might impede judicial progression and advancement, particularly for those with caring responsibilities (often women). Workplace flexibility may promote judicial recruitment, satisfaction and retention.[123] Indeed, in the '2014 UK Judicial Attitude Survey', the inability to work flexible hours was a factor that would prompt early retirement for 17 per cent of respondents;[124] conversely, the opportunity to work part-time would make 34 per cent of respondents more likely to remain in the judiciary until retirement age, and increased flexibility in working hours would influence 25 per cent to remain.[125]

A focus on part-time working represents a limited view of what constitutes 'flexible work'. Other forms of flexibility include shorter working hours, job sharing, gradual retirement or 'bridge' jobs for older judges, sabbaticals, increased unpaid or paid leave, and leave for caring or family responsibilities.[126] It is unclear whether these more creative options are being adopted by courts and tribunals.

Retirement

Judges and tribunal members are some of the few workers in the UK who are still subject to mandatory retirement ages. Most judicial officers now

---

120 Thomas (n 89) 52.

121 Ibid.

122 Ibid, 57.

123 Hartlapp, M. and Schmid, G. (2008) 'Labour market policy for "active ageing" in Europe: expanding the options for retirement transitions', *Journal of Social Policy*, 37(3): 409–31, DOI:10.1017/S0047279408001979, at 417.

124 Thomas (n 93) 46.

125 Ibid, 51.

126 Fogg, S. (2001) *Counting on Experience: A Review of Good Practice in the Employment of Mature Workers*. Sydney: NSW Committee on Ageing, 34.

have a mandatory retirement age of 75,[127] increased in 2022 from age 70.[128]

Mandatory retirement can open up space for new judicial appointments, and this may help to increase judicial diversity. In a survey I conducted of appointment and retirement announcements posted on the Courts and Tribunals Judiciary's website, I found that 67 more women were appointed to the bench as a result of judicial retirements and resignations from 1 November 2013 to 16 August 2015.[129] This implies that progress is being made towards gender diversity at least partly due to judicial retirements, some of which occur at the mandatory retirement age. Thus, mandatory retirement is one means of facilitating judicial turnover and increasing diversity; that said, its overall impact on diversity is relatively small.

Fixed judicial retirement ages can also deter some people from seeking judicial appointment: those with disrupted or nonlinear career paths may prefer to remain in roles with no fixed retirement age rather than seek a judicial appointment with a fixed retirement age. Now that mandatory retirement has been abolished for many roles, judicial retirement ages may deter more diverse applicants who prefer to continue working, either due to lost years in child rearing or due to a need for income.[130] Retirement ages stop some people from '[reaching] the highest levels of the judiciary, however talented or experienced they might be, because their career paths have taken too long'.[131] Adopting higher retirement ages, or removing them entirely, may be 'particularly beneficial to those who started on the career ladder later in life, perhaps after taking a career break to have children'.[132] Removing or extending judicial retirement ages may actually make the judiciary a more attractive career path for nontraditional office holders.[133]

---

[127] Public Service Pensions and Judicial Offices Act 2022 (UK), s 121, sch 1; see Judicial Pensions and Retirement Act 1993 (UK), s 26, sch 6 ('JUPRA').

[128] Cowie, G. (2021) 'Judicial retirement: plans to move from 70 to 75', Insight, House of Commons Library, UK Parliament [online], 12 March. Available from: https://commons library.parliament.uk/judicial-retirement-plans-to-move-from-70-to-75/ [Accessed 25 June 2021].

[129] Blackham, A. (2018) 'Judicial diversity and mandatory retirement: obstacle or route to diversity?', in G. Gee and E. Rackley (eds) *Debating Judicial Appointments in an Age of Diversity*, Abingdon: Routledge, 183–97.

[130] Campbell, S. (1979) 'Delayed mandatory retirement and the working woman', *The Gerontologist*, 19(3): 257–63, DOI:10.1093/geront/19.3.257.

[131] Select Committee on the Constitution (n 9) para 195.

[132] Ibid.

[133] Genn, H.G. (2008) 'The attractiveness of senior judicial appointment to highly qualified practitioners: report to the judicial executive board', Directorate of Judicial Offices for England and Wales. Available from: http://www.ucl.ac.uk/laws/judicial-institute/files/The_Attractiveness_of_Senior_Judicial_Appointment_Research_Report.pdf [Accessed 31 March 2015], 29.

These effects are exacerbated by judicial pension arrangements. Under the Judicial Pensions and Retirement Act 1993 (JUPRA) pension system,[134] those appointed as judges after the age of 50 are unlikely to earn a full judicial pension. The New Judicial Pension Scheme (introduced in 2015) further reduces judicial pensions. This may lead to a shortage of individuals willing to enter judicial office.[135] Alternatively, it may lead to more wealthy (and often white male) lawyers 'consider[ing] the High Court as a hobby to pursue for a few years', as they do not need the remuneration or pension from a judicial appointment.[136] This may seriously undermine judicial diversity, and poses a particular challenge for women, who are more likely to take career breaks to look after children, reducing their overall income and financial wellbeing prior to being appointed to the bench,[137] and potentially slowing their career progression and ability to be appointed to the bench at an earlier age.[138]

Pensions and retirement provisions – taken together – may prevent good candidates from accepting an appointment to the bench[139] and impede progress towards diversity. Changes to pensions and pay may also impair judicial retention. The '2014 Judicial Attitude Survey' found that pension and pay entitlements were highly influential on judicial behaviour, at least once individuals were occupying judicial posts: 68 per cent of respondents said they would likely leave the judiciary due to reductions in pension benefits.[140] Conversely, 58 per cent said a settled position on pension entitlements would help to keep them in their posts.[141] A clear majority – 76 per cent – said they would discourage suitable applicants from applying to become a judge given the likelihood of further pension reductions.[142] This may seriously affect the judicial appointments process, including for more diverse candidates.

---

[134] Judicial Pensions and Retirement Act 1993 (UK).

[135] Jack, A. (2015) 'Very empty benches', *Counsel*, November. Available from: http://www.counselmagazine.co.uk/articles/very-empty-benches [Accessed 7 April 2016].

[136] Jack, A. (2015) 'Empty benches', *Counsel*, July. Available from: http://www.counselmagazine.co.uk/articles/empty-benches [Accessed 7 April 2016].

[137] HC Deb 3 December 1992, vol 215, col 432 (Sir Ivan Lawrence). See also col 464 (Sir Ivan Lawrence).

[138] HC Deb 3 December 1992, vol 215, col 449 (Mr Byers).

[139] HL Deb 30 June 1992, vol 538, col 691 (Lord Benson). See also HL Deb 30 June 1992, vol 538, col 696 (Viscount Bledisloe); HC Deb 3 December 1992, vol 215, col 465 (Sir Ivan Lawrence).

[140] Thomas (n 93) 46.

[141] Ibid, 51.

[142] Ibid, 57.

The future of judicial diversity

Securing the future of judicial diversity therefore requires concerted action, across the areas of recruitment, retention and retirement. Current initiatives are not sufficient; more needs to be done. In designing new interventions and initiatives, though, we need better data around diversity, particularly for grounds other than gender and ethnicity. The Courts and Tribunals Judiciary's 'Judicial Diversity and Inclusion Strategy 2020–2025' makes it clear that better data gathering and reporting is key to promoting judicial diversity:

> we must improve the diversity data we hold and our reporting on diversity in the judiciary. Better data will mean that we can identify areas where we have become more diverse and take focused action, on an evidence led basis, on the areas where progress to date has not been sufficient. We will use the data we collect to inform and improve policies, procedures and practices in the judiciary, and to drive strategies directed at improving the personal and professional diversity of the judiciary and supporting a more inclusive culture.[143]

The strategy puts forward four core objectives for achieving diversity:

- creating an environment in which there is greater responsibility for, and reporting on, progress in achieving diversity and inclusion;
- supporting and building a more inclusive and respectful culture and working environment within the judiciary;
- supporting and developing the career potential of existing judges;
- supporting greater understanding of judicial roles and achieving greater diversity in the pool of applicants for judicial roles.[144]

These are all worthy objectives, but we also need to review judicial pensions and pay, fundamentally challenge prevailing ideas of 'merit', promote and encourage flexible working, and introduce more effective positive action measures, such as quotas.

More generally, too, a focus on judicial diversity requires us to focus on diversity in the legal profession, as most judges are drawn from those working as barristers and solicitors.[145] Thus, more diverse voices in the

[143] Courts and Tribunals Judiciary (n 13) 10.

[144] Ibid.

[145] Lord Sumption (n 63) 10.

judiciary require us to include diverse voices in the legal profession and in legal education.

Further reading

Blackham, A. (2019) 'Reconceiving judicial office through a labour law lens', *Federal Law Review*, 47(2): 203–30.

Courts and Tribunals Judiciary (2020) 'Judicial diversity and inclusion strategy 2020–2025', London: Judicial Office. Available from: https://www.judiciary.uk/wp-content/uploads/2020/11/Judicial-Diversity-and-Inclsuion-Strategy-2020-2025.pdf [Accessed 22 June 2021].

Gee, G. and Rackley, E. (eds) (2018) *Debating Judicial Appointments in an Age of Diversity*, Abingdon: Routledge.

Hunter, R. (2015) 'Judicial diversity and the "new" judge', in H. Sommerlad, S. Harris-Short, S. Vaughan and R. Young (eds) *The Futures of Legal Education and the Legal Profession*, London: Bloomsbury, 79–96.

Malleson, K. (2003) 'Justifying gender equality on the bench: why difference won't do', *Feminist Legal Studies*, 11: 1–24.

PART II

The Individual and the State

7

The *Begum* Case, Discretion and Parliamentary Sovereignty: Unmaking the Constitutional Subject

Devyani Prabhat

Introduction

This chapter examines the intersection between constitutional law and citizenship frameworks to unpack how rights arise for constitutional subjects. Constitutional subjects can be of two kinds. First, constitutional subjects are people who can make constitutional claims. Second, constitutional subjects may be topics that are covered by the constitution. In this sense, these are the subject matter of the constitution. Both these meanings are interrelated, as without people to raise claims, there is no point in having constitutional subject matters. This chapter uses the opportunity to examine the cancellation of citizenship case brought in 2021– *Begum v Secretary of State for the Home Department*[1] – to exemplify the operation of fundamental principles of British constitutional and immigration law. The tensions in this field are manifold.[2] Having additional nationalities has often been perceived as an advantage and a privilege of globalisation.

1 *R (Begum) v Secretary of State for the Home Department* [2021] UKSC 7.

2 In the US context, see Motomura, H. (1996) 'Whose alien nation? Two models of constitutional immigration law', *Michigan Law Review*, 94(6): 1927–52. For more on the comparative context, see Golder, B. and Williams, G. (2006) 'Balancing national security and human rights: assessing the legal response of common law nations to the threat of terrorism', *Journal of Comparative Policy Analysis*, 8(1): 43–62.

However, as nationality through migrant connections becomes a racialised category, it also creates precariousness and lack of voice. Cancellation cases affect minority ethnic citizens more than others through their ancestry and/or ethnicity – so-called 'heritage' links. These dynamics push some members of society to the fringes of citizenship – they become 'accidental citizens' and a hierarchy or typology of constitutional claims becomes prevalent rather than equal justice for all. This chapter firstly establishes the links between cancellation powers and effects on minority ethnic citizens through the *Begum* case. It then examines parliamentary sovereignty and its interplay with issues of discretion and deference. It also analyses the specific barriers to review for national security matters with the associated adverse effects on minority rights, eventually concluding that those with multiple nationality connections are particularly at risk of becoming lesser or merely accidental citizens.

Cancellation, the *Begum* case and minority ethnicity citizens

Cancellation cases are increasingly used to prevent the re-entry of 'problematic' citizens for the purposes of counterterrorism. The manner in which the legislative provisions for cancellation of citizenship are structured places minority ethnic citizens at greater risk of loss of citizenship. By losing citizenship, they are rendered foreign and thus citizenship stripping has become a new way of migration control. As stripping citizenship is permitted by an Act of Parliament – section 40 of the British Nationality Act 1981 – any challenges to cancellation provisions are difficult because of parliamentary sovereignty and the discretion given by statute to the Secretary of State in recognition of executive competence in the field of national security.[3] This chapter examines the operative constitutional principles and doctrines, such as parliamentary sovereignty, the rule of law and the separation of powers, that intersect with the lives of citizens with migrant connections (dual nationals, and those with connections with, or claims to, other kinds of national citizenship) in the scenario of cancellation of citizenship.

In the case of citizens born in the UK, if they do not hold another nationality, they cannot be left stateless through cancellation of their British citizenship because of the UK's commitments to conventions that prevent

[3] For details on cancellation laws, see the following parliamentary briefing: Gower, M. and McGuinness, T. (2017) 'Deprivation of British citizenship and withdrawal of passport facilities', London: House of Commons Library, 9 June. Available from: https://researchbriefings.files.parliament.uk/documents/SN06820/SN06820.pdf [Accessed 24 December 2022].

Table 7.1: Cancellation of British citizenship for reasons of conduct

British citizen born in the UK?	Any other nationality?	Can British citizenship be cancelled for conduct?	Can be rendered stateless as per current law?
Yes	No	No	No
Yes	Yes	Yes	There is no risk of statelessness
No	Yes	Yes	There is no risk of statelessness
No	No	Yes	Yes

statelessness (the 1954 Convention relating to the Status of Stateless Persons and the 1961 Convention on the Reduction of Statelessness). Those who hold another nationality are categorised as being at no risk of statelessness and therefore their citizenship can (arguably) be cancelled without violating these Convention obligations. Table 7.1 (prepared by this author) summarises how this operates differentially for those with multiple nationalities and depending on the pathway by which they became citizens. It demonstrates that the present British approach in the UK puts those without another nationality – not born in the UK – at risk of statelessness. The table illustrates conceptual differences between citizenship pathways, nationality holdings, and risk of statelessness.

The fourth column in Table 7.1 illustrates how and when a person could potentially be rendered stateless by a cancellation order. For those who naturalise, there is a risk of statelessness as they can be stripped of British citizenship even without another nationality in place.[4] This can happen if they have no other nationality, but whether or not there is any alternative existing nationality is often disputed in court. There are instances when the Home Office raises claims that individuals have national connections with other countries through ethnicity or parental links which might provide them eligibility for that other country's citizenship. One such instance is that of British-born Shamima Begum, who has now been stripped of her British citizenship on the grounds of national security.

[4] Anderson, D. (2016) 'Citizenship removal resulting in statelessness: first report of the independent reviewer on the operation of the power to remove citizenship obtained by naturalisation from persons who have no other citizenship.' April, 11041601, London: The Stationery Office. Available from: https://assets.publishing.service.gov.uk/government/uploads/system/uploads/attachment_data/file/518120/David_Anderson_QC_-_CITIZENSHIP_REMOVAL__web_.pdf [Accessed 6 March 2023].

Begum, a 15-year-old British schoolgirl who left the UK for Syria in 2015, was found in a camp in Syria in 2019. The then Home Secretary removed her British citizenship soon afterwards, arguing that Begum was eligible for Bangladeshi nationality through her parents and would therefore not be rendered stateless. Yet, on 20 February 2019, Bangladesh issued a statement saying Begum did not have Bangladeshi nationality and would not be allowed into Bangladesh.[5] In May 2019, Bangladesh stated it would seek the death penalty in a criminal trial for Begum if she ever visited Bangladesh because of her connection with terrorism. Ironically, this means that whether a cancellation measure survives a court challenge by affected people largely depends on the text and interpretation of Bangladeshi nationality provisions and case law. But the fact that Bangladesh says she has no claim to Bangladeshi citizenship now means that she is effectively stateless in Syria and elsewhere.[6] An immediate implication of the *Begum* case is that anyone with any other national connection is now at greater risk of losing their British citizenship and becoming effectively stateless.[7] The situation raises concerns for migrants who naturalised to citizenship as well as second-generation migrants who were born in the UK. Indeed, in many instances migrants may not even be aware of any eligibility they may have to their parents' countries of origin. Some South Asian countries have provided increased access to their national citizenships to descendants of their overseas nationals in order to facilitate greater links with the diaspora. The diaspora is a source of remittances and return migration or continued business links, so such changes incentivise continued investment in the Global South. However, an unintended consequence is that these efforts to enhance links with parental countries of origin may put British minority ethnic

---

5 Addley, E. and Redwan, A. (2019) 'Shamima Begum will not be allowed here, says Bangladesh', *The Guardian* [online], 20 February. Available from: https://www.theguardian.com/uk-news/2019/feb/20/rights-of-shamima-begums-son-not-affected-says-javid [Accessed 24 December 2022].

6 Gjevori, E. (2019) 'What Shamima Begum's case says about the future of Muslims in the UK', *TRT World* [online], 11 March. Available from: https://www.trtworld.com/magazine/what-shamima-begum-s-case-says-about-the-future-of-muslims-in-the-uk-24381 [Accessed 24 December 2022].

7 There are many symbolic elements of cancellation, especially in Begum's deprivation. For example, see ibid. There are also severe consequences of loss of citizenship for individuals. For instance, some British nationals were stripped of citizenship and then killed by drone attacks: see Woods, C. and Ross, A. (2013) 'Former British citizens killed by drone strikes after passports revoked', *The Bureau of Investigative Journalism* [online], 27 February. Available from: https://www.thebureauinvestigates.com/stories/2013-02-27/former-british-citizens-killed-by-drone-strikes-after-passports-revoked [Accessed 6 March 2023].

nationals at higher risk of losing their British citizenship and render them voiceless in the legal system; many would find appealing from outside the country an inaccessible process. Indeed, this seems to be the thrust of the Begum situation.

Begum, now an adult, wants to return to the UK so that she can effectively challenge the removal of her citizenship, but the Supreme Court has refused permission for her to return, reversing a decision in her favour from the Court of Appeal.[8] The grounds on which the Court of Appeal had permitted Begum to return were primarily that the Special Immigration Appeals Commission (SIAC)[9] that heard her case on appeal from the decision of the Home Secretary should have reviewed the merits of her case rather than limiting its scope of review. While the case raised complex legal issues, by the time it was heard by the Supreme Court, the central issue was the appropriate standard of review in the various court proceedings below. Some of the proceedings related to the Minister's decision to cancel Begum's citizenship, while others addressed the refusal of leave to enter (LTE), which is an immigration decision. Begum would require LTE to return to the UK to challenge her deprivation order, so both deprivation and LTE refusal are linked but distinct legal issues. In Begum's cross-appeal the judges were also clear that any unfairness occasioned by her absence from the UK would not automatically result in the SIAC's decision being overturned on appeal. This argument made on behalf of Begum was the weakest element in Begum's case and it is possible that it negatively impacted the other issues.

Despite the permutations and combinations of the pathways, subject matter and parties raising the issues in question, the Supreme Court arrived at a strangely uniform view on judicial oversight over decisions in the area of deprivation matters in all instances. In every consideration it appears that the court is of the view that no court (including the SIAC, a Divisional Court or the Court of Appeal) can fully review the Home Secretary's decision making. The result in the *Begum* case was that Begum remained excluded from participation in her appeal against cancellation of her citizenship. The wide discretionary powers conferred on the Secretary of State were upheld as valid and Begum's fair trial rights remained suspended for reasons not disclosed to the public.

In 2023 (at the time of editing this chapter) the SIAC has finally given its decision on Begum's appeal to her citizenship cancellation without her

8 *Begum* (n 1).

9 The SIAC is a court that deals with appeals from persons deported by the Home Secretary under various statutory powers, and usually related to matters of national security. Appeals from cancellation of citizenship are heard by the SIAC.

being present in person. It agreed with the Home Secretary and dismissed Begum's appeal. However, it also said that there is 'a credible suspicion that Ms Begum was recruited, transferred and then harboured for the purpose of sexual exploitation'.[10] This decision indicates that it would be nearly impossible to challenge the discretion of the Home Secretary in cancelling people's citizenship on the basis of any human rights issues; even egregious violations such as trafficking of minors.

Such concentration of executive power is potentially problematic. When executive power is not scrutinised by other institutions (through checks and balances), there is scope for discrimination to remain unchecked.[11] Yet ministerial and executive discretion are also required to respond flexibly and effectively to matters of policy and practice. Further, Parliament has the authority to determine and delimit the scope of the use of such discretion. Thus, this is an area where there can be debate about the extent to which executive power should be scrutinised in the interests of justice and fairness. Overall, the *Begum* case and the area of cancellation provide insights into some age-old constitutional dilemmas and tensions on the rule of law, parliamentary sovereignty, human rights and the rights of citizens in a highly contentious contemporary context. In order to unpack the various elements, let us turn to the controversies surrounding parliamentary sovereignty.

Parliamentary sovereignty and judges

In the absence of a single codified constitutional document, the UK's parliamentary democracy is partly governed by long-established constitutional conventions. The importance of Parliament in this context is greater than in other countries where the rights and duties of a government and its people are more clearly demarcated and set out in a document that occupies superior legal status. Here in the UK, rights issues often arise against the backdrop of parliamentary sovereignty.[12] The doctrine of parliamentary sovereignty provides the foundational rules that govern the creation and ordering of legal norms in the UK. It dictates that Parliament can make or unmake any law and no other body can override Parliament's

[10] *Begum* (n 1) para 219.

[11] Sutherland, E.E. (2006) 'Undue deference to experts syndrome', *Indiana International & Comparative Law Review*, 16(2): 375–422.

[12] For example, see Hardman, H. (2020) 'In the name of parliamentary sovereignty: conflict between the UK government and the courts over judicial deference in the case of prisoner voting rights', *British Politics*, 15(2): 226–50.

actions in this regard.[13] Yet judges have a duty derived from common law to assess the legality of governmental decisions and acts. Traditionally, primary statute has been considered the domain for primacy of parliamentary action, whereas secondary legislation, rules and other kinds of decisions have been areas of judicial oversight. These demarcations changed considerably with the expanded adjudicative and interpretative powers conferred on judges through the Human Rights Act 1998 (HRA) which gives effect to the European Convention on Human Rights (ECHR).[14] While judges still cannot strike down primary legislation, they can now interpret it in a manner compatible with Convention rights or, if this is not possible, declare provisions in primary statute to be incompatible with the HRA through the Act's statutory scheme (sections 3 and 4).[15] These developments have meant that courts can now engage much more closely with rights determinations and examine primary statute as well as all other relevant materials for this purpose. Indeed, section 6 of the HRA requires courts and tribunals to act compatibly with Convention rights. The judicial duties and powers under the Act enable judges to adjudicate on rights issues through a proportionality analysis. Thus, in the HRA context, the duty to review becomes a heightened duty as judges have to assess individual rights and freedoms while ensuring democracy is not undermined. The changed landscape of rights determinations does not mean that Parliament and its authority have been undermined, however.

Parliamentary sovereignty is about the source and effect of the law as it is premised on a democratic basis for law which is superior to all other potentially conflicting sources for rules. In some ways, this makes parliamentary sovereignty the primary rule of recognition for all laws in a nation state and the very foundation of the constitution. Yet modern constitutionalism also requires a system of checks and balances which is achieved through the separation of powers and judicial independence as a part of the balance of powers. In theory, the doctrine of the separation of powers provides the judiciary with an independent supervisory role in the structure of governance. The powers and functions of different institutions such as the legislature, the executive and the judiciary are separate and supreme, and yet intertwined and interdependent. Judges cannot become

[13] Dicey, A.V. (1996) *Introduction to the Study of the Law of the Constitution* (8th edn), London: Macmillan, 38.

[14] See, Klug, F. (2003) 'Judicial deference under the Human Rights Act 1998', *European Human Rights Law Review*, 125–33.

[15] For an assessment of this mechanism, see Young, A. (1998) *Parliamentary Sovereignty and the Human Rights Act*, Oxford: Hart Publishing, and Young A. (2011) 'Is dialogue working under the Human Rights Act 1998', *Public Law*, 4: 773–800.

primary law makers in this scheme, but they can interpret law and oversee how law is administered.[16]

There are many contradictions and tensions in the evolving role of the judiciary with respect to parliamentary sovereignty. The boundaries between interpretation and law-making are not always clear-cut as in order to understand the scope of a law, judges may need to revisit what Parliament intended in the statute.[17] Further, common law provides many grounds for judicial review of executive action. Executive action is usually statutorily permitted (whether directly through primary legislation or through delegated provisions), so judicial review deals with the nature and scope of statute directly or indirectly in many instances.[18] An example of how this operates is seen in immigration law, where a person may challenge their deportation from the UK on the basis of their right to a private and family life (Article 8 ECHR).[19] Courts try to determine through a proportionality analysis how individual rights can be protected without breaching the requirements of the separation of powers.

Yet, judicial review of ministerial discretion occurred prior to the HRA scheme. In the past judges have given effect to parliamentary intent when reviewing official decisions by determining whether such decisions fall within the four corners of the law (the *ultra vires* theory). Under the strict *ultra vires* doctrine, the judicial review court was seen as simply policing the limits of the powers granted to the decision maker by Parliament. The more expansive *ultra vires* approach differs from this as it goes beyond specific intent to including wider consideration of judicial review grounds. The modified approach is not just about the four corners of the law, but would also have regard to factors that are important for the rule of law. Oversight of these factors by courts would be included as essential for the rule of law.[20]

For assessments on rights, especially for those who are unpopular or disfavoured in society (for example, fair trial rights of criminal suspects) and those who are underrepresented in Parliament (such as minority ethnic groups), the judiciary arguably plays a countermajoritarian balancing

[16] Elliott, M. (2004) 'United Kingdom: parliamentary sovereignty under pressure', *International Journal of Constitutional Law*, 3(2): 545–627.

[17] Bogdanor, V. (2012) 'Imprisoned by a doctrine: the modern defence of parliamentary sovereignty', *Oxford Journal of Legal Studies*, 32(1): 179–95.

[18] Craig, P. (2013) 'The nature of reasonableness review', *Current Legal Problems*, 66(1): 131–67.

[19] For example, see the House of Lords in *Huang v Secretary of State for the Home Department* [2007] UKHL 11 on Article 8 and proportionality.

[20] Lakin, S. (2008) 'Debunking the idea of parliamentary sovereignty: the controlling factor of legality in the British Constitution', *Oxford Journal of Legal Studies*, 28(4): 709–34.

function to the executive and the legislature.[21] As we have seen in matters of cancellation of citizenship, there are greater impacts on minority ethnic groups. Cancellation cases also have symbolic effects as they make statements about the extent to which rights are valued, and the meaning and content of citizenship and belonging in the heterogeneous population of modern Britain. Thus, the judicial countermajoritarian function is vital in this sphere of judicial review that concerns minority rights.[22] If minority rights become fragile and subject to majoritarian tolerance, majoritarian democracy may acquire elements of authoritarianism. Thus, contrary to the pronouncements in the *Begum* case (which will be discussed subsequently), judicial oversight is necessary to prevent unchecked abuse of power.

The *Begum* case, discretion, deference and institutional competence (expertise)

In the *Begum* case the main right at stake before the Supreme Court was the right to a fair trial as Begum was unable to enter the country to participate in the proceedings before the SIAC. Her lawyers had submitted that they were unable to contact her and take instructions from her from the camps in war-torn Syria. The Court of Appeal had found this situation compelling and allowed Begum to return, but on appeal, the Supreme Court refused to permit her return and stated that the right to a fair trial was subject to public safety.[23] The Supreme Court stayed Begum's appeal indefinitely and observed that 'if a vital public interest – in this case, the safety of the public – makes it impossible for a case to be fairly heard, then the courts cannot ordinarily hear it'.[24] Applying this to Begum's situation, the Supreme Court suggested that: 'The appropriate response to the problem in the present case is for the appeal to be stayed until Ms Begum is in a position to play an effective part in it without the safety of the public being compromised. That is not a perfect solution, as it is not known how long it may be before that is possible. But there is no perfect solution to a dilemma of the present kind.'[25]

What created this uneasy situation that would result in an indefinite stay to Begum's right to fair trial? Although the right was at stake, the Supreme

[21] Bui, D.T. (2015) 'How many tiers of criminal justice in England and Wales? An approach to the limitation on fair trial rights', *Commonwealth Law Bulletin*, 41(3): 439–46.

[22] Forsyth, C. and Elliott, M. (2003) 'The legitimacy of judicial review', *Public Law*, 286–307.

[23] Not surprisingly when foreigners find it challenging to obtain fair trials and this is even more so when this involves issues linked to entering or being sent out of a country. See Arnell, P. (2018) 'The contrasting evolution of the right to a fair trial in UK extradition law', *International Journal of Human Rights*, 22(7): 869–87.

[24] *Begum* (n 1) para 135.

[25] *Begum* (n 1) para 135.

Court did not focus on the nature and extent to which this right was engaged in the case and eventually decided the case on applicable standards of review. In the coversheet to the judgment, we find a note on which point three is: 'The steps taken on behalf of the Secretary of State and Her Majesty's Government to facilitate Ms Begum's involvement in the deprivation appeal, as described in the Witness Statements of Lauren Cooper dated 12 October 2020 and 5 November 2020, shall be confidential and no party or other person shall publish or disclose the same.' Given that confidentiality, in the interests of national security, permeates each aspect which could potentially relate to the issue of fair trial, we are only given this tantalising glimpse into future possibilities (such as steps that may be taken by the government). It is impossible to gauge what may change in Begum's situation in the future, as information on government action is not divulged in publicly available documents.

In order to justify why an appeal, which ordinarily has a more expansive remit than a judicial review proceeding, cannot adopt a close scrutiny of the deprivation decision, Lord Reed relied on an understanding that a proceeding which is called an appeal is not necessarily one in which an appellate review (full merits review) will always take place.[26] Here the subject matter is of critical importance according to Lord Reed. The Supreme Court opined that appeals, such as that before the SIAC, can be restricted by inherent limitations to review powers such as those placed on courts by the separation of powers doctrine. Courts have to respect executive authority in matters of national security and thereby rely on the discretion of the Home Secretary. Further, the Supreme Court drew on unreasonableness as a standard of review for the exercise of ministerial discretion. Unreasonableness is much maligned because its restrictive nature in administrative review sets a very high bar for any challenge.[27] The right to fair trial is at the core of being able to raise other rights in judicial proceedings. In the *Begum* situation, being left without citizenship in a Syrian camp could entail risk to life and risk of torture. To use the unreasonableness standard, especially in the context of rights which are of an absolute (or unqualified) nature, such as Articles 2 and 3 of the ECHR, is a severe limitation on human rights in the context of national security.[28]

In the past, the SIAC has rarely engaged in full factual analysis, at least in rulings which it makes public. Several human rights issues, such as the right to life, the right to be free from torture and the right to

---

[26] *Begum* (n 1) para 69.

[27] Dindjer, H. (2021) 'What makes an administrative decision unreasonable?', *Modern Law Review*, 84(2): 265–96.

[28] Jowell, J. and Lester, A. (1988) 'Beyond *Wednesbury*: substantive principles of administrative law', *Commonwealth Law Bulletin*, 14(2): 858–87.

family life, have not been fully evaluated on their merits by the SIAC in cancellation cases.[29] However, now such issues are even less likely to be agitated or seriously considered in the SIAC as the Supreme Court judges disagreed with the Court of Appeal on the SIAC's role in national security matters. The Court of Appeal had reminded the SIAC that it is an appeals court which should conduct a full review by assessing all the facts in a case itself rather than relying on the decisions of other courts or bodies. But the Supreme Court decided that the SIAC could not do so in the current instance as the sole discretion in cancellation decisions is with the Home Secretary. Not surprisingly, following this approach, the Home Secretary becomes the sole custodian of the evidence and details of the decision making. The 2023 decision of the SIAC in the *Begum* case demonstrates how this operates with the SIAC no longer willing to consider the rights linked issues.

The *Begum* resolution is inconsistent with earlier judicial approaches such as in the landmark case of *Padfield v Minister of Agriculture, Fisheries and Food*.[30] In this leading case on the examination of ministerial discretion, judges set out how discretion conferred by statute should be examined. This case was about the power of the Minister under section 19(3) of the Agriculture Marketing Act 1958 to appoint a committee of investigation into the operation of milk marketing schemes. The Act provided for a committee of investigation to consider and report on certain kinds of complaint 'if the Minister in any case so directs'; the question was whether these words gave the Minister absolute discretion or whether it was subject to review and, if so, on what grounds. Lord Reid explained that such discretion was not unfettered and had to be reviewed in accordance with the intention of the statute. The intention would be inferred from the Act read as a whole and thus was about close scrutiny of statute. The court in *Padfield* did exactly that. The judges examined the relevant statutory provisions and decided on the purpose and scope of the Minister's discretion, and about the reasons given by the Minister for his decision not to appoint a committee. Following *Padfield*, it seems logical that a similar approach to reviewing ministerial discretion should have been adopted in other cases of ministerial discretion. However, it is likely that *Begum* was given very different treatment by the Supreme Court judges because of its national security context, which creates additional barriers to review.

Another case where ministerial discretion was raised in court – in the context of tax credits rather than national security – was *R (SC, CB and 8*

---

[29] Prabhat, D. (2020) 'Political context and meaning of British citizenship: cancellation as a national security measure', *Law, Culture and the Humanities*, 16(2): 294–312.

[30] [1968] UKHL 1.

Children) v Secretary of State for Work and Pensions and Others,[31] where the court adjudicated on whether a two-child limit on child tax credits was compatible with the ECHR, as given effect by the HRA. The court concluded that the two-child limit has an objective and reasonable justification, notwithstanding its greater impact on women, because it pursues a legitimate aim: to protect the economic wellbeing of the country by achieving savings in public expenditure and thus contributing to reducing the fiscal deficit.[32]

According to the judgment, Parliament took account of the impact of the limitation on the interests of affected children, and decided that the impact was outweighed by the reasons for introducing it.[33] The court reasoned that if there was evidence that the original decision maker carried out a proportionality analysis, the judges would not step in to reconsider the decision. Thus, there was no need for the court to re-examine if Parliament made the right choice. A reassessment, in such circumstances, would be a political question and would likely stir up intense political controversy.[34] The court based the limitations of its review on the doctrine of the separation of powers as this was an area for Parliament and not for legal reasoning.[35] This is similar to the court's approach to ministerial discretion on national security in the *Begum* case. In *SC, CB* as well as *Begum*, institutional competence and respect for separation of powers are given priority by judges. However, in *SC, CB* the court examined whether the original decision maker had carried out a proportionality review, whereas in the *Begum* case there was no review of the original decision. The *Begum* decision therefore both deviates from the earlier *Padfield* approach and offers more deference to the original decision maker than the judgment in *SC, CB*.

National security: special barriers to review

While judges defer to executive decision making based on the need to respect the executive's autonomy, the *Begum* case arises in the context of national security and thus occasioned additional deference to executive decision making. A past example can be found in the 1980s, when any and all employees of the Government Communications Headquarters (GCHQ) were prohibited from joining any trade union. This decision was justified based on the potential threat to national security, and enforced using an Order

31 [2021] UKSC 26.

32 Ibid, paras 190–3.

33 Ibid, para 207.

34 Ibid, paras 208 and 209.

35 See also Allan, T.T. (2010) 'Deference, defiance, and doctrine: defining the limits of judicial review', *University of Toronto Law Journal*, 60(1): 41–60.

of Council, which is an exercise of the Royal Prerogative power. In the GCHQ case, the House of Lords held that the Royal Prerogative was subject to judicial review, just like statutory instruments.[36] However, on national security grounds, the action of restricting the trade union was justified. This approach of a special treatment for national security is consistent with other precedent in this area, for example, *Secretary of State for the Home Department v Rehman (AP)*.[37] In the *Rehman* case the court examined the deportation order of a national security suspect. The SIAC had decided in the case that there was no national security threat from the suspect, but the House of Lords[38] found that the suspect could be deported as the SIAC should have deferred more to the decision of the Secretary of State in a national security-related decision. Yet, there are three distinctions between the *Rehman* and *Begum* cases. First, Rehman was a foreign suspect (Pakistani-born) whose right to remain in the UK was much less secure than that of Begum, who was born a British citizen. Second, the court was deciding the case in the immediate aftermath of the devastating events of 9/11, but subsequent cases have evidenced a shift in approach. For instance, in *A v Secretary of State for the Home Department*,[39] when the court examined the indefinite detention of foreign suspects pursuant to post-9/11 legislation, it found the measure incompatible with human rights obligations, thereby showing a departure from the *Rehman* view on national security. Third, even in *Rehman*, the House of Lords acknowledged that the SIAC could determine its own facts, but found the degree of deference to the original decision maker (the Minister) inadequate. In *Begum*, the Supreme Court appears to regard the SIAC as precluded from conducting its own examination of the national security situation leading to citizenship stripping by the Secretary of State. In paragraph 66 of the decision, the Supreme Court judges looked at section 40(2) of the British Nationality Act 1981 to determine the scope of discretionary power given to the Secretary of State. Section 40(2) provides: '(2) The Secretary of State may by order deprive a person of citizenship status if the Secretary of State is satisfied that deprivation is conducive to the public good.' According to the Supreme Court:

> The opening words ('The Secretary of State may …') indicate that decisions under section 40(2) are made by the Secretary of State in the

36 *Council of Civil Service Unions v Minister for the Civil Service* [1984] UKHL 9.

37 [2001] UKHL 47.

38 At that time, the House of Lords was the highest court in the land. In October 2009, the Supreme Court replaced the Appellate Committee of the House of Lords as the highest court in the UK.

39 [2004] UKHL 56.

> exercise of his discretion. The discretion is one which Parliament has confided to the Secretary of State. In the absence of any provision to the contrary, it must therefore be exercised by the Secretary of State and by no one else. There is no indication in either the 1981 Act or the 1997 Act, in its present form, that Parliament intended the discretion to be exercised by or at the direction of SIAC.

Further, in paragraph 67, the Court makes a distinction between the discretion of the SIAC and the discretion of the Secretary of State:

> The statutory condition which must be satisfied before the discretion can be exercised is that 'the Secretary of State is satisfied that deprivation is conducive to the public good'. The condition is not that 'SIAC is satisfied that deprivation is conducive to the public good'. The existence of a right of appeal against the Secretary of State's decision enables his conclusion that he was satisfied to be challenged. It does not, however, convert the statutory requirement that the Secretary of State must be satisfied into a requirement that SIAC must be satisfied.

The Supreme Court recognises that there is some leeway for the SIAC in its review function but the standard for the review is of unreasonableness on the part of the first decision maker. That is a high bar as this standard requires that no reasonable decision maker would have acted in a similar way. There is scope to assess:

> whether he has taken into account some irrelevant matter or has disregarded something to which he should have given weight, or has erred on a point of law: an issue which encompasses the consideration of factual questions, as appears, in the context of statutory appeals, from *Edwards (Inspector of Taxes) v Bairstow [1956] AC 14*. They must also determine for themselves the compatibility of the decision with the obligations of the decision maker under the Human Rights Act, where such a question arises.[40]

Owing to the sovereignty of Parliament in terms of drafting legislation and delegating power, the Court clarifies in paragraph 68 that 'appellate courts and tribunals cannot generally decide how a statutory discretion conferred upon the primary decision-maker ought to have been exercised, or exercise the discretion themselves, in the absence of any statutory provision authorising them to do so'. These reasons for excluding intensive review

[40] *Begum* (n 1) para 68.

of statutorily conferred executive discretion only become heightened in national security matters, where the executive has to act under extraordinary conditions of urgency and emergency. Terrorism threatens the basic right to life. A flexible and expeditious approach is required, so executive discretion has been viewed as the best means through which to engage in counterterrorism. Counterterrorism also includes border control, which is a state function. The argument is often made that courts do not have the institutional competence or expertise to fully appreciate national security needs, and this has framed the courts' approach.[41]

The extent of relative institutional competence is itself a matter for judicial determination. Lord Hoffmann, in the *ProLife Alliance* case , said that deference is not the correct word to use as it is not about civility and manners, but about a legal assessment of the situation which courts are best placed to undertake.[42] This means that even if courts decide not to review a decision, they need to make a legal determination of the reasons for or against a review. Institutional competence is not just about questions of security; there are also issues of rights that need to be assessed. Courts often possess the best expertise to assess impacts on rights and to evaluate whether less restrictive means could have been used. Further, the idea of majoritarian democracy is not necessarily in the spirit of true democracy. Courts are institutions established by democracies and therefore do not suffer from institutional legitimacy gaps in their role as independent bodies.[43] Normally a codified constitutional document makes a ready reference to this role but in the UK this role comes under stress because of the absence of a document that sets out such specified functions. Instead, rule of law principles, which are widely accepted in the UK's constitutional sphere, guide courts, and these principles, distilled over time, do not direct courts to abdicate unquestioningly to any other branch of the state. Lord Bingham's famous list of rule of law principles includes the avoidance of unexamined discretion. Drawing on Dicey, Bingham writes that one of the core rule of law principles is that '[q]uestions of legal right and liability should ordinarily be resolved by the exercise of the law and not the exercise of discretion'.[44] This view is reinforced by Lord Hope's statement in the *Jackson* case that: 'The rule of law enforced by the courts is the ultimate controlling factor on which our constitution is based.'[45]

41 Deference on national security matters is a global phenomenon. See Scheppele, K. (2012) 'The new judicial deference', *Boston University Law Review*, 92(1): 89–170; Chesney, R.M. (2009) 'National security fact deference', *Virginia Law Review*, 95(6): 1361–436.

42 *R (ProLife Alliance) v BBC* [2003] UKHL 23, paras 74–7.

43 Schlink, B. (2011) 'Proportionality in constitutional law: why everywhere but here?', *Duke Journal of Comparative & International Law*, 22: 291–302, at 300.

44 Bingham, T. (2011) *The Rule of Law*, London: Penguin, 48.

45 See *R (Jackson) v Her Majesty's Attorney-General* [2005] UKHL 56, para 107.

Yet for national security, it is not just domestic courts that appear to defer to the executive and legislature. Even the European Court of Human Rights (ECtHR) has an equivalent international law doctrine, which is the doctrine of the margin of appreciation in the ECHR system. The doctrine is prominent in terrorism cases. Although the ECtHR is not affected by the doctrine of parliamentary sovereignty and by the strict theory of the separation of powers between state organs, the Court's judgments are affected by issues of legitimacy and institutional competence in dealing with deprivation of liberty in terrorism cases. This is most apparent when judges examine Article 15 ECHR on derogation – a process of exemption from the obligation to secure a specific Convention right. National authorities are accountable to the people in defending national security against terrorism and arguably an international court should not interfere with the government's decisions. In deciding a terrorism case under the Article 5 right to liberty, the Court considers that its democratic legitimacy stems from the jurisdiction granted by the contracting parties in deciding human rights cases. However, Article 15 has the effect of withdrawing part of the jurisdiction in emergency situations. When derogations are filed, national authorities withdraw the sovereignty previously granted to the ECtHR. For example, the ECtHR offered wide latitude to the UK government in the decision of *Brannigan and McBride*, where it was held that a wide margin of appreciation meant it should not 'substitute its view as to what measures were most appropriate or expedient … in dealing with an emergency situation for that of the Government which has direct responsibility for establishing the balance between the taking of effective measures to combat terrorism on the one hand, and respecting individual rights on the other'.[46]

However, this reasoning is not something that should guide British courts, as they do not have to think of domestic sovereignty issues. The ECtHR is an international court, which was given specific jurisdiction by member states to protect fundamental rights. British courts always have a constitutional mandate to protect rights and that cannot be taken away by a national government. UK courts have greater legitimacy than the ECtHR in deciding terrorism cases involving personal freedom because of this domestic mandate. In *A v Secretary of State for the Home Department* (the Belmarsh case) the judges held that the indefinite detention of foreign prisoners without trial under section 23 of the Anti-terrorism, Crime and Security Act 2001 was incompatible with the ECHR.[47] The judges refused to grant wide deference to the executive. Expertise and parliamentary authorisation to deal with national security issues normally lead courts to

[46] *Brannigan and McBride v UK* App No 14553/89; 14554/89 (ECHR, 25 May 1993), para 59.
[47] *A* (n 39).

grant wide deference, but Lord Hoffmann emphasised the importance of personal liberty and refused to grant wide discretion to the government in declaring a public emergency. Lord Bingham added that for political issues, the government will have greater relative institutional competence, but if the issues involve more legal content, there is justifiably more involvement by the courts.[48] Thus, in the arena of rights and legal adjudication relating to rights, courts will have superior institutional competence as the legal question is more important here than the political content.

By contrast, in *Begum*, the Supreme Court admonished the Court of Appeal for misunderstanding the role of the SIAC.[49] It also pointed out that the Court of Appeal had made its own assessment of the requirements of national security and preferred it to that of the then Home Secretary, and it had wrongly done so despite the absence of any relevant evidence before it, or any relevant findings of fact by the court below. Again, reminiscent of 'deference', the word 'respect' is used when the Supreme Court chided the Court of Appeal saying that: 'Its approach did not give the Home Secretary's assessment the respect which it should have received, given that it is the Home Secretary who has been charged by Parliament with responsibility for making such assessments, and who is democratically accountable to Parliament for the discharge of that responsibility.'[50]

Perhaps the *Begum* case is indicative of a larger trend of deference to ministers and the government by judges. In a case in 2021, *R (AB) v Secretary of State for Justice*,[51] the court was examining the solitary confinement of a young offender, prisoner AB. The court refused to consider every aspect of AB's treatment and the compatibility of such treatment with Article 3 of the ECHR because such examination would be unfair to the then Secretary of State. Instead, the Supreme Court decided that the ECtHR itself had not adopted any bright line rule that the solitary confinement of a person under 18 is automatically a violation of Article 3. A minimal approach to rights and a reluctance to scrutinise ministerial discretion appears to be a common theme. In *Begum*, the Supreme Court opted for a solution that neither protected rights nor guaranteed a long-term national interest by staying Ms Begum's appeal until 'she would be in a position to play an effective part in it without the safety of the public being compromised'.[52] A failure to take a stance that protects rights at the highest level is a compromise that is not just about Ms Begum, who was only a child when she left Britain, but one that

[48] Ibid, para 29.
[49] *Begum* (n 1) para 133.
[50] Ibid, para 133.
[51] [2021] UKSC 28.
[52] *Begum* (n 1) para 135.

lets down many others who have no other effective means of representation in a majoritarian parliamentary democracy. In many ways the deference shown in the *Begum* case is also a throwback to the wartime decision of *Liversidge*, where, cognisant of the national security context, judges refused to examine the reasons for indefinite detention of a British subject.[53]

Unlocking sovereignty for minority rights

When courts review executive action based on statutory provisions, they cannot decide on legality without examining the relevant legislation. So, an assessment of unlawfulness would also have to involve a careful analysis of legislation in order to understand the basis of the discretion and how it should be exercised. Indeed, in the *Begum* case the Supreme Court had to determine statutory intent. It also looked closely at policy to decide that the Court of Appeal had mistakenly treated the then Home Secretary's policy, intended for her own guidance in the exercise of the discretion conferred upon her by Parliament, as if it were a binding directive.[54]

Looking at statutory intent and executive discretion thus requires a willingness by judges to also look at the wider political context, as law is not wholly separate from politics. As Griffith writes in his famous lecture on the Political Constitution 'the constitution is no more and no less than what happens'.[55] It is unduly restrictive to place the role of judges within the narrow confines of formal legalism and risks undermining fairness as a cornerstone of the rule of law. However, too much judicial discretion can affect another principle of the rule of law: that of legal certainty. Thus, prudence dictates that in the sliding scale of use of review powers, important executive decisions are given more weight in judicial determinations.

With that caution in mind, given the latitude and democratic role of courts in providing a voice for disfavoured minority ethnic groups, it may be time to rethink the language of sovereignty prevalent in British constitutional law. Instead of the language of parliamentary sovereignty which distracts from citizenship, rights and good governance, and concentrates power in only one locus, it may be better to abandon the concept of a single sovereignty. Allan and other public lawyers have developed a concept of shared sovereignty instead, which recognises the checks and balances required for democracy to protect minority rights.[56] As democracy in the UK is only of a representative nature,

[53] *Liversidge v Anderson* [1941] UKHL 1.

[54] *Begum* (n 1) para 137.

[55] Griffith, J.A.G. (1979) 'The political constitution', *Modern Law Review*, 42(1): 1–21, 19.

[56] For instance, see Allan, T.T. (2006) 'Human rights and judicial review: critique of due deference', *Cambridge Law Journal*, 65(3): 671–95.

it should not take on the engorged status of direct democracy. Representative democracy does not represent everyone and does not necessarily reflect detailed consent from 'the people' for every ministerial decision or action. Indeed, Parliament itself does not get to scrutinise all legislative provisions or executive decisions, so if majoritarian consent becomes the basis of democracy, a legitimacy gap emerges in democratic institutions.

People with possible multiple nationalities or citizenship will have such links through migration, having migrated themselves or being connected to family members who migrated in the past. Although some estimates of people with such connections are in the millions, such numbers are likely to always remain in the minority in a society where most people gain citizenship by birth and blood links with long-settled ancestors.[57] Equating parliamentary democracy with majoritarian democracy therefore risks further marginalising the racial and minority ethnic populations in the UK through their links with other nationalities.

Conclusion

The courts, as exemplified in the *Begum* case, are deferential to the discretionary powers of the then Home Secretary on matters pertaining to national security and are also cognisant of parliamentary sovereignty. Yet, they appear to fail to recognise their own competence and expertise on issues of rights and their supervisory role as a check on ministerial discretion.

It is important to recognise that the *Begum* decision of the Supreme Court is a limited one which is not based on an assessment of the merits of Begum's deprivation case. It is only a pronouncement on whether she has to be given permission to return to the UK to participate in an effective and fair manner in the immigration appeal. However, the reach of the judgment is wide, as through its highly restrictive approach, it renders courts impotent on the issue of review of ministerial discretion and action, particularly in the context of national security.[58] Preoccupation with parliamentary sovereignty and a majoritarian idea of democracy implemented through this broad view of discretion adds to the present-day insecurity of citizenship.

[57] For example, see the following study: van der Merwe, B. (2021) 'British citizenship of six million people could be jeopardised by Home Office plans', *New Statesman* [online], 1 December. Available from: https://www.newstatesman.com/politics/2021/12/exclusive-british-citizenship-of-six-million-people-could-be-jeopardised-by-home-office-plans [Accessed 24 December 2022].

[58] Precedent creation is a complex story. It is unclear to what extent the *Begum* case will be a precedent for other cases. See Goodhart, A.A. (1934) 'Precedent in English and continental law', *Law Quarterly Review*, 50(1): 40–65.

The unchecked approach of the government means that citizenship stripping becomes another mechanism of migration control as it is used to prevent the re-entry of citizens, mostly minority ethnic groups, who are treated as accidental citizens by the state. The exercise of general human rights is not possible unless a person can re-enter a country drawing on their nationality. If the link of nationality is broken, it leaves people without recourse to many remedies. The constitutional subject is expelled from constitutional protection and becomes a non-entity for the state.

Further reading

Allan, T.T. (2010) 'Defence, defiance, and doctrine: defining the limits of judicial review', *University of Toronto Law Journal*, 60(1): 41–60.

Bogdanor, V. (2012) 'Imprisoned by a doctrine: the modern defence of parliamentary sovereignty', *Oxford Journal of Legal Studies*, 32(1): 179–95.

Craig, P. (2013) 'The nature of reasonableness review', *Current Legal Problems*, 66(1): 131–67.

Golder, B. and Williams, G. (2006) 'Balancing national security and human rights: assessing the legal response of common law nations to the threat of terrorism', *Journal of Comparative Policy Analysis*, 8(1): 43–62.

Klug, F. (2003) 'Judicial deference under the Human Rights Act 1998', *European Human Rights Law Review*, 125–33.

Prabhat, D. (2020) 'Political context and meaning of British citizenship: cancellation as a national security measure', *Law, Culture and the Humanities*, 16(2): 294–312.

8

Racialisation in UK Counterterrorism Law and Policy

Tufyal Choudhury

Introduction

Terrorism is a contested concept covering a diverse range of actors and groups defying international definition because at its heart lies 'difficult questions of when violence is justified or legitimate, by whom, and for what purposes'.[1] Britain's use of the label of terrorism has its roots in the description of actions by groups resisting colonial rule.[2] Many contemporary counterterrorism policies and practices have their origins in British counterinsurgency measures deployed against anti-colonial movements in Ireland, Palestine, Malaya and Kenya.[3] Surveying practices of population relocation and mass detention in the counterinsurgency measures of Western states, Khalili finds that: 'Racialization of the enemy is crucial to liberal counter-insurgency, in that ultimately a racial hierarchy resolves the tensions between illiberal methods and liberal discourse, between bloody hands and honeyed tongues, between weapons and war and emancipatory hyperbole.'[4]

This chapter examines the ways in which processes of racialisation are embedded within the exercise and implementation of the domestic

[1] Saul, B. (2018) 'Minorities and Counter-Terrorism Law', *European Yearbook of Minority Issues Online*, 15(1): 1–22, at 5.

[2] McQuade, J. (2021) *A Genealogy of Terrorism: Colonial Law and the Origins of an Idea*, Cambridge: Cambridge University Press.

[3] Razack, S.H. (2008) *Casting out: The Eviction of Muslims from Western Law and Politics*, Toronto: Toronto University Press; Mackinlay, J. (2009) *The Insurgent Archipelago*, London: Hurst & Co.

[4] Khalili, L. (2013) *Time in the Shadows: Confinement in Counterinsurgencies*, Stanford: Stanford University Press, 4–5.

counterterrorism laws and policies deployed in the UK in response to violence connected to ISIS and Al-Qaeda. Such processes of racialisation are counter to constitutional commitments to the rule of law, including equality before the law and non-discrimination, which are fundamental features in the self-presentation of modern liberal states. While the emergence of political liberalism from the 17th century onwards sat (un)easily alongside support for systems of racial chattel slavery, segregation and discrimination,[5] the post-war period of human rights and constitutionalism stressed commitments to equality. In the UK, Parliament incrementally prohibited discrimination in key spheres of life. Nevertheless, the public functions of the state, including policing and national security, remained outside the scope of anti-discrimination laws.[6] It was only after the passage of the Human Rights Act 1998 and the Race Relations (Amendment) Act 2000 that some protection was provided against discrimination in counterterrorism legislation, policy and practice. However, this is not comprehensive; the activities of the Security Services remain largely untouched. This chapter examines the ways in which, notwithstanding commitments to equality and non-discrimination, processes of racialisation and racial discrimination permeate counterterrorism laws, policies and practices in oblique ways. Counterterrorism's contribution to racialisation is revealed through consideration of the cumulative impact of four interconnected issues: the definition of terrorism; the development of pre-emptive criminal offences; the emerging frame of radicalisation as a way to explain and understand why people turn to violence; and the evolution of the government's strategy for preventing radicalisation. An examination of these issues reveals how processes of racialisation often remain beyond the reach of public law review. This analysis shows the limits of public law as a tool of social change when state actions operate against a broader backdrop of discriminatory narratives and ideas that are sufficiently normalised so as to go unnoticed and unchallenged.

Racialisation

Before examining specific aspects of counterterrorism, it is necessary to understand what is meant by 'race', racism and racialisation. Our everyday use of 'race' and racism conceals diverse meanings attached to these terms. Perhaps the most widespread understanding of 'race' suggests a biological division of humans into separate genetic racial groups. However, this pseudo-science of 'race', which underpinned eugenics, drove fears of racial contamination and paved the way to practices of racial protection and

[5] Losurdo, D. (2011) *Liberalism: A Counter-History*, London: Verso.

[6] See also Chapter 9 in this volume.

cleansing, only gained prominence in the 19th century.[7] This enduring understanding of 'race', rooted in 'race science' and biological essentialism, provides a limited understanding of how 'race' has configured the modern international order.[8] Understanding 'race' in purely biological terms ignores the preceding centuries of racial chattel slavery and colonial racial rule in which differences rooted in culture and religion, rather than genes, played a central role. This longer historical perspective reveals that 'race' and supposed racial differences are constructed through a broad set of signifiers and is central to European theories of white superiority. It 'is above all else a project of colonial distinction and a system of legitimation to justify oppressive and discriminatory practices'.[9]

Racism emerges from the construction of groups into a hierarchy based on characteristics that are used to signal innate difference and inferiority to white people. In this context racism cannot be reduced to the aggregate result of individual prejudice, but is also the consequence of structures and processes that sustain the hierarchy and reproduce racial difference. A structural understanding of racism helps explain why racial inequality endures in societies committed to anti-racism and persists even as racist attitudes decline.[10] It recognises that racism and racist outcomes do not require racist intentions; racism is not reduced to racial hatred or violence. These, rather, are the extreme manifestation of structural processes that reveal themselves more readily in indicators of economic, social and cultural exclusion; through differential outcomes in criminal justice,[11] education, employment and housing, and in exclusionary narratives of national identity.[12]

Racialisation is a process that brings 'race' into being.[13] Importantly, it is not limited to colour or physical characteristics alone, but can be constructed through cultural traits that include religious clothing and practice; such 'characteristics emerge as "racial" as an outcome of the process'.[14]

---

[7] Saini, A. (2019) *Superior: The Return of Race Science*, London: Fourth Estate.

[8] Goldberg, D.T. (2009) *Racist Culture: Philosophy and the Politics of Meaning*, Chichester: John Wiley & Sons.

[9] Lentin, A. (2020) *Why Race Still Matters*, Cambridge: Polity Press, 5.

[10] Bonilla-Silva, E. (2018) *Racism without Racists: Color-Blind Racism and the Persistence of Racial Inequality in America*, Lanham: Rowman & Littlefield.

[11] Lammy, D. (2017) 'The Lammy Review: An Independent Review into the Treatment of, and Outcomes for, Black, Asian and Minority Ethnic Individuals in the Criminal Justice System', September, London: Ministry of Justice.

[12] Byrne, B., Alexander, C., Khan O., Nazroo, J. and Shankley, W. (eds) (2020) *Ethnicity, Race and Inequality in the UK: State of the Nation*, Bristol: Policy Press.

[13] Barot, R. and Bird, J. (2001) 'Racialization: The Genealogy and Critique of a Concept', *Ethnic and Racial Studies*, 24(4): 601–18.

[14] Garner, S. and Selod, S. (2015) 'The Racialization of Muslims: Empirical Studies of Islamophobia', *Critical Sociology*, 41(1): 9–19, at 12.

A long shared history, cultural traditions as well as a common religion and experiences of oppression were identified as key factors in holding that Jews[15] and Sikhs[16] constituted an 'ethnic or racial group' for the purpose of the Race Relations Act 1976. While Muslims were held not to constitute an 'ethnic or racial group',[17] Islamophobia, in the context of counterterrorism policing, can be seen as a form of racism as it involves a 'set of ideas and practices that amalgamate all Muslims into one group and the characteristics associated with Muslims (violence, misogyny, political allegiance/disloyalty, incompatibility with Western values, etc.) are treated as if they are innate'.[18]

Resistance to suggestions that religious practices, beliefs or identities can be a constitutive element of 'race' reflects the continuing hold of biological notions of race. When the All-Party Parliamentary Group (APPG) on British Muslims defined Islamophobia as 'a type of racism that targets expression of Muslimness or perceived Muslimness',[19] the National Police Chiefs' Council (NPCC) countered that using the term 'racism' was misleading as there can be 'what some might see as legitimate criticism of the tenets of Islam – a religion'.[20] This claim that Islamophobia cannot be racism because Muslims are not a 'race' draws on biological accounts that only 'races' can be the real subjects of racism, ignoring that race is a social construct and that religions can be racialised. Unintentionally acknowledging the extent to which racialisation of Muslims feature in counterterrorism policing practices, the NPCC warned that the APPG's definition could 'undermine counter-terrorism powers, which seek to tackle extremism or prevent terrorism'.[21] Their concern implies that any acknowledgement that religious practices and expressions of religious identity can be implicated in processes of racialisation will constrain the exercise of counterterrorism powers.

Regulating the exercise of discretion and decision-making processes in modern states operating through complex bureaucracies remains a central

[15] *Seide v Gillette Industries Ltd* [1980] IRLR 427.

[16] *Mandla (Sewa Singh) v Dowell Lee* [1983] 2 AC 548.

[17] *Nyazi v Rymans Ltd* [1988] EAT/6/88.

[18] Ibid, 13.

[19] All-Party Parliamentary Group on British Muslims (2017); 'Islamophobia Defined: The Inquiry into a Working Definition of Islamophobia', 11. Available from: https://static1.squarespace.com/static/599c3d2febbd1a90cffdd8a9/t/5bfd1ea3352f531a6170ceee/1543315109493/Islamophobia+Defined.pdf [Accessed 24 December 2022].

[20] Basu, N. (2019) 'NPPC lead for counter terrorism calls for changes to proposed definition of Islamophobia', National Police Chiefs' Council [online] 15 May. Available from: https://news.npcc.police.uk/releases/npcc-lead-for-counter-terrorism-calls-for-changes-to-parliamentary-definition-of-islamophobia [Accessed 6 March 2023].

[21] Quoted in Dodd, V. (2019) 'Police Chiefs in Row over Definition of Islamophobia', *The Guardian* [online] 15 May. Available from: https://www.theguardian.com/news/2019/may/15/police-chiefs-in-row-over-definition-of-islamophobia [Accessed 11 March 2022].

concern for public law. Lord Bingham, identifying the core principles of the rule of law, stated that questions of legal right and liability should ordinarily be resolved by the application of the law, not the exercise of discretion.[22] In liberal states committed to equality, processes of racialisation are oblique and implicit, operating through the exercise of discretion and processes of selection. In countering terrorism, security officials develop profiles and create categories and groups to inform policing efforts. The repeated and continuous exercise of state power against 'suspect' groups normalises the focus on them. State power can be deployed through raids, arrests, covert surveillance, informal questioning and even initiatives for partnerships and collaboration. Discourses of race-neutrality and anti-discrimination that permeate counterterrorism policing further diffuse processes of racialisation.[23] Legal challenge is difficult as these actions operate against a backdrop in which the evidential threshold needed to bring discrimination claims is difficult to meet.[24] Anti-discrimination laws, emphasising redress for individual instances of race discrimination, can sustain rather than reveal and challenge racism embedded into race-neutral structures of state laws, policies and practices.[25]

The following sections show how the UK counterterrorism laws and policies create spaces for the exercise of discretion that nurture what Sentas refers to as a racialised 'common sense' of who should be the 'proper' focus of counterterrorism policing and counter-radicalisation policies.[26] This begins with the British state's definition of terrorism.

The definition of terrorism

A legal definition of terrorism is not necessary to prosecute terrorists for harmful violent acts. These are covered by criminal law offences relating to people, property and the use or possession of explosives and weapons. The legal definition of terrorism serves other functions. First, it has a denunciatory role, expressing societal condemnation of the use of violence to influence political changes and enabling higher sentences for crimes connected to terrorism. This moral signification function creates challenges for critique and opposition to counterterrorism measures. Those who question or oppose

---

22 Bingham, T. (2010) *The Rule of Law*, London: Allen Lane.

23 Sentas, V. (2015) *Traces of Terror: Counter-Terrorism Law, Policing and Race*, Oxford: Oxford University Press.

24 Amnesty International (2021) *A Human Rights Guide for Researching Racial and Religious Discrimination in Counter-Terrorism in Europe*, London: Amnesty International. See also Chapter 9 in this volume.

25 Atrey, S. (2021) 'Structural Racism and Race Discrimination', *Current Legal Problems*, 74(1):1–34.

26 Sentas (n 23).

counterterrorism laws or policies risk being accused of 'enabling terrorism'.[27] Second, it can authorise the use of an extensive range of powers that are not ordinarily available to the police. For example, authorised officers can search and question a person at border ports to determine whether a person is a terrorist without requiring any reasonable suspicion for believing the person might be a terrorist;[28] likewise, arresting a person under section 41 of the Terrorism Act 2000 (TA 2000) allows a suspect to be held in pre-charge detention for up to 14 days,[29] compared to three days for normal arrests,[30] and to have access to their lawyer delayed.[31] Third, even if there is insufficient evidence for prosecution, information connecting an individual to terrorism-related activities provides the basis for exercising extraordinary executive powers that constitute significant interferences with fundamental rights. These include Terrorism Prevention and Investigation Orders that restrict where a person can live, who they can associate with and how many hours each day they can leave their home.[32] Fourth, the criminal law has been expanded to cover an increasing number of terrorism-related offences that constitute a significant departure from the normal principles for imposing criminal culpability on individuals.[33] Fifthly, terrorist offenders are subject to more stringent conditions on release from prison. For example, for at least ten years after release, ex-offenders must provide information relating to their passport, payment and identity cards, details of vehicles they use and overseas travel plans.[34] Thus, in state-mandated efforts to counter terrorism, ever-expanding powers have been instituted. Whether a person's behaviour falls within the scope of this framework rests on the state's definition of terrorism.

Under section 1 of the TA 2000, terrorism entails the 'use or threat of action' that is 'designed to influence the government', 'an international governmental organisation' or 'the public or a section of the public'. Furthermore, the use or threat of action must be 'made for the purposes of advancing a political, religious, racial, or ideological cause'. Thus, the purpose of the action is pivotal in turning an action into a terrorist act. The need for evidence of a 'purpose' places a further burden on the prosecution, requiring evidence that the action was aimed at advancing a relevant cause. This necessitates collecting evidence

[27] Jenkins J., Perry D. and Stott, P. (2022) *Delegitimising Counter-Terrorism: The Activist Campaign to Delegitimise Prevent*, London: Policy Exchange, 6.

[28] Terrorism Act 2000, sch 7.

[29] Ibid, sch 8, para 36(3).

[30] Police and Criminal Evidence Act 1984, s 42.

[31] TA 2000, sch 8, para 8.

[32] Terrorism Prevention and Investigation Measures Act 2011.

[33] This is examined further in the discussion on 'pre-emptive offences' later in this chapter.

[34] Counter-Terrorism Act 2008, Part 4.

about beliefs and so brings expressions of ideas that suggest a religious cause under investigation, surveillance and suspicion.[35]

The range of 'actions' that can be deemed terrorist acts is also wide. A terrorist act is not limited to life-threatening actions or acts of serious violence against a person, but also includes 'serious damage to property' and 'creating serious risk to the health and safety of the public'.[36] Further, 'action taken for the benefit of a proscribed organisation' is also deemed to be an 'action for the purposes of terrorism'.[37] The range of potential action that can be terrorist acts is also broadened by the territorial scope of the legislation. It does not limit terrorism to actions or threats within the UK, but extends it to any actions or threats directed at any government. The Supreme Court rejected a narrower reading of the territorial scope, accepting that the definition 'was indeed intended to be very wide'.[38]

An expansive definition of terrorism leaves significant discretion to executive bodies in determining which acts fall within its scope. The dangers of this were highlighted by David Anderson KC, then Independent Reviewer of Terrorism Legislation, when he expressed concern that the broad definition 'may encourage a tendency – itself potentially discriminatory – to reserve the word for categories of perpetrators with which it is stereotypically associated'.[39] This, he cautions, risks creating 'a tendency to categorise Islamist-inspired violence as terrorism more readily than what is still often referred to as "domestic extremism"'.[40] Determining whether actions should be treated as terrorism seems to depend on whether the activities are assessed as posing a threat to 'national security'.[41] With no legal definition of national security, this adds a further layer of opaqueness and uncertainty. Furthermore, 'terrorism' itself is identified as a threat to national security. This circularity

---

35 Roach, K. (2007) 'The Case for Defining Terrorism with Restraint and without Reference to Political or Religious Motive', in A. Lynch, E. MacDonald and G. Williams (eds) *Law and Liberty in the War on Terror*, Sydney: Federation Press, 39–48.

36 TA 2000, s 1(2).

37 Ibid, s 1(5).

38 *R v Gul* [2013] UKSC 64, para 38.

39 Anderson, D. (2014) 'The Terrorism Acts in 2013: Report of the Independent Reviewer on the Operation of the Terrorism Act 2000 and Part 1 of the Terrorism Act 2006', July, London: The Stationery Office, 80. Available from: https://assets.publishing.service.gov.uk/government/uploads/system/uploads/attachment_data/file/335310/IndependentReviewTerrorismReport2014.pdf [Accessed 6 March 2023].

40 Ibid.

41 HM Government (2018) 'CONTEST: The United Kingdom's Strategy for Countering Terrorism', Cm 9608, June, London: The Stationery Office, 21. Available from: https://assets.publishing.service.gov.uk/government/uploads/system/uploads/attachment_data/file/716907/140618_CCS207_CCS0218929798-1_CONTEST_3.0_WEB.pdf [Accessed 3 April 2023].

has led another Independent Reviewer, Jonathan Hall KC, to conclude that 'traditional labelling of whether something is or is not terrorism may conceal inequalities in treatment of equally harmful phenomena'.[42]

The broad definition of terrorism is also pivotal to the definition of a 'terrorist', as a person who 'is or has been concerned in the commission, preparation or instigation of acts of terrorism'.[43] Built upon this are powers enabling officials at border ports to stop, search and detain anyone to determine if they are a terrorist.[44] Without the need for reasonable suspicion, the primary constraint on the exercise of discretion is the requirement that any stop should be for the purpose permitted by legislation. The broad discretionary nature of this power creates spaces that enable selective enforcement shielded from scrutiny. The Code of Practice prohibits discrimination, stating that religion and ethnicity alone or in combination cannot be used as the 'sole reason' for examining a person; however, they can be taken into account if combined with other relevant factors.[45] This therefore makes it hard to prove discretion is exercised illegitimately on the grounds of religion or ethnicity alone.

Confronted with the difficulty of detecting discrimination, courts have focused on the *risk* of arbitrariness rather than finding actual arbitrary or discriminatory use. Widely drawn powers that create an intolerable risk of arbitrary application may fail to meet the requirement in the European Convention on Human Rights (ECHR) that an interference must be 'prescribed by law'. However, close scrutiny of counterterrorism powers is curtailed by the considerable judicial deference paid to the executive's assessment on matters of national security. Acceptance of the democratic legitimacy and institutional capacity of executive decision making informed Lord Slynn's conclusion that the Home Secretary 'is undoubtedly in the best position to judge what national security requires even if his decision is open to review. The assessment of what is needed in the light of changing circumstances is primarily for him'.[46] This deference was apparent in the

---

[42] Hall, J. (2021) 'The Terrorism Acts in 2019: Report of the Independent Reviewer of Terrorism Legislation on the Operation of the Terrorism Acts 2000 and 2006', March, London: The Stationery Office, 34. March. Available from: https://assets.publishing.service.gov.uk/government/uploads/attachment_data/file/972261/THE_TERRORISM_ACTS_IN_2019_REPORT_Accessible.pdf [Accessed 6 March 2023].

[43] TA 2000, s 40(1).

[44] Ibid, sch 7, para 2(1).

[45] Home Office (2015) 'Examining Officers and Review Officers under Schedule 7 to the Terrorism Act 2000: Draft of Practice', June, London: The Stationery Office. Available from: https://assets.publishing.service.gov.uk/government/uploads/system/uploads/attachment_data/file/890266/CCS207_CCS0320264954-001_Examining_Officers_and_Review_Officers_Web_Accessible.pdf [Accessed 6 March 2023].

[46] *Secretary for the Home Department v Rehman* [2001] UKHL 47, para 26.

Supreme Court's willingness to accept claims regarding the necessity of Schedule 7 powers as a tool for countering terrorism, without careful examination of the evidence for such claims. The majority focused on the evidence of executive restraint in the exercise of these powers.[47] However, Lord Kerr, dissenting, recognised that the risk of the arbitrary use of unfettered powers is not remedied by its careful use, as '[a] power on which there are insufficient legal constraints does not become legal simply because those who may have resort to it, exercise self-restraint'.[48]

As will be evidenced in the following sections, the wide definition of terrorism and the limits of judicial review standards help create conditions for processes of racialisation to flourish.

'Pre-emptive' offences

The expansion of 'pre-emptive' terrorism offences has been a key feature of both national and international counterterrorism since 2001.[49] In the aftermath of the July 2005 London bombings, the British government proposed a raft of new pre-emptive offences, introduced in the Terrorism Act 2006 (TA 2006). This included the preparation of terrorist acts,[50] the indirect encouragement of terrorism,[51] the dissemination of terrorist publications,[52] training for terrorism[53] and attending a place used for terrorist training.[54]

The pre-emptive offences contribute to processes of racialisation in two ways. First, some of the arguments put forward to justify the rebalancing of counterterrorism policy towards greater pre-emption draw on characterisations of the terrorist threat that are inscribed with racialised orientalist tropes. Second, as these offences criminalise conduct that is itself neutral, culpability often rests on establishing a general intent to engage in terrorism. This is achieved by carefully threading together an individual's ideological or religious beliefs, their association with suspected extremists, and evidence of online search activities.

---

[47] Lennon, G. (2021) 'All-Risks Counter-Terrorist Policing', in G. Lennon, C. King and C. McCartney (eds) *Counter-Terrorism, Constitutionalism and Miscarriages of Justice: A Festschirft for Professor Clive Walker*, Oxford: Hart Publishing, 167–84.

[48] *Beghal v DPP* [2015] UKSC 49, para 103.

[49] Ginsborg, L. (2021) 'Moving toward the Criminalization of "Pre-crime": The UN Security Council's Recent Legislative Action on Counterterrorism', in A. Vedaschi and K.L. Scheppele (eds) *9/11 and the Rise of Global Anti-terrorism Law: How the UN Security Council Rules the World*, Cambridge: Cambridge University Press, 133–54.

[50] TA 2006, s 5.

[51] Ibid, s 1.

[52] Ibid, s 2.

[53] Ibid, s 6.

[54] Ibid, s 8.

In proposing a new approach to counterterrorism, including through expansive pre-emptive offences, the then Prime Minister Tony Blair argued that the scale of violence and the nature of the threat posed by 'Islamist extremism' differed qualitatively from nationalist terrorism and, as a consequence, the 'rules of the game' had changed.[55] This echoed the contentious 'new terrorism' thesis, which posits religiously motivated terrorism as driven by irrational fanaticism.[56] Furthermore, framing Al-Qaeda's violence as an attack on 'our values' locates counterterrorism at the frontline in the defence of civilisation against 'barbarism'. It reinforces the idea that 'their' violence is uniquely monstrous and fails to recognise that both state and nonstate actors have shown themselves capable of degrading violence.[57]

To appreciate the expansive reach of pre-emptive terrorism offences, it is necessary to understand how far they diverge from ordinary criminal offences. As noted earlier, existing laws are sufficient to prosecute violent terrorist attacks. Incomplete or inchoate offences also enable prosecutions before harms occur; it attaches liability to attempting, assisting, encouraging or aiding and abetting another in committing an offence. A commitment to respecting individual autonomy means that liability for incomplete offences ordinarily attaches where an individual demonstrates a determination to commit an offence. Culpability should not be imputed where there remains an opportunity for an individual to change their mind. An 'attempt' requires actions that are more than 'merely preparatory': you may leave your home intending to rob a bank, and even approach the bank, but until you enter the bank, the possibility of changing your mind remains and your conduct is viewed as preparatory rather than an attempt.[58] While the boundaries between an attempt and preparatory conduct are contested, pre-emptive terrorism offences introduced by the TA 2006 extend the temporal reach of the law to include actions viewed as preparation for terrorism.[59] Walker warns that 'the broad nature of "preparations" comes close to penalizing criminal thoughts rather than harms and leaving no possibility of withdrawal'.[60] The indirect encouragement[61] and terrorism training[62] offences criminalise

[55] Brown, C. and Wolf, M. (2013) 'Rights Laws to Be Overhauled as Blair Says "the Game Has Changed', *The Independent* [online], 29 April. Available from: https://www.independent.co.uk/news/uk/politics/rights-laws-to-be-overhauled-as-blair-says-the-game-has-changed-304031.html [Accessed 5 January 2022].

[56] Laqueur, W. (1998) 'Terror's New Face: The Radicalisation and Escalation of Modern Terrorism', *Harvard International Review*, 20(4): 48–51.

[57] See Elkins, C. (2022) *Legacy of Violence: A History of the British Empire*, London: Penguin.

[58] *R v Campbell* (1990) 93 Cr App R 350.

[59] TA 2006, s 5.

[60] Walker, C. (2011) *Terrorism and the Law*, Oxford: Oxford University Press, 225.

[61] TA 2006, s 1.

[62] Ibid, s 6.

activities in the absence of directly harmful culpable conduct. Indirect encouragement fails to meet the normal requirements of harm demanded by criminal law, as it criminalises conduct that may not be harmful and only 'tenuously causally related to the consummate harm', particularly as the harm may arise from the subsequent conduct of a third party.[63]

Pre-emptive offences criminalise a huge swathe of activities as 'terrorist actions'. However, only a fraction of the individuals who could be charged are in fact subject to prosecution. Prosecutorial discretion therefore constrains the use of the legislation and could counteract the definitional breadth of the offences.[64] However, case law analysis suggests that executive discretion has not always limited prosecutions, and judicial interpretation has extended the scope of some offences beyond the original legislative goal.[65] Reliance on the exercise of executive discretion to limit prosecutions to those who are the 'real terrorists' constitutes an admission that the definitions are too broad and also risks creating a discretionary space in which racialised profiles of the 'real' terrorist can inform the basis for selection for prosecution. Broad offences may facilitate the prosecution of real terrorists, but by shielding from the courts the reason a person is selected for prosecution, they oust the court's ability to adjudicate fairly as they deny defendants the opportunity to challenge the real reason for their prosecution. Furthermore, those who are not 'real terrorists' cannot challenge inappropriate prosecutions as the trial process is confined to considering whether the elements of the offence charged are met.[66]

The potential for racialised profiling is acute in pre-emptive offences that criminalise otherwise neutral actions. This concern relates not only to offences which can be committed recklessly – that is, without requiring the accused to form any terrorism-related intention – but even when a terror-related intention is required, this does not entail an intention fixed upon a specific plan.[67] Rather, it calls for evidence that the individual has a general mindset to engage in terrorism. Without evidence demonstrating the intention to carry out a particular terrorist act, circumstantial evidence

63 Ashworth, A. and Zender, L. (2014) *Preventative Justice*, Oxford: Oxford University Press, 180.

64 Anderson, D. (2011) 'Report on the Operation in 2010 of the Terrorism Act 2000 and of Part 1 of the Terrorism Act 2006', July, London: The Stationery Office. Available from: https://assets.publishing.service.gov.uk/government/uploads/system/uploads/attachment_data/file/243552/9780108510885.pdf [Accessed 6 March 2023], 29.

65 Cornford, A. (2020) 'Terrorist Precursor Offences: Evaluating the Law in Practice', *Criminal Law Review*, 8: 663–85.

66 Edwards, J. (2010) 'Justice Denied: The Criminal Law and the Ouster of the Courts', *Oxford Journal of Legal Studies*, 30(4): 725–48.

67 TA 2006, s 5(2).

from a wide range of actions and activities may be knitted together to show that an accused possesses the required general intention to commit terrorism. Thus, evidence of possession of extremist materials and associating with known terrorists could be used to position a defendant as a person with the mindset and characteristics of a person who is likely to engage in terrorist violence in the future unless stopped in the present.[68] The breadth of pre-emptive offences leaves room for discretionary prosecutions and selective enforcement of the law against those already deemed suspect because of beliefs that suggest their commitment to a political or religious cause. This potential for the criminalisation of 'guilty minds' rather than 'guilty acts' usurps the principle that people should be accountable for their bad actions, not bad thoughts.

The scope of reinforcing racialised discriminatory processes through the exercise of discretion is exacerbated by the fact that evidence for pre-emptive offences is increasingly driven by the targeting decisions of intelligence and policing agencies of those they already think likely to be involved in terrorism. The Farooqi case provides an example. This case involved the prosecution of four individuals for the preparation of acts of terrorism, possession of terrorist materials and solicitation for murder. It was based on evidence carefully gathered through an extensive undercover policing investigation. Farooqi ran an Islamic bookstall, from which he sought to persuade passers-by of the justice and virtue in travelling to South Asia to fight with the Taliban against the Afghan government and North Atlantic Treaty Organization (NATO) forces, including British soldiers. This meticulous undercover operation found no evidence of a specific terrorist plot or attack, but did gather evidence of the defendant's belief in 'violent jihad'. The officers witnessed the defendant's attempts to persuade them and others that fighting against British troops in Afghanistan was a religious obligation. After the return of guilty verdicts, the police admitted that they 'did not recover any blueprint, attack plan or endgame for these men'; nevertheless, they stated that 'what we were able to prove was their ideology'.[69] Their belief in 'violent jihad' became evidence of their commitment to terrorism. Analysis of prosecutions in Australia also found that pre-emptive offences relied on the accused's commitment to extremist beliefs as evidence of 'incipient violence', so that holding lawful but extremist

[68] Cornford, A. and Petzsche, A. (2019) 'Terrorism Offences', in K. Ambos, A. Duff, J. Roberts, T. Weigend and A. Heinze (eds) *Core Concepts in Criminal Law and Criminal Justice*, Cambridge: Cambridge University Press, 172–209.

[69] BBC (2011) 'Munir Farooqi Given Four Life Sentences for Terror Charges', *BBC News* [online], 9 September. Available from: https://www.bbc.co.uk/news/uk-england-manchester-14851811 [Accessed 5 January 2022].

beliefs is presented as evidence of 'planning to do *something violent*'.[70] The centring of ideology in understanding and explaining why people engage in terrorism draws on the notion of radicalisation that has become the dominant frame for the analysis of terrorism since 2001. Radicalisation and the development of policies to prevent radicalisation provide a further site in which processes of racialisation operate.

Radicalisation

Radicalisation, which is defined as 'the process by which a person comes to support terrorism and forms of extremism leading to terrorism', emerged as the dominant frame for understanding the pathway by which a person becomes a terrorist shortly after 2001.[71] It rapidly inserted itself into national and international counterterrorism strategies[72] and spread beyond security policy into other areas, including criminal and even family law.[73] Despite its ubiquity, its utility and scientific value remain deeply contested.

A key criticism of radicalisation theories is their focus on the role of ideology and theology as a cause of violence. Neumann, while distinguishing between 'cognitive' and 'behavioural' radicalisation, maintains that understanding ideology remains important in understanding terrorism.[74] Contrasting violence by the Irish Republican Army (IRA) in Northern Ireland with nonviolent resistance in Tibet, he argues that the differences in approach adopted by these movements reflect their differing ideologies. For Crenshaw, it is the method rather than identity or ideology that usually 'determines whether or not an action can be defined as terrorism'.[75] Opposition to the use of violence can be ideological, and terrorism may be intrinsic to some ideologies, or a justification for violence can be embedded into the doctrines of some groups. But for many movements that engage in violence, shifts from violence to nonviolence reflect changes in tactical calculations rather than ideological positions.

---

70 Sentas (n 23) 6 (emphasis in original).

71 HM Government (2011) 'The Prevent Strategy' (Cm 8092), London: The Stationery Office, 108. Available from: https://assets.publishing.service.gov.uk/government/uploads/system/uploads/attachment_data/file/97976/prevent-strategy-review.pdf [Accessed 3 April 2023].

72 Hayes, B. and Kundnani, A. (2018) *The Globalisation of Countering Violent Extremism Policies: Undermining Human Rights, Instrumentalising Civil Society*, Amsterdam: Transnational Institute.

73 Ahdash, F. (2018) 'The Interaction between Family Law and Counter-Terrorism: A Critical Examination of the Radicalisation Cases in the Family Courts', *Child and Family Law Quarterly*, 30(4): 389–413.

74 Neumann, P. (2013) 'The Trouble with Radicalization', *International Affairs*, 89(4): 873–93.

75 Crenshaw, M. (2011) *Explaining Terrorism, Causes, Processes and Consequences*, Abingdon: Routledge, 207.

Understanding terrorism through the prism of radicalisation centres the individual as the primary unit of analysis, and delves into their mind and personal history for explanations. The attention in radicalisation theories on individual psychology is criticised for shifting focus away from wider societal and political contexts, and the role of state actions that generate political violence.[76] Former Prime Minister David Cameron emphasised the centrality of ideology in driving radicalisation, placing this above other factors such as discrimination, poverty or anger at foreign policy.[77] He dismissed the latter, arguing that many people experience poverty or discrimination or are angry with foreign policy without turning to violence. However, this logic also applies to those holding extremist beliefs, since '[m]ost people who hold radical ideas do not engage in terrorism, and many terrorists – even those who do lay claim to a "cause" – are not deeply ideological and may not radicalize in any traditional sense'.[78]

For many policy makers and practitioners, the value of radicalisation is in the promise that the radicalisation models can enable preventative interventions. Yet, the various models have so far been inadequate at identifying which of the individuals holding radical ideas will cross the line into terrorist violence.[79] With no clear way to identify terrorists, counter-radicalisation policies posit 'indicators' that are said to make individuals 'vulnerable to' or 'at risk' of radicalisation. However, the lack of control groups in the research developing indicators erodes their value and validity.[80] The Royal College of Psychiatrists warns that 'current tools and methodologies should be treated with caution', particularly as 'methodologies that seek to predict rare events, such as acts of terror, yield consistently poor results'.[81] Despite these caveats, indicators play a pivotal role in the strategy to prevent radicalisation. Indicators of risk, provided by the government as guidance to schools in England, included a desire for adventure and excitement, a search for answers to questions of identity, faith and belonging or the wish to enhance self-esteem or improve

---

[76] Githens-Mazer, J. and Lambert, R. (2010) 'Why Conventional Wisdom on Radicalization Fails: The Persistence of a Failed Discourse', *International Affairs*, 86(4): 889–901.

[77] Cameron, D. (2011) 'PM's Speech at Munich Security Conference', 5 February. Available from: https://www.gov.uk/government/speeches/pms-speech-at-munich-security-conference [Accessed 5 January 2022].

[78] Borum, R. (2012) 'Radicalization into Violent Extremism I: A Review of Social Science Theories', *Journal of Strategic Security*, 4(4): 7–36, at 8.

[79] Kundnani, A. (2012) 'Radicalisation: The Journey of a Concept', *Race and Class*, 54(2): 3–25.

[80] Sageman, M. (2016) *Misunderstanding Terrorism*, Philadelphia: University of Pennsylvania Press.

[81] Royal College of Psychiatrists (2016) *Counter-Terrorism and Psychiatry, Position Statement PS04/16*, London: Royal College of Psychiatrists, 5–6.

'street cred'.[82] While these indicators could apply to anyone, by operating through a Prevent Strategy that initially focused only on Muslims, they enabled and embedded suspicion of the activities, behaviours and beliefs of Muslims.

The Prevent strategy

Intended 'to stop people becoming terrorists or supporting terrorism', Prevent is one of the four strands of the overall counterterrorism strategy (CONTEST).[83] It came to prominence after the 2005 London bombings when policy concerns about 'home-grown' terrorism came to the fore. The initial strategy, in place from 2007 to 2011, focused exclusively on 'international terrorism', leaving domestic terrorism and terrorism related to Northern Ireland outside its scope. As a consequence, it focused on British Muslim communities. Following a review in 2010, a revised strategy refocused Prevent in two crucial ways. It now covered 'all forms of terrorism' and extended Prevent from concern with violent extremism to the more widely defined 'extremism', with greater emphasis on challenging ideas that it argued underpinned radicalisation. Crucially, it defined extremism as 'vocal and active opposition to fundamental British values', which were identified as including 'democracy, the rule of law, individual liberty and mutual respect and toleration of different faiths and beliefs'.[84] A further recalibration in the delivery of the 2011 strategy came with the introduction of a statutory Prevent duty on specific authorities to show 'due regard to the need to prevent people being drawn into terrorism'.[85] Analysis of the strategy's development reveals an evolution of processes of racialisation.

Engaging moderate Muslims while searching for extremist Muslims

Until 2011, the Prevent strategy explicitly and unambiguously targeted Muslims. One government performance measure for the delivery of Prevent, 'National Indicator 35', was 'understanding of, and engagement with Muslim communities'. Local Prevent funding was initially based on the size of the local Muslim population, implying that the presence of Muslims was a

82 Department for Children, Schools and Families (2008) 'Learning Together to Be Safe: A Toolkit to Help Schools Contribute to the Prevention of Violent Extremism', Nottingham: DCSF, 17–18.

83 HM Government (n 41) 6. The others strands of CONTEST are Pursue, Protect and Prepare.

84 Ibid, 107.

85 Counter-Terrorism and Security Act 2015, s 26.

legitimate measure of risk.[86] Furthermore, the Prevent Violent Extremism (PVE) national pathfinder fund supported actions and activities to help Muslim communities 'build *their* resilience to violent extremist messages and to voice *their* condemnation of violent extremism',[87] thus implying that the problem was the failure of Muslim communities to condemn terrorism and their potential to succumb to violent extremist messages. Under Prevent, the government set up Muslim Youth and Muslim Women's Advisory Boards. Over £45 million was spent on local activities, engaging over 50,000 young Muslims. The strategy targeted theology, funded roadshows of Islamic scholars and supported setting up the Mosques and Imams Advisory Board to improve mosque governance. This concentration on Muslims and Islam embedded racialisation at the genesis of Prevent. Through this emphasis on engagement with Muslims, Islamic religious institutions and community organisations, the Prevent strategy confirmed Muslim communities as the natural subject of counterterrorism and counter-radicalisation policies.[88] The need to work with Muslim communities reinforced the notion that Islam is both the 'cure and cause of radicalisation'.[89]

Sensitive to charges of unfairly targeting Muslims, politicians and policy makers argued that their attention was on those groups and communities that were targeted for recruitment by Al-Qaeda and that the issue was not Islam, but Islamism and Islamist extremism.[90] The then Prime Minster Blair stressed that Al-Qaeda's justification of its actions was a 'perversion of Islam' and that 'extremism is not the true voice of Islam'.[91] The strategy's

---

86 Kundnani, A. (2009) 'Spooked! How Not to Prevent Violent Extremism', London: Institute of Race Relations.

87 Department for Communities and Local Government (2007) 'Preventing Violent Extremism Pathfinder Fund: Guidance Notes for Government Offices and Local Authorities in England', February, London: Department for Communities and Local Government. Available from: https://webarchive.nationalarchives.gov.uk/ukgwa/20091003055312mp_/http://www.communities.gov.uk/documents/communities/pdf/320330.pdf [Accessed 6 March 2023] 7 (emphasis added).

88 Baker-Beall, C. (2016) *The European Union's Fight against Terrorism: Discourse, Policies and Identity*, Manchester: Manchester University Press, 148.

89 Brown, K.E. (2018) 'Introduction: Radicalisation and Securitisation of Muslims in Europe', *Journal of Muslims in Europe*, 7: 139–45, at 139.

90 The Prevent strategy defines Islamism as 'a philosophy which, in the broadest sense, promotes the application of Islamic values to modern government. There are no commonly agreed definitions of "Islamism" and "Islamist", and groups or individuals described as Islamist often have very different aims and views about how those aims might be realised. Some militant Islamists would endorse violence or terrorism to achieve their aims. Many Islamists do not' (HM Government (n 71), 108).

91 Blair, T. (2006) 'Speech to the Foreign Policy Centre', *The Guardian* [online], 21 March 2006. Available from: https://www.theguardian.com/politics/2006/mar/21/iraq.iraq1 [Accessed 24 December 2022].

engagement with Muslims purported to support and strengthen moderate Muslims against the extremists within their community. Through this approach, the strategy brought into being one of the central tropes of the global war on terror: the moderate Muslim who comes into being against the extremist or radical Muslim.[92]

By differentiating moderate Muslims from extremists, police and policy makers sought to focus on extremists without being seen to openly profile on the grounds of race or religion. However, scholars of race highlight ways in which counterterrorism policies and practices intensify and extend existing processes of racialisation of Muslims.[93] The notion of the 'radical Islamist' resonates as it is inscribed on to existing orientalist tropes and stereotypes of Muslim men and Islam as innately violent and aggressive.[94] Such tropes persist in claims that the 'new terrorism' of Al-Qaeda, driven by 'religious fanaticism', is decoupled from wider geopolitical conflicts and differs qualitatively from the other forms of political violence.[95]

Consequently, both extremist and moderate Muslims are objects of policing and policy. They exist on a continuum; both are the objects of state intervention and control. As Sentas accurately observes, 'counter-terrorism law and policing, in their different modes bring into existence policed subjects who are the objects of counter-terrorism: the extremist and the moderate Muslims'.[96] While identification of a person as 'moderate' is clearly not criminalisation, it nevertheless involves a 'racialized process of being made a *policed subject*'.[97]

The moderate/extremist and Islam/Islamism binaries reinforce the perception that the problem of terrorist violence lies within Islam. As the moderate and the extremist exist at different points on the same continuum, in which there is a fluidity of movement, it leaves Muslims having to display 'safe identities' to show to others through their appearance, behaviours and expressed opinions that they are not the 'wrong' type of Muslim.[98] Thus: 'In

---

[92] Abdel-Fattah, R. (2020) 'Countering Violent Extremism, Governmentality and Australian Muslim Youth as "Becoming Terrorist"', *Journal of Sociology*, 56(3): 372–87, at 378.

[93] See Garner, S. and Selod, S. (2015) 'The Racialization of Muslims: Empirical Studies of Islamophobia', *Critical Sociology*, 41(1): 9–19; Cainkar, L. and Selod, S. (2018) 'Review of Race Scholarship and the War on Terror', *Sociology of Race and Ethnicity*, 4(2): 165–77; Abu-Bakare, A. (2020) 'Counterterrorism and Race', *International Politics Reviews*, 8: 79–99.

[94] Said, E. (1978) *Orientalism: Western Concepts of the Orient*, London: Routledge.

[95] Laqueur, W. (1999) *The New Terrorism: Fanaticism and the Arms of Mass Destruction*, Oxford: Oxford University Press.

[96] Sentas (n 23) 22.

[97] Ibid, 177.

[98] Mythens, G., Walklate, S. and Khan, F. (2009) '"I'm a Muslim, But I'm Not a Terrorist": Victimization, Risky Identities and the Performance of Safety', *British Journal of Criminology*, 49(6): 736–54.

the war on terror, every Muslim is infected with the dormant virus and must offer an immunisation record, a reassurance that the strain of Muslimness they contain is safe.'[99] One antidote against the infection of extremism offered in the Prevent strategy is an education in 'fundamental British values' (FBV).

Fundamental British values

Under the revised 2011 Prevent strategy, FBV became a key terrain in which racialisation acted. For the then Prime Minster Cameron, the failure to promote these values had allowed violent and nonviolent extremism to flourish.[100]

While support for the rule of law, democracy, liberty and tolerance is difficult to object to, their racialised coding arises from the push to promote FBV as a response to the so-called 'Trojan Horse' affair.[101] This centred on allegations of a conspiracy by some Muslim parents to control and subvert secular state schools in Birmingham with large numbers of Muslim students. A local authority commissioned review found no evidence of a concerted plot.[102] An investigation for the Department for Education, led by ex-counterterrorism police chief Peter Clarke, while discovering no evidence of support for violent extremism, claimed there were attempts to introduce an 'aggressive Islamic ethos' and conservative Islamic practices in some schools.[103] This report laid the foundations for the promotion of 'fundamental British values' to become an integral part of Britain's approach to countering radicalisation. In this context, a vague notion of shared values has been deployed to control 'Muslim mobilisation and claims-making'.[104]

---

[99] Abdel-Fattah, R. (2019) 'Managing Belief and Speech as Incipient Violence: "I'm Giving You the Opportunity to Say That You Aren't"'. *Journal of Policing, Intelligence and Counter Terrorism*, 14(1): 20–38, at 21.

[100] Cameron, D. (2014) 'British Values', 15 June. Available from: https://www.gov.uk/government/news/british-values-article-by-david-cameron [Accessed 5 January 2022].

[101] See Holmwood, J. and O'Toole, T. (2018) *Countering Extremism in British Schools? The Truth about the Birmingham Trojan Horse Affair*, Bristol: Policy Press.

[102] Kershaw, I. (2014) 'Investigation Report: Trojan Horse Letter: Report of Ian Kershaw of Northern Education for Birmingham City Council in Respect of Issues Arising as a Resule of Concerns Raised in a Letter Dated 27 November 2013, Known as the Trojan Horse Letter', Northern Education. Available from: https://www.birmingham.gov.uk/downloads/file/1579/investigation_report_trojan_horse_letter_the_kershaw_report [Accessed 5 January 2022].

[103] Clarke, P. (2014) 'Report into Allegations Concerning Birmingham Schools Arising from the "Trojan Horse" Letter', July, HC 576, London: HMSO, 14.

[104] Breen, D. and Meer, N. (2019) 'Securing Whiteness?: Critical Race Theory (CRT) and the Securitization of Muslims in Education', *Identities*, 26(5): 595–613.

In the narrative of the good empire, liberty, democracy and the rule of law are characterised as inherently British values. This tells one strand of British history while ignoring centuries during which it led the world in trading slaves and colonising; overlooking the structural and institutional forms of racism that continue to shape the lives of minority ethnic groups.[105] This narrative contributes to conceptualising terrorists as uniquely barbaric and enables the framing of the war on terror as one between the forces of civilisation and barbarism.[106] The embarrassment and contention surrounding the identification of democratic values as inherently British values, reported among those tasked with promoting these in multicultural educational settings, is one indication of the way in which their racial coding is felt and understood.[107]

Racialised surveillance

Concerns that Prevent was being used for covert surveillance and stigmatised Muslim communities led to its labelling as a 'toxic brand' and accelerated disengagement from and opposition to it in sections of the UK Muslim communities.[108] Their growing weariness towards Prevent may have contributed to its shift on to frontline professionals after 2011 and the introduction of the Prevent duty in 2015. At the core of the duty is the training of frontline workers across an array of public services to identify individuals considered vulnerable to radicalisation, and refer them to the government's counter-radicalisation mentoring programme 'Channel'. Surveillance for signs of radicalisation is fundamental to the duty. The need for vigilance is intensified by guidance that stressed both the apparent ubiquity of the threat, as 'there is no single way of identifying an individual who is likely to be susceptible to a terrorist ideology', and warnings that those at risk may conceal any signs.[109] A crucial part of surveillance is the 'coding'

---

[105] Runnymede Trust,(2021), 'England Civil Society Submission to the United Nations Committee on the Elimination of Racial Discrimination', London: Runnymede Trust. Available from: www.runnymedetrust.org/uploads/CERD/Runnymede%20CERD%20report%20v3.pdf [Accessed 5 January 2022].

[106] Crawford, C. (2017) 'Promoting "Fundamental British Values" in Schools: A Critical Race Perspective', *Curriculum Perspectives*, 37(1): 197–204.

[107] Busher, J., Choudhury, T., Thomas, P. and Harris, G. (2017) 'What the Prevent Duty Means for Schools and Colleges in England: An Analysis of Educationalists' Experiences', July, London: The Aziz Foundation.

[108] Halliday, J. and Dodd, V. (2015) 'UK Anti-radicalisation Prevent Strategy a "Toxic Brand"', *The Guardian* [online], 9 March. Available from: https://www.theguardian.com/uk-news/2015/mar/09/anti-radicalisation-prevent-strategy-a-toxic-brand [Accessed 5 January 2022].

[109] Department for Education (2015) 'The Prevent Duty: Departmental Advice for Schools and Childcare Providers', June, London: Department for Education, 6.

of that which is 'normal' and that which is 'abnormal' or 'dangerous'.[110] Research into the duty's implementation finds that everyday Islamic practices or expressions of Muslim identity become marked as signs of potential danger by frontline workers unfamiliar with them.[111]

Younis argues that the risk of racialisation arises from the very banality of the indicators of radicalisation combined with Prevent training that empowers frontline staff to trust their instincts or, if there is any doubt, to report along the referral process anyway. The problem is that intuition and instinct operate against a backdrop of a racialised conception of 'the terrorist' and a common-sense understanding of who the real threat is. Thus, 'the reliance on intuition is foundational in explaining how racial prejudice enters the picture'.[112] Everyday intuition is informed by broader political discourses of nationalism and national identity that are racially coded.[113]

A total of 95 per cent of formal Prevent referrals are 'false positives'; this means the individuals are ultimately found not to present a risk of vulnerability to radicalisation requiring a Channel referral.[114] Analysis of Prevent referral data suggests possible discrimination in the referral process, as those making referrals are significantly better at identifying appropriate referrals for right-wing extremism than Islamist extremism.[115] Despite the numerous potential human rights violations that a Prevent investigation and referral could entail,[116] there have been very few legal challenges to individual referrals. The breadth of the indicators and the broad discretion conferred on professionals in reaching a judgement make it difficult to contest any referral. Other obstacles to mounting public law challenges include the vulnerability of those under investigation; the majority of referrals are of young people.

[110] Fiske, J. (1998) 'Surveilling the City: Whiteness, the Black Man and Democratic Totalitarianism', *Theory, Culture & Society*, 15(2): 67–88, at 72.

[111] Heath-Kelly, C. and Strausz, E. (2017) 'Counter-Terrorism in the NHS: Evaluating Prevent Safeguarding in the NHS', Coventry: University of Warwick; and Busher et al (n 107).

[112] Younis, T. (2021) 'Counter-Radicalisation, Public Health and Racism: A Case Analysis of Prevent', in K. Bhui and D. Bhugra (eds) *Terrorism, Violent Radicalisation and Mental Health*, Oxford: Oxford University Press, 203–16, at 209.

[113] Younis, T. (2020) 'The Psychologisation of Counter-Extremism: Unpacking PREVENT', *Race and Class*, 62(3): 37–60.

[114] Holmwood, J. and Aitlhadj, L. (2022) *The People's Review of Prevent*, London: Prevent Watch, 3.

[115] Busher, J., Choudhury, T. and Thomas, P. (2023) 'Surveillance and Preventing Violent Extremism: The Evidence from Schools and Further Education Colleges in England', in M. Kwet (ed) *The Cambridge Handbook of Surveillance and Race*, Cambridge: Cambridge University Press, 267–87.

[116] Holmwood and Aitlhadj (n 114).

The socioeconomically marginalised positions of British Muslims[117] means that most families will lack the resources needed to mount a legal case. This is exacerbated by the intense fear, anxiety and stigma that accompanies coming under any terrorism-related investigation.[118]

Conclusion

This chapter has sought to detail how processes of racialisation operate through counterterrorism laws, policies and practices. In doing so it reveals how these processes are both enabled by law and remain beyond the reach of public law and constitutional commitments to equality and nondiscrimination. This evasion begins with the broad definition of terrorism, upon which are built wide pre-emptive offences. Beyond this lie counter-radicalisation strategies that enrol swathes of the public sector into remaining vigilant for signs of radicalisation based on vague and unproven indicators. These laws, policies and practices combine to generate unjust spaces for discretionary and selective enforcement, where judgements are made within a social, political and cultural context in which anti-Muslim conspiracy theories and tropes, once relegated to fringe groups, are increasingly accepted as part of mainstream political discourse.[119]

The ability to confront and counter discrete and concealed processes of racialisation through public law remains limited. For example, although the Prevent strategy had been in place for over a decade, the introduction of the Prevent duty in 2015 was the first time that an aspect of the strategy was placed on a statutory footing. Setting out the requirements of the duty in legislation and statutory guidance offers the potential for greater transparency and consistency as well as opening the door for legal challenge and subjecting the policy to 'the values of constitutionalism which lie behind the application of law'.[120] However, public law scrutiny of the processes of racialisation is curtailed by the diffuse ways in which race is inscribed into its everyday practices. As Saher Aziz notes in her reflection on security, race and rights on the twentieth anniversary of 9/11, 'law alone cannot solve racialized counterterrorism because it is in essence a cultural problem …

[117] Muslim Council of Britain (2015) 'British Muslims in Number: A Demographic, Socio-economic and Health Profile of Muslims in Britain Drawing on the 2011 Census', January, London: Muslim Council of Britain. Available from: https://www.mcb.org.uk/wp-content/uploads/2015/02/MCBCensusReport_2015.pdf [Accessed 5 April 2022].

[118] Sabir, R. (2022) *The Suspect: Counterterrorism, Islam and the Security State*, London: Pluto.

[119] Mulhall, J. (2017) 'Going Mainstream: The Mainstreaming of Anti-Muslim Prejudice in Europe and North America', Mini-Report Issue 1, February, London: Hope Not Hate.

[120] Walker, C. and Cawley, O. (2022) 'The juridification of the UK's counter terrorism prevent policy', *Studies in Conflict & Terrorism,* 45(11): 1004–29, at 1007.

regardless of how neutral laws may be on their face, their enforcement will continue to be racist (among other disparate outcomes) so long as racism permeates … society'.[121]

Further reading

Abu-Bakare, A. (2020) 'Counterterrorism and Race', *International Politics Reviews*, 8: 79–99.

Cainkar, L. and Selod, S. (2018) 'Review of Race Scholarship and the War on Terror', *Sociology of Race and Ethnicity*, 4(2): 165–77.

Sentas, V. (2015) *Traces of Terror: Counter-Terrorism Law, Policing and Race*, Oxford: Oxford University Press.

Shabbir, R. (2022) *The Suspect: Counterterrorism, Islam, and the Security State*, London: Pluto.

Younis, T. (2021) 'Counter-Radicalisation, Public Health and Racism: A Case Analysis of Prevent', in K. Bhui and D. Bhugra (eds) *Terrorism, Violent Radicalisation and Mental Health*, Oxford: Oxford University Press, 203–16.

[121] Aziz, S. (2021) 'Reflections of Security, Race and Rights 20 Years after 9/11', *Journal of National Security Law and Policy*, 12: 135–51, at 137.

9

Racism, Law and the Police: Over 50 Years of Anti-discrimination Law and Policing

Ben Bowling and Shruti Iyer

Introduction

Policing is one of the most contentious aspects of British 'race relations' and a key area for students of public law. Although the police were persistently accused of racism throughout the 20th century, their coercive powers were exempt from anti-discrimination law until the new millennium. Taking anti-discrimination law and policing practice in Britain as a case study, we seek to contribute to understanding how police powers are regulated by public law, and in particular the relationship between 'black letter' law 'in the books' and 'blue letter' law 'in action' by the police.[1] We draw on Grimshaw and Jefferson's environmental theory of policework, which contends that law is an overarching structure, in that it makes the police use of coercive powers possible and permissible; yet it is not a dominant structure, because it does not control the use of police power in any given situation. Grimshaw and Jefferson show that law is necessary to explain police practice, but that it is insufficient without examining police working culture and democratic accountability mechanisms. This insight allows us to consider how public law is shaped, over time, by everyday discriminatory attitudes and beliefs, and places an analysis of legal changes in conversation with the forces of broader social change.

---

1 Bowling, B., Reiner, R. and Sheptycki, J. (2019) *The Politics of the Police*, Oxford: Oxford University Press; Dixon, D. (1997) *Law in Policing*, Oxford: Oxford University Press.

In this chapter, we ask four questions:

1. Why did it take 35 years after the introduction of the first Race Relations Act in 1965 for discrimination on the grounds of 'race' in police operational practice to be made unlawful?[2]
2. How do the police discriminate on the basis of race in everyday practice?[3]
3. What were the political, economic and cultural forces that led to police powers being subject to the 'full force' of the Race Relations (Amendment) Act 2000?
4. What impact has anti-discrimination law had on police operational practice since the 1960s?

These are questions for public law scholars because they concern the application of anti-discrimination law as a means to regulate the actions of the state and its agents. For 35 years, racialised minority ethnic groups in the UK were unable to hold the state to account for discrimination in policework, even though they could hold private persons and bodies to account. The failure to control police racism and hold the state accountable for the disproportionate use of coercive power against people of colour is of deep concern because it tacitly condones a violation of stated commitments to the democratic values of fairness, equality and liberty. This chapter examines the relationship between policing and anti-discrimination law using a historical lens and demonstrates that public law, as it is shaped in practice, is subject to a range of structural, institutional, cultural, economic and political forces. Our focus here – on the failure of anti-discrimination law to reduce racism in policing – is offered as a case study that can be applied to other areas of equality and human rights law; often the law is changed in the books, but little progress is made in action. This reveals the complex and fluid relationship between legal change and social change, and that deployment of public power in a democratic state is subject to these forces and is also a site at which they can be contested.

---

2 By 'race', we refer to the police practice of using physical characteristics – for example, skin colour or hair texture – as markers of racial group, ethnic or national origin. For a history of this use, see Bowling, B. (1999) *Violent Racism*, Oxford: Oxford University Press, 33.

3 While there is good evidence that the police in this period failed to protect Black and minority ethnic victims of crime and racist violence, this chapter considers only the impact of the exemption on the use of police coercive powers evidenced through the use of stop-and-search powers. We also restrict our analysis to anti-discrimination law in regulating coercive powers and do not cover employment law or human rights law.

Understanding racism and policework: a theoretical framework

Police are often referred to as 'officers of the law', charged with law enforcement and held accountable to law. This begs the following question: how, if at all, does the law shape police practice? We follow Grimshaw and Jefferson's 'environmental model' in understanding everyday policework as a complex product of three specific elements: law, work and democracy.[4] Law, in this model, is the 'determinant but not dominant' structure of policework. Law specifies what actions can and cannot be taken, but not which actions *will* be taken, against whom and how often. Understanding the formal legal framework, its precision and permissiveness, the level of discretion it allows for, and its relationship to other structures is important to explain the role of public law in policework. Work – Grimshaw and Jefferson's second environmental element – has two dimensions. The first is the vertical dimension of rules, policies and commands that influence everyday practice. The second is the horizontal dimension of the occupational culture, values and routines of the police organisation and the officers who work within it. This occupational environment institutionalises norms and attitudes that shape the interpretation of law.

In turn, the actions of the police, as well as changes in law, are affected by a third environmental element: politics. This 'democratic relation' refers to the ways in which members of society, as individuals or groups or through public institutions, influence police practice.[5] Obvious examples include members of Parliament and civil servants; central and local government elected representatives and officials; pressure groups, nongovernmental organisations and the news media. Grimshaw and Jefferson assert that policework is not isolated from the larger social system and, in order to understand it, we must attend to 'the relationship between all the elements within a given social formation' and 'materially, in relation to the foundations of the social formation as a whole'.[6] They rely on the concept of hegemony to understand this relationship. From this perspective, the ruling class does not rule merely through repression, using the police as its blunt instrument, but by winning consent for its programme from those it subordinates.

In policing, these domains also produce contesting explanations for racism and racial discrimination in policework. A structural theory emphasises how discriminatory police practices stem from broader socioeconomic inequalities. A disciplinary theory, by contrast, locates the cause of racism as

4 Grimshaw, B. and Jefferson, J. (1987) *Interpreting Policework*, London: Allen & Unwin.

5 Ibid, 38.

6 Ibid, 14.

'institutional': a collective failure as an organisation to provide a fair service. A cultural understanding may point to both the occupational culture of the police and widely held stereotypes about minority ethnic groups. An interpersonal perspective would focus on direct and explicit discrimination between a police officer and an individual. Each sphere, however, is intrinsically linked – structural and disciplinary elements underpin the 'interpersonal' ways in which police officers relate to people of colour, while changing attitudes to racial discrimination may spur institutional change.

Law: linking immigration law and 'race relations' law

The beginnings of immigration control

Even before the Second World War, concerns were raised in the political sphere about the perceived damaging effects of so-called 'coloured immigration'.[7] The first legislation came as British colonies began to declare their independence. The 1948 British Nationality Act established Commonwealth citizens as British subjects who retained the right to enter, settle and work in Britain. The British government had little desire to limit migration, fearing that this might aggravate independence negotiations and inflame anti-colonial sentiment.[8]

Extensive migration did not begin until the late 1950s and, by then, calls for immigration control were growing.[9] Immigration was increasingly linked in public discourse to 'race' and the social problems believed to be caused by the so-called immigrants.[10] Surveys of popular opinion showed that a significant proportion of the British population saw Black people as 'uncivilized', 'backward', ignorant, illiterate and lacking proper education.[11] The question arose of how the entry of Black and Asian people from British colonies could be controlled despite their legal rights to travel freely within the Empire.[12] A contradiction thus emerged: on the one hand, the economy needed migrants due to a shortage of workers, particularly in low-wage jobs; on the other hand, migrants were framed as socially undesirable, partly due to a shortage of housing but also to tropes that positioned people of colour as inferior and as 'a problem' that required management and control.[13] As

7 Ramdin, R. (1987) *The Making of the Black Working Class in Britain*, Aldershot: Gower.

8 Bashi, V. (2004) 'Globalized Anti-Blackness: Transnationalizing Western Immigration Law, Policy, and Practice', *Ethnic and Racial Studies*, 27(4): 584–606, at 595.

9 Spencer, I.R.G. (1997) *British Immigration Policy since 1939: The Making of Multi-racial Britain*, London: Routledge, 47–55.

10 Gilroy, P. (1987) *There Ain't No Black in the Union Jack*, London: Hutchinson.

11 Richmond, A.H. (1955) *The Colour Problem: A Study of Racial Relations*, Harmondsworth: Penguin.

12 Hiro, D. (1973) *Black British, White British*, Harmondsworth: Penguin.

13 Solomos, J. (1993) *Race and Racism in Britain* (2nd edn), London: Macmillan.

demand for labour declined, racist violence against the new Commonwealth settlers grew, making urban areas sites of struggle.[14] Widespread racism and the difficulty of obtaining loans forced immigrants into the least desirable neighbourhoods.[15] After the 1958 anti-Black riots in Nottingham and Notting Hill, these tensions could no longer be ignored.[16] The Civil Rights movement in the US deepened British politicians' fears – in 1961 Rab Butler, then Home Secretary, declared that immigration control was necessary to avoid a replication of the US 'colour problem'.[17] With this in mind, the British government established immigration controls to deal with the perceived socially undesirable consequences of unrestricted migration and settlement of people of colour.

The Commonwealth Immigrants Act 1962 established a de facto 'white Britain policy'.[18] The Act required those seeking to enter the UK for settlement to be issued with a job voucher.[19] The then Home Secretary Butler said, candidly, that the 'great merit' of the labour vouchers scheme was that:

> it can be presented as making no distinction on grounds of race and colour ... although the scheme purports to relate solely to employment and to be non-discriminatory, its aim is primarily social and its restrictive effect is intended to and would operate on coloured people almost exclusively.[20]

Despite the restrictions, demands for harsher controls from politicians and the general public intensified. In the general election of 1964, a Conservative candidate won the safe Labour seat of Smethwick on the back of the slogan: 'If you want a n★★★★r for a neighbour, vote Labour'.[21] In 1967 East African Asians possessed passports not subject to the 1962 Act. Unsure of their future under African majority rule in the newly independent countries of Tanzania, Uganda and Kenya, 10,000 of them entered the UK in the last two weeks of February 1968.[22] The second

14 Gordon, P. (1983) *White Law*, London: Pluto; Bowling (n 2).

15 Sivanandan, A. (1982) *A Different Hunger*, London: Pluto, 103; Smith, S. (1989) *The Politics of Race and Residence: Citizenship, Segregation and White Supremacy in Britain*, Cambridge: Polity.

16 Hiro, D. (1973) *Black British, White British*, Harmondsworth: Penguin.

17 Bashi (n 8) 596.

18 Gordon (n 14).

19 Spencer (n 9) 129.

20 Quoted in Dean, D. (1993) 'The Conservative Government and the 1961 Commonwealth Immigration Act: The Inside Story', *Race and Class*, 35(2): 57–74, at 68.

21 Bowling (n 2) 35.

22 Hansen, R. (1999) 'The Kenyan Asians, British Politics, and the Commonwealth Immigrants Act, 1968', *Historical Journal*, 42(3): 809–34.

Commonwealth Immigrants Act was then rushed through Parliament, limiting British citizenship to those with a parent or grandparent born in the UK. This effectively equated British citizenship with British ancestry and white skin. The infamous 'Rivers of Blood' speech by Conservative MP Enoch Powell in 1968 further propelled the racialised discourse on migration. Powell spoke of what he saw as the dangers of Commonwealth immigration filled with the foreboding of a 'total transformation' of British society and the 'nation busily engaged in heaping up its own funeral pyre'.[23]

The 1971 Immigration Act and 1981 British Nationality Act went further, abolishing the nominal right of citizenship for Commonwealth citizens. This consolidated the idea that immigration was undesirable, and allowed Britain access to cheap labour without what were considered the 'social costs' associated with settlement.[24] Those who were not ordinarily resident after the Act came into force were subject to deportation.[25] Police officers were empowered to arrest without warrant anyone suspected to have entered the country unlawfully, to have overstayed or to have failed to observe rules attached to their permit, such as working.[26] Subjecting citizens of the colonies to immigration control legitimised state coercion against people of colour. Because it was impossible to distinguish legal from illegal migrants on the basis of physical appearance alone, state officials suspected anyone who *appeared to be* an immigrant.[27]

Linking 'race relations' law and immigration controls

The political issue at the heart of the race and immigration debate was not 'the volume of black settlement but rather its character and its effects'.[28] The logic linking immigration law with race relations law was expressed in the infamous 'Hattersley formula', named after the Labour Home Secretary at the time, Roy Hattersley, who said: 'without integration, limitation is inexcusable; without limitation, integration is impossible'.[29] The Race Relations Act 1965 therefore sought to legitimise immigration control by legislating against overt forms of discrimination.

---

[23] Enoch Powell, Conservative MP for Wolverhampton South West, speech, 20 April 1968, Conservative Political Centre, Birmingham.

[24] Gordon (n 14) 12.

[25] Gordon (n 14); Gordon, P. (1985) *Policing Immigration: Britain's Internal Controls*, London: Pluto.

[26] Sivanandan (n 15) 27.

[27] Gordon (n 14) 17.

[28] Gilroy (n 10) 85.

[29] Hansard vol 709, cols 378–85.

The 1965 Act made racial discrimination illegal in 'places of public resort'. This was a response to the widespread 'colour bar', an informal ban on access to public places (akin to Jim Crow laws in the US and South African Apartheid) that prevented people of colour from renting homes or visiting hotels, clubs and pubs. The Act outlawed the refusal to provide services on the grounds of race, relying on citizen groups to ensure compliance.[30] The Race Relations Act 1968 went further by prohibiting racial discrimination in employment, housing, credit and insurance. It introduced the Race Relations Board as a regulatory body, although this had no powers of enforcement and could merely seek damages and an injunction against discriminatory practices. Crucially, state agencies, including the police, courts, prisons and immigration service, were exempt from these laws.

Within a decade it had become clear that the 1965 and 1968 Acts were insufficient to prevent racist discrimination.[31] The response was the Race Relations Act 1976, which made indirect discrimination[32] unlawful and created the Commission for Racial Equality (CRE) to investigate cases. Police powers, however, still remained exempt from its scope, and the 1976 Act failed to have a significant impact. Few legal actions were successful. Police impunity from laws intended to prohibit discrimination became more obviously problematic after widespread rioting in 1981. The most serious event, the Brixton uprising, was triggered by Operation Swamp, during which 943 people were stopped and 118 arrested, over half of them Black and most of them under 21.[33] Lord Scarman, in his report on the unrest, pointed to the failure of race relations legislation and called for strengthened community relations.[34] Nonetheless, the government refused to bring the police within the scope of anti-discrimination law.[35]

Explaining the exemption of the police from the Race Relations Acts

The Immigration Act 1971 created a system of *internal* immigration controls to add to conventional *external* controls, such as issuing visas and checking passports.[36] Internal controls included surveillance of people of colour within

[30] Freeman, G.P. (1979) *Immigrant Labor and Racial Conflict in Industrial Societies*, Princeton: Princeton University Press, 146.

[31] Gordon (n 14) 18.

[32] Indirect discrimination occurs where a condition or requirement is applied equally to different racial groups, but the proportion of a racial group that can comply is considerably smaller than that of another group.

[33] Gordon (n 14) 26.

[34] 'The Brixton Disorders, 10–12 April 1981: Report of an Inquiry by the Rt Hon The Lord Scarman', OBE, November, Home Office, Cmnd 8427, London: HMSO.

[35] Solomos (n 13) 72.

[36] Gordon (n 25).

domestic territory, including workplaces, railway stations and hospitals, as well as passport raids and routine street policing. People who had entered the country 'illegally' or had overstayed their visa were actively sought out, and employers who knowingly hired them were penalised.[37] At the border, authorities scrutinised non-white migrants in particular.[38] As controls were explicitly designed to limit the numbers of 'coloured immigrants', being an immigrant was equated with having black or brown skin.[39] Racism and racial stereotyping became an inherent part of both immigration control and everyday policework.[40]

The Immigration Act 1971 granted police officers the power to detain, question and arrest those suspected of being in breach of immigration law, and provided the legal basis for passport raids throughout the 1970s and 1980s.[41] A review of these operations in 1980 reasserted the police power to carry out raids and demand to see passports.[42] Over 5,000 people were held in custody under the Act, many for long periods. After a series of particularly harsh raids in 1980, the general secretaries of the Transport and General Workers' Union and General and Municipal Workers' Union warned that such operations were producing a situation akin to the pass-laws[43] that were integral to South African Apartheid.

The government exempted all powers of government, including those of the police, from the scope of the Race Relations Act 1976. Although this seems astonishing with the benefit of hindsight, in the context of stringent internal immigration controls it was arguably impossible for the state to bring the police within the scope of anti-discrimination laws. The police were tasked with enforcing domestic immigration controls and this task *required* racial discrimination. It explicitly used 'ethnic appearance' – the preferred police term – as the basis for targeting immigrants.[44] In a Cabinet discussion on including the police within the scope of the Race Relations

---

37 Sivanandan (n 15) 28, 134.

38 Smith, E. and Marmo, M. (2014) *Race, Gender and the Body in British Immigration Control*, Basingstoke: Palgrave Macmillan.

39 Gordon (n 25); Weber, L. and Bowling, B. (2008) 'Valiant Beggars and Global Vagabonds: Select, Eject, Immobilize', *Theoretical Criminology*, 12(3): 355–75.

40 Hall, S., Critcher, C., Jefferson, T., Clarke, J. and Roberts, B. (1978) *Policing the Crisis: Mugging, the State, and Law and Order*, London: Macmillan; Weber, L. and Bowling, B. (2004) 'Policing Migration: A Framework for Investigating the Regulation of Global Mobility', *Policing & Society*, 14(3): 195–212; Gordon (n 14); Gordon (n 25).

41 Gordon (n 25); Weber and Bowling (n 40).

42 Gordon (n 14) 37.

43 'Pass laws' were an internal passport system used in Apartheid South Africa restricting largely African men to designated areas. They entitled the police to demand, at any time, that Africans show a valid pass or face detention/arrest.

44 Gordon (n 25); Weber and Bowling (n 40).

Act 1968, Harold Wilson, the then Prime Minister, said: 'There is no doubt that the immigrants believe that the police discriminate against them, and the Chancellor [Roy Jenkins] thinks that a number of policemen agree with Mr Enoch Powell's views on race.'[45] Nonetheless, James Callaghan, the then Home Secretary, bowed to pressure to exempt the police from the Act, saying: 'The opposition of the Police Federation to amending the code has been intense and deep-seated. And the Police Advisory Board has been unanimous in advising me not to proceed.'[46] After the Lawrence Inquiry – to which we return later on – Callaghan admitted that yielding to pressure on the issue was a mistake. As the Stephen Lawrence case demonstrated, failing to hold the police accountable for racism would have fatal consequences.

Work: police practice while exempt from anti-discrimination law

Grimshaw and Jefferson's environmental theory of policing draws attention to the ways in which the police 'working environment' shapes operational practice. While law is the determinant element, it must be understood in the context of how law is interpreted and translated into action. Police occupational culture – norms, stereotypes and working knowledge of the job – helps explain which laws are enforced and against whom.

In 1970s and 1980s public discourse, racialised ethnic minority groups were framed as a socially undesirable problem.[47] This was particularly evident within police occupational culture. Studies in this period found widespread use of racist language, negative views of Black and Asian people, and support for far-right political parties. Smith and Gray found that 'racial prejudice and racialist talk … [were] pervasive … expected, accepted and even fashionable'.[48] A study of attitudes and perceptions of police officers in the late 1980s found that Black people were characterised as prone to violent crime and drug abuse, incomprehensible, suspicious, hard to handle, 'naturally excitable', aggressive, lacking brainpower, troublesome and 'tooled up'.[49] The police emphasised Black criminality and dangerousness in order to improve their own standing and increase their resources and powers.[50]

---

45 BBC (1999) 'Callaghan: I Was Wrong on Police and Race', *BBC News* [online], 8 January. Available from: http://news.bbc.co.uk/1/hi/special_report/1999/01/99/1968_secret_history/244320.stm [Accessed 24 December 2022].

46 Ibid.

47 Hall et al (n 40); Gilroy (n 10).

48 Smith, D. and Gray, J. (1985), *Police and People in London,* London: Gower, 388–9.

49 Graef, R. (1989), *Talking Blues*, London: Collins Harvill.

50 Hall et al (n 40) 96, 111; Institute of Race Relations (1987) *Policing against Black People*, London: Institute of Race Relations, 52.

One important example of how racial stereotypes shaped police practice was the use and abuse of 'stop and search' powers. Black and minority ethnic communities consistently complained that questioning under immigration law, passport checks and routine stop and search were used disproportionately against them. The police were deployed to Black and minority ethnic neighbourhoods even where local crime rates did not justify disproportionate attention; these neighbourhoods were regarded as intrinsically criminal and a threat to public order.[51] The police used section 4 of the Vagrancy Act 1824 (popularly called the 'sus' law) – the arrestable criminal offence of being a suspected person loitering with intent to commit a crime – to harass young Black people. The Institute of Race Relations noted that stopping Black people driving cars was the most common pretext: 'The police seem to assume that no black person can own a decent car … if you come from a black area (and particularly if you are driving into a white one), you must be up to no good.'[52]

Targeting young people was an important part of the process of criminalising minority ethnic communities.[53] A person stopped by police was automatically checked against a register of wanted people, including those alleged to have breached the terms of the Immigration Act. For the reasons explained earlier, when Black or brown people came into contact with the police, most often in a stop-and-search encounter, but even as victims of crime or as witnesses, their immigration status was immediately called into question. There were recorded instances of people of colour being taken to a police station for not having their passport on them when stopped in the street. In 1973, passport checks in Birmingham were so widespread that many people routinely carried their passports for 'protection from the police'.[54] The systematic suspicion of minority ethnic people significantly increased the rate at which they came to the attention of the authorities, which was used to justify harsher policing.[55] In 1979, Home Office research demonstrated that Black people were 14–15 times more likely than white people to be arrested for 'sus' or 'robbery and other violent thefts'.[56] Stereotyping was an integral element of police culture that had an impact on police practice.

'Sus' was repealed in 1981 after a protracted community campaign. The Police and Criminal Evidence Act (PACE) was introduced in 1984 to

51 Ibid, 12.

52 Ibid.

53 Gordon (n 14) 33.

54 Institute of Race Relations (n 50) 15.

55 Bowling, B., Parmar, A. and Phillips, C. (2008) 'Policing Ethnic Minority Communities', in T. Newburn (ed) *Handbook of Policing* (2nd edn), Cullompton: Willan Publishing, 611–41, 611.

56 Stevens, P. and Willis, C. (1979) 'Race, Crime and Arrests', Home Office Research Research Report No 58, London: Home Office.

regulate police powers, and its Code of Practice A stipulates that reasonable grounds for suspicion must have an objective basis and cannot be based on stereotypical images of certain groups.[57] But since stop and search is exercised with high levels of discretion and low levels of accountability, legal regulation has largely failed to prevent abuse.[58] Officers believed that 'if you see four black youths in a car, it's worth giving them a pull, as at least one of them is going to be guilty of something or other'.[59]

Democracy: the public demand to hold the police accountable

The third element of Grimshaw and Jefferson's environmental theory is the democratic relationship with the public. This element focuses on the way that political structures and actors influence police practice. In seeking to understand the impact of anti-discrimination law on police practice, key actors include national, local and international political figures, the news media, public inquiries and bodies such as the CRE (now integrated into the Equality and Human Rights Commission [EHRC]). Their work should also be situated in the context of the changing political economy of the period.

The impetus for legislative change occurred within the context of a more fundamental restructuring of the public sector around the notions of service provision and privatisation. Citizens were encouraged to think of themselves as consumers, and institutions were focused on achieving measurable results. Neoliberalism as an economic doctrine demanded the devolution of the welfare state and smaller government.[60] As a result, the public sector was pushed towards managerialism, notably through the Police and Magistrates' Courts Act 1994, which made the police more business-like.[61] The restructuring of the police took place amid annual crime control

57 The police are empowered to stop and search under: s 1 of the Police and Criminal Evidence Act 1984, s 23 of the Misuse of Drugs Act 1971, s 60 of the Criminal Justice and Public Order Act 1994, s 47 of the Firearms Act 1968 and s 44 of the Terrorism Act 2000 (now repealed and replaced with s 47). See Bowling B. and Phillips C. (2007) 'Disproportionate and Discriminatory: Reviewing the Evidence on Police Stop and Search', *Modern Law Review*, 70(6): 936–61.

58 Bowling and Phillips (n 57); Bowling, Reiner and Sheptycki (n 1) chapter 6.

59 Cashmore, E. (2001) 'The Experiences of Ethnic Minority Police Officers in Britain: Under-Recruitment and Racial Profiling in a Performance Culture', *Ethnic and Racial Studies*, 24(4): 642–59.

60 Wacquant, L. (2010), 'Crafting the Neoliberal State: Workfare, Prisonfare, and Social Insecurity', *Sociological Forum*, 25(2): 197–220.

61 McLaughlin, E. and Murji, K. (1997), 'The Future Lasts a Long Time: Public Policework and the Managerialist Paradox', in P. Francis, P. Davies and V. Jupp (eds) *Policing Futures: The Police, Law Enforcement and the Twenty-First Century*, London: Macmillan, 80–103, 98.

targets and objectives, and an expanding role for private policing. Construing the police as a service like any other – subject to rigorous market discipline, with targets to meet and vulnerable to cuts – weakened the argument that they should be exempt from anti-discrimination legislation.

In *Amin*, the House of Lords ruled that police officers should be held liable for discrimination when acting outside their law enforcement role.[62] This created a distinction between regulatory activities – specifically the use of coercive powers – and the provision of services.[63] This was expanded further in *Farah*.[64] In this case, the complainant had summoned police assistance after being subject to a racist attack, but instead of attempting to detain her attackers or help her, the police charged her with affray, common assault and causing suffering to the dog that had been unleashed by her attackers. The House of Lords held that the services the complainant sought from the police came within the scope of the test set out in *Amin* as similar to an act that may be performed by a private person. Further, the argument was accepted that section 20 of the Race Relations Act 1976 covered duties involving assistance to the public. This clearly seems to be a law enforcement power, where police power was used to 'overpolice' and criminalise a victim, yet it was brought under the scope of the Act. Although the claim that chief officers should have vicarious liability for the actions of their officers failed (so only individual officers could be held liable), the *Farah* case eroded the justification for exempting the police from anti-discrimination law.

Britain also underwent a profound change in the politics of multiculturalism. Lord Scarman's report on the Brixton riots called for a radical programme to tackle racial inequality, and the CRE joined the chorus of voices calling for reform.[65] It became more assertive, publishing several reviews calling for anti-discrimination law to be strengthened. It also asked for an amendment to overrule the *Amin* judgment and extend the scope of the Race Relations Act 1976 to actions taken by government and public bodies.

The CRE also pushed for an independent public inquiry into the application of immigration rules to individuals, particularly members of non-white minorities.[66] The Home Office launched a legal challenge, arguing in *Home Office v Commission for Racial Equality* that the Race Relations Act was not applicable to government institutions and powers. Counsel for the Home Office argued with extraordinary candour that such use of the CRE's powers could not have been Parliament's intention:

---

62 *R v Entry Clearance Officer (Bombay) ex parte Amin* (1983) 2 AC 818.

63 Fiddick, J. and Hicks, J. (2000) *The Race Relations Amendment Bill [HL]*. Research Paper 00/27, House of Commons Library, 10.

64 *Farah v Commissioner of Police of the Metropolis* [1998] QB 65.

65 Solomos (n 13) 92.

66 Smith and Marmo (n 38) 112.

> The policy of immigration control, as described in the Immigration Act 1971, is, *by its very nature, based on racial discrimination* in that it discriminates against people on the ground of their nationality. *It is the function of the immigration service to ensure that such discrimination is enforced.*[67]

The essence of the Home Office's legal argument is that it was absurd to suggest that the Race Relations Act 1976 was intended to apply to the police or immigration control or that they be subject to scrutiny or regulation of this kind. The government's own lawyers argued that immigration policing *required racial discrimination*. Over time, the police were further drawn into immigration work, from large-scale raids and forced deportations to monitoring asylum applicants.[68]

The CRE won the right to investigate allegations of racial discrimination, though the Home Office was not obliged to cooperate. The tide was turning in favour of the CRE: once it was permitted to investigate immigration control, it became harder to argue that the police should remain exempt from anti-discrimination law. The CRE's demands finally materialised in the Race Relations (Amendment) Act 2000. However, under the Immigration and Asylum Act 1999, which passed into law shortly beforehand, immigration officers were granted constabulary powers within domestic space rather than having powers restricted to ports and airports. Henceforth, specialist immigration police, accountable only to the Home Secretary, were empowered to use reasonable force to arrest suspects, or enter and search premises and persons without a warrant. This shift in immigration policing was explained both by the broader restructuring of the public sector and the creation of a purpose-built immigration police force.[69]

Another vital element of the political context was the public inquiry into the racist murder of Stephen Lawrence. Between the time of Lawrence's murder in 1993 and the Lawrence Inquiry's report in 1999, sustained press coverage and support for the family's campaign from prominent civil society members, including Nelson Mandela, persuaded the New Labour government to commission a public inquiry. The Inquiry's report, and the research evidence submitted to it, showed that the Metropolitan Police had conducted an incompetent investigation and were institutionally racist.[70] Faced with this evidence, exempting the police from the Race

---

[67] [1982] QB 385, [1981] 2 WLR 703, emphasis added.

[68] Weber and Bowling (n 40) 205.

[69] Bowling, B. and Westenra, S. (2020) 'A Really Hostile Environment: Adiaphorization, Global Policing and the Crimmigration Control System', *Theoretical Criminology*, 24(2): 163–83.

[70] Macpherson of Cluny, Sir William (1999), 'The Stephen Lawrence Inquiry', February, CM 4262-I, London: Home Office; Cathcart, B. (1999) *The Case of Stephen Lawrence*, London: Penguin; Bowling (n 2).

Relations Act became untenable. The police response to the murder showed that they saw neither Stephen Lawrence nor his friend Duwayne Brooks as victims of a crime to whom they had to provide a fair service. The then Home Secretary's Stephen Lawrence Action Plan accepted the inquiry's recommendation that the 'full force of Race Relations legislation should apply to all police officers' and that 'Chief Officers of Police should be made vicariously liable for the acts and omissions of their officers relevant to that legislation'.[71] Following the publication of the report, the government brought all public services and functions within the scope of anti-discrimination legislation through the Race Relations (Amendment) Act 2000. It placed a general duty on specified public authorities to promote race equality, made chief officers liable for compensation, costs and expenses, and required them to take reasonable steps to ensure their officers did not racially discriminate.

Shifting internal immigration law enforcement away from domestic police forces to a bespoke agency paved the way for the police to be subject to anti-discrimination legislation. This finally reconciled the tension between policing and race relations law, which arose from the fact that the police were required to discriminate in order to enforce immigration law. Immigration authorities remained exempt under section 19B of the Race Relations (Amendment) Act 2000. Discrimination on the grounds of nationality, national origin and ethnicity remains permissible where immigration legislation requires it or where a minister has authorised it. Such authorisations are rarely transparent; there is no obligation to disclose them, and internal instructions prohibit any reference to them when recording decisions.[72] The only way for someone to find out whether a ministerial authorisation has affected them is to compel disclosure in legal proceedings.[73]

Today's UK Border Force is 'a true immigration police force'.[74] It has the full range of coercive and intrusive powers of the police, but fewer regulatory safeguards (such as PACE) to monitor these powers.[75] The dual-interventionist mechanism of internal and external immigration controls now falls largely within the remit of the immigration authorities.[76] Although the domestic police

[71] Home Office (1999) 'Stephen Lawrence Inquiry: Home Secretary's Action Plan', March, London: Home Office Communication Directorate, 11.

[72] See FOI request 17943.

[73] Clayton, G. (2016) *Textbook on Immigration and Asylum Law*, Oxford: Oxford University Press, 214.

[74] MacDonald, I. and Toal, R. (eds) (2010) *MacDonald's Immigration Law and Practice*, London: LexisNexis.

[75] Weber and Bowling (n 40) 206–7; Bowling, B. and Westenra, S. (2018) 'Racism, Immigration and Policing', in M. Bosworth, A. Parmar and Y. Vázquez (eds) *Race, Criminal Justice and Migration Control: Enforcing the Boundaries of Belonging*, Oxford: Oxford University Press, 61–77.

[76] Gordon (n 14) 16.

are still actively involved in policing immigration, and have recently cemented close links with the immigration service (for example, in Operation Nexus), this involves a focus on 'high harm' criminality and not immigration status per se.[77]

Hegemony: the failures of anti-discrimination law

The legacy of institutional racism, sexism and homophobia in British policing is manifest in in Baroness Casey's 2023 report on the culture and standards of behaviour in the Metropolitan police. The Casey Review found that the Met fails to reflect the community that it serves, that many officers experience discrimination at work, racism and racial bias are reinforced within police systems. It showed that the organisation is permissive of racist attitudes, has weak misconduct procedures and lacks transparency and accountability. Casey concluded that Black Londoners 'have been under-protected and over-policed for too long'.[78] According to Whitfield, 'in this country at least, racial discrimination is not a field in which Government action can make much difference.[79] This scepticism appears justified, at least in relation to policing. A detailed assessment of the impact of the Race Relations (Amendment) Act 2000 (and subsequent equalities legislation) is beyond the scope of this chapter, but there is little reason to believe that public law has contributed to fairness, justice and equality in policing or to improving police–community relations. Figures released in October 2015 under the Freedom of Information Act 2000 revealed that the Metropolitan Police had received over 240 complaints of racial discrimination between March 2014 and February 2015, none of which were upheld.[80] Several officers had multiple allegations against them, but none resulted in any action.[81] Bringing a successful claim against the police appears as difficult as ever. Early in 2017, in response to a Freedom

[77] Parmar, A. (2020) 'Arresting (Non)Citizenship: The Policing Migration Nexus of Nationality, Race and Criminalization', *Theoretical Criminology*, 24(1): 28–49. 'Operation Nexus' placed immigration officers in police custody suites, subjecting suspected foreign nationals to enhanced immigration checks from the very moment they are booked into custody.

[78] Baroness Casey of Blackstock (2023) 'An Independent Review into the Standards of Behaviour and Internal Culture of the Metropolitan Police Service: Final Report'. London: Metropolitan Police, 19.

[79] Whitfield, J. (2007) 'The Historical Context: Policing and Black People in Post-War Britain', in M. Rowe (ed) *Policing beyond Macpherson: Issues in Policing, Race, and Society*, Cullompton: Willan Publishing, 1.

[80] Taylor, M. and Dodd, V. (2015), 'No Racial Discrimination Complaints against Met Police Upheld', *The Guardian* [online], 12 October. Available from: https://www.theguardian.com/uk-news/2015/oct/12/no-racial-discrimination-complaints-upheld-met-police [Accessed 24 December 2022].

[81] Full data available from: https://londonagainstpoliceviolence.files.wordpress.com/2015/10/discrimination-complaints-mar14-feb15.pdf [Accessed 24 December 2022].

of Information request, the Metropolitan Police admitted to passing details of victims and witnesses of crime to immigration enforcement if there were concerns over their immigration status.[82] Clearly, the disciplinary impulse to police immigration through a variety of state institutions continues.[83]

Many cases of racial discrimination are settled out of court, such as *Smith v Commissioner of Police for the Metropolis*.[84] This civil action against the police for racial discrimination, false imprisonment, trespass to property and harassment arose from 18 separate stops, none of which resulted in an arrest or the discovery of prohibited items. Racial discrimination is difficult to prove in court; under the European Convention on Human Rights, the Article 14 prohibition of discrimination on the grounds of race is contingent on proving the violation of another Convention right (usually Article 5 or Article 8). In *Roberts*,[85] for example, the High Court and the Court of Appeal refused to consider statistical evidence on the discriminatory impact of suspicionless searches under section 60 of the Criminal Justice and Public Order Act 1994, on the basis that they were 'controversial' and gave rise to 'difficult issues of interpretation'.[86] The Supreme Court, too, refused to take into evidence reports from the EHRC that documented racial profiling.[87] The appellant was limited to arguing that the power had insufficient safeguards and dropped the claim of racial discrimination.[88] This speaks to the difficulty of constructing a claim of racial discrimination in court: it is often difficult to prove that an individual has been treated in a racist manner by a police officer or other public official. The courts tend to exclude statistical evidence

[82] Jeraj, S. and Bloomer, N. (2017), 'Met Police Hands Victims of Crime over to the Home Office for Immigration Enforcement', *Politics.co.uk* [online], 5 April. Available from: http://www.politics.co.uk/news/2017/04/05/met-police-hands-victims-of-crime-over-to-the-home-office [Accessed 24 December 2022].

[83] Parmar (n 77).

[84] Central London County Court, Claim no 5CL107102. Settled through mediation, 5 April 2007.

[85] *R (Roberts) v Commissioner of Police of the Metropolis* [2015] UKSC 79.

[86] Delsol, R. and Wissow, L. (2014) 'Case Watch: UK Appeals Court Disregards Evidence That Stop and Search is Discriminatory', *Open Society Justice Initiative* [online], 16 February. Available from: https://www.justiceinitiative.org/voices/case-watch-uk-appeals-court-disregards-evidence-stop-and-search-discriminatory [Accessed 24 December 2022].

[87] The EHRC is a nongovernmental body set up under the Equality Act 2006. It subsumed the CRE and is responsible for promoting and enforcing equality laws in England, Scotland and Wales.

[88] Marks, E. (2016a) 'Suspicionless Searches in the Supreme Court', *King's Law Journal*, 27(2): 137–44; Marks, E. (2016b) 'Unjustified Assumptions: The Supreme Court and Section 60', *Stopwatch* [online], 29 February. Available from: https://www.stop-watch.org/news-opinion/unjustified-assumptions-the-supreme-court-and-section-60/ [Accessed 24 December 2022].

of systematic or structural patterns of discrimination, and it is very difficult to show conclusively that a state official *intended* to discriminate without some evidence that points to racial animus in the defendant's mind.

The closest that anti-discrimination legal action has come to changing police practice was in 2010, when the EHRC threatened legal action under the Equality Act 2006 (which subsumed the Race Relations Acts). The Commission identified seven police forces with the highest rates of racial disproportionality and initiated legal enforcement action against two forces. Although the action was not pursued as far as the courts, this work fed into a broader process of legal, cultural and political change that reshaped the use of police powers. In this instance, there was significant change: the use of stop and search declined markedly between 2010 and 2016, and suspicionless searches fell even more rapidly.[89] Although evidence of racial discrimination and discussions about racism were integral to the debates, anti-discrimination law did not play a significant part in changing police practice. It is perhaps an obvious point, but where the law is highly permissive, difficult to invoke or unenforceable in practice, it cannot play much of a role in shaping police action. This demonstrates how any analysis of public law – particularly anti-discrimination law – must be embedded within a wider analysis of the social, historical and political processes within which law operates. Changing the way in which the police and other state agencies exercise their powers is more often brought about through politics than through law and policy.

In this wider context, government policy underpins and exacerbates new forms of racism.[90] Widespread anti-immigrant sentiment in British public life makes it impossible for anti-discrimination law to be effective. State policy permits overt discrimination in immigration policy and practice while arguing that discrimination is wrong; racial profiling and discrimination have been funnelled into immigration enforcement, which remains exempt from anti-discrimination law. The move from immigration control to 'induced repatriation'[91] continues through the systemic stigmatisation of asylum seekers.[92] The burden of immigration control is now diffused through a variety of authorities under 'hostile environment' policies: health services, educational institutions and private landlords are now all expected to check immigration status, thereby contributing to immigration law enforcement.[93]

89 Bowling, B. and Marks E. (2017), 'The Rise and Fall of Suspicionless Searches', *King's Law Journal*, 28(1): 62–88.

90 Burnett, J. (2012) 'After Lawrence: Racial Violence and Policing in the UK', *Race & Class*, 54(1): 91–8, at 95.

91 Sivanandan (n 15) 131.

92 Bosworth, M. and Kellezi, B. (2014) 'Citizenship and Belonging in a Women's Immigration Removal Centre', in C. Phillips and C. Webster (eds) *New Directions in Race, Ethnicity, and Crime*, Abingdon: Routledge, 80–96.

93 Bowling and Westenra (n 69).

The institutional racism of the police force is now supplemented by the lack of accountability of private corporations involved in immigration control. The case of Jimmy Mubenga, who was forcibly restrained and asphyxiated by two private security guards during his deportation in 2010, is a shocking reminder that racism is alive and well. The guards were found not guilty of manslaughter, though an inquest jury found in 2013 that Mr Mubenga was unlawfully killed.[94] The disciplinary control of people of colour is buttressed by the ongoing drive to control immigration and the cultural narrative that immigrants are undesirable.

The dynamic set in motion in the 1970s continues: immigration control calls for racism, and racism calls for more immigration restrictions. Unsurprisingly, the overpolicing of Black and minority ethnic people continues. In 1999, Black people were six times more likely to be stopped under PACE; in 2009–10, this had risen to seven times more likely. As of 2018, Black people are nine times more likely to be stopped and searched than white people, and people of colour are, collectively, four times more likely to be searched.[95]

Public law in this area has been more aspirational than practical; it sets standards of equality, fairness and anti-discrimination 'in the books' that have little relationship to the political and economic processes that perpetuate racism. The structural and cultural factors that drive and legitimise racism and anti-immigrant sentiment show no sign of abating, nor does the disciplinary power of state institutions targeting migrants. One reason to be hopeful is the emergence of civil society organisations attempting to hold the police to account and mounting campaigns for justice. These include organisations that work with the police (such as the Metropolitan Black Police Association, the EHRC and His Majesty's Inspectorate of Constabulary and Fire and Rescue Services), the mass media, and activist groups such as Liberty, State Watch, Institute of Race Relations, StopWatch and Black Lives Matter. The immense support that family campaigns have attracted after the death of loved ones at the hands of the police is evidence that activism can change the culture of a society that sanctions discriminatory policing. While this still depends on individuals prying justice from the hands of the state, it can force a shift in public opinion and in police practice – much like the

[94] BBC (2013) 'Jimmy Mubenga: Heathrow Deportee "Unlawfully Killed"', *BBC News* [online], 9 July. Available from: https://www.bbc.com/news/uk-england-23244203 [Accessed 24 December 2022].

[95] Home Office (2018) 'Police Powers and Procedures, England and Wales, Year Ending 31 March 2018', Statistical Bulletin 24/18 [online], 25 October, Lonndon: Home Office. Available from: https://assets.publishing.service.gov.uk/government/uploads/system/uploads/attachment_data/file/751215/police-powers-procedures-mar18-hosb2418.pdf [Accessed 6 March 2023].

democratic shift that propelled the Race Relations (Amendment) Act 2000 on to the statute books.

Despite their obvious limitations, these laws stimulate further action and advocacy, and form an important part of the moral demands that are made for a fairer and more equal society. There *is* still a place for law in this story of social change. *Gillan*,[96] a case decided by the European Court of Human Rights, challenged the use of suspicionless searches under the Terrorism Act 2000. Although the Court did not explicitly engage with the question of discrimination, its judgment led to a dramatic reduction in the use of stop-and-search powers, reducing the impact of racist policing on minority ethnic communities.[97] Law is a dynamic and fluid force running through the elements of work, democracy and hegemony. While it can have tactical and strategic uses,[98] it is essential to examine the context within which law operates and exerts its effects.

Conclusion

Drawing on Grimshaw and Jefferson's environmental theory of policing, we have answered the four questions about the relationship between anti-discrimination law and police practice that we posed in the introduction.[99] First, British police forces were granted immunity from 'race relations' law between 1965 and 2000 because they had an essential role in immigration law enforcement that was designed to discriminate against people of African, Caribbean and Asian origin. The police were required *by law* to discriminate on the grounds of 'race'. This made the application of anti-discrimination law against immigration enforcement impossible, and it was fiercely resisted by the Home Office and the police. Second, the consequence of this exemption was that the police were given licence to discriminate against people of colour throughout the 20th century, including the power to stop and search and to question people about their immigration status. Compounded by prejudice and stereotyping, the result was the systemic overpolicing of people of colour.[100] Third, the key processes and events in British society that led to the police being brought within the scope of anti-discrimination law include the neoliberal restructuring of the public sector, the more assertive role taken by the CRE, the Lawrence Inquiry

---

96 *Gillan v United Kingdom* (2010) 50 EHRR 1105.

97 See Bowling and Marks (n 89); Marks (2016b) (n 88).

98 For the distinction between strategy and tactics, see Knox, R. (2010) 'Strategy and Tactics', *Finnish Yearbook of International Law*, 21: 193–229.

99 Grimshaw and Jefferson (n 4).

100 Bowling et al (n 55).

and the granting of constabulary powers to the immigration service in 1999. Fourth, the long-awaited application of the 'full force' of the Race Relations Act to the police has achieved little: the law has rarely been used; racism in immigration enforcement remains unchecked; and stop-and-search rates continue to be disproportionately high for Black and minority ethnic communities. This pessimistic conclusion is tempered only by the hope that there are other ways than law to improve the quality of policework, such as activist campaigns for justice and strengthening accountability mechanisms. To achieve fairness and justice for all, we should understand that public and private law are embedded within these broader structures, and direct our energy towards more radical cultural, social and political change.

Further reading

Bowling, B., Parmar, A. and Phillips, C. (2003), 'Policing Ethnic Minority Communities', in T. Newburn (ed) *Handbook of Policing*, Cullompton: Willan Publishing, 611–41.

Bowling, B., Reiner, R. and Sheptycki, J. (2019) *The Politics of the Police*, Oxford: Oxford University Press.

Gordon, P. (1983) *White Law*, London: Pluto.

Sivanandan, A. (1982) *A Different Hunger*, London: Pluto.

Smith, E. and Marmo, M. (2014) *Race, Gender and the Body in British Immigration Control*, Basingstoke: Palgrave Macmillan.

Solomos, J. (1993) *Race and Racism in Britain* (2nd edn), London: Macmillan.

10

The Administration of Social Security Benefits: Gendered Implications

Ciara Fitzpatrick

Introduction

The social security system – the distribution of cash transfers to individuals – is a considerable cog in the governmental wheel and is the single largest area of expenditure.[1] Yet, the system's cost, its extensive complexity and the breadth of its reach mean that it is often misunderstood and frequently challenged.[2] It has been the site of frequent government-led 'welfare reform', which has equated to significant cuts in expenditure. Incremental reform over the last half century has eroded the system's ability to prevent poverty. Rather than a vehicle for redistribution, the contemporary social security system is designed to promote full-time participation in the labour market through the pursuit of 'welfare conditionality', which requires a benefit claimant to meet work-related obligations set out in a contractual agreement with the state before receiving benefits.[3] Under the current

1 The expenditure on benefit, pension and social fund payments in 2018–19 was £191 billion. See Annually Managed Expenditure, Department for Work and Pensions (2020) 'Annual Report and Accounts 2019–20 for the Year Ended 31 March 2020', HCC 401, London: The Stationery Office. Available from: https://assets.publishing.service.gov.uk/government/uploads/system/uploads/attachment_data/file/896268/dwp-annual-report-and-accounts-2019-2020.pdf [Accessed 4 June 2021] 16.

2 Millar, J. and Sainsbury, S. (2018) 'Social Security: The Landscape', in *Understanding Social Security* (3rd edn), Bristol: Policy Press, 1.

3 Dwyer, P. and Wright, S. (2014) 'Ubiquitous Conditionality and its Implications for Social Citizenship', *Journal of Poverty and Social Justice*, 22(9): 27–35.

system of Universal Credit (UC), this agreement is termed the 'claimant commitment'.[4] If an individual fails to meet the terms of the claimant commitment, which involves arduous job search requirements, they will be liable to receive a sanction.[5] This is a pause in the 'standard allowance' of a benefit payment. This financial penalty has triggered debt, rent arrears and foodbank use, and can lead to claimants becoming destitute, homeless and suicidal.[6] In the contemporary system, paid employment is valorised, while the value and legitimacy of other contributions, such as unpaid work in the domestic sphere (which continues to fall predominantly on the shoulders of women), is undermined.[7]

The adjudication of social security law is one of the less well-recognised areas of public law practice, mainly owing to the system's great complexity,[8] encompassing a myriad of benefits with different purposes, different eligibility criteria, and means-tested and contributory provision. Yet, citizens' participation in social security tribunals is one of the central ways in which they interact and feel the reach of UK public law in their everyday lives as they seek a legal remedy.[9] It is also an area of social welfare law where litigation is increasingly making its way to the Supreme Court. There have been a number of high-profile legal challenges regarding those social security

---

4 Welfare Reform Act 2012, c 5 (14).

5 Department for Work and Pensions (2022) 'Guidance: Universal Credit and Your Claimant Commitment'. Available from: https://www.gov.uk/government/publications/universal-credit-and-your-claimant-commitment-quick-guide/universal-credit-and-your-claimant-commitment [Accessed 8 April 2022].

6 Dwyer, P. (2018), 'Punitive and Ineffective: Benefit Sanctions within Social Security', *Journal of Social Security Law*, 25: 142–57; Dwyer, P. (2018) 'Final Findings: Overview, Research Report', Welfare Conditionality, University of York, York. Available from: http://www.welfareconditionality.ac.uk [Accessed 4 June 2021]; Watts, B. and Fitzpatrick, S. (2018) *Welfare Conditionality*, Abingdon: Routledge; Adler, M. (2018) *Cruel, Inhuman or Degrading Treatment? Benefit Sanctions in the UK*, Basingstoke: Palgrave Macmillan.

7 Freedland, M. and King, D. (2003) 'Contractual Governance and Illiberal Contracts: Some Problems of Contractualism as an Instrument of Behaviour Management by Agencies of Government', *Cambridge Journal of Economics*, 27: 465–77, at 466; Dwyer, P. (2016) 'Citizenship, Conduct and Conditionality: Sanction and Support in the 21st Century UK Welfare State', in M. Fenger, J. Hudson and C. Needham (eds), *Social Policy Review 28: Analysis and Debate in Social Policy 2016*, Bristol: Policy Press, 41–62, at 42.

8 Harris, N. (2013) *Law in a Complex State: Complexity and Structure in the Law and Structure of Welfare*, Oxford: Hart Publishing.

9 For example, in the last quarter of 2021, Her Majesty's Courts and Tribunal Service (HMCTS) recorded 25,254 cases of social security and child support receipts (with 19,000 cases disposed of) between October and December 2021. See HMCTS (2022) 'Tribunal Statistics Quarterly: October to December 2021'. Available from: https://www.gov.uk/government/statistics/tribunal-statistics-quarterly-october-to-december-2021 [Accessed 4 April 2022].

measures that have had a retrogressive impact on the rights of women and their dependants – chiefly the 'two-child limit'[10] and the 'benefit cap'.[11] The two-child limit legislates for the limitation of the child element of UC, and Child Tax Credit, to a family's first two children born after 6 April 2017, and the benefit cap limits the household income that can be received from social security benefits. Unfortunately, the litigation has thus far achieved little success.

It is the nexus between gender, the increasingly conditional social security system and social citizenship that will be explored in this chapter. It will begin by considering women's access to the social security system from a historical perspective, focusing on the development of the post-war welfare state and specifically the failure of UC to address the prevalent 'male breadwinner' model. The subsequent section of the chapter will examine the introduction of the 'two-child limit', the 'benefit cap' and the legal challenges that followed. This discussion is intended to deepen the reader's understanding of the executive's use of constitutional power in this sphere of public law to regulate the behaviour of those women viewed as having 'less eligibility' for the self-determination of their rights.

Social citizenship rights, gender and the male breadwinner model

Social citizenship rights 'can be understood as the specific interpretation and concretisation of the more abstract and universalisable human rights'.[12] In the same way as human rights, the triad of civil, political and social citizenship rights as theorised by T.H. Marshall in the early post-war period are indivisible and interdependent.[13] Marshall's conception of citizenship was primarily concerned with the relationship between social class and social integration, and has been criticised for excluding gender. His theory conceives of social citizenship as the opportunity for every individual in society to access a right to 'a modicum of economic welfare and security to enjoy the life of a civilised being according to the standards prevailing'.[14]

---

[10] *R (SC and Others) v Secretary of State for Work and Pensions and Others* [2018] EWHC 864 (Admin); *R (SC and Others) v Secretary of State for Work and Pensions and Others* [2019] EWCA Civ 615; *R (SC and Others) v Secretary of State for Work and Pensions and Others* [2021] UKSC 26.

[11] *R (DA and Others) v Secretary of State for Work and Pensions* [2018] EWCA Civ 504; *R (DA and Others) v Secretary of State for Work and Pensions* [2019] UKSC 21.

[12] Lister, R. (2021) *Poverty* (2nd edn), Cambridge: Polity Press, 185.

[13] Lister, R. (1990) *The Exclusive Society: Citizenship and the Poor*, London: CPAG.

[14] Marshall, T.H. and Bottommore, T. (1992) *Social Class and Citizenship*, London: Pluto, 8.

Interaction with the social security system is an important site of social citizenship for women, but women's engagement with the social security system has always been different from that of men. The development of the welfare state, based primarily on wage replacement benefits, is a gender construct in that it defines who is entitled to social security in gendered ways and consequently reinforces gendered assumptions about work and caring roles.[15] The post-war social security system was based on the stereotypical picture of a male breadwinner and his dependant wife and children. This stance is best illustrated by William Beveridge who said in his groundbreaking report (1942): 'The attitude of the housewife to gainful employment outside the home is not and should not be the same as single women: she has other duties.'[16] While single women could access social citizenship alongside men, most married women paid reduced National Insurance contributions and therefore depended on their husbands to access benefits.[17] In essence, a non-earning wife's access to the social security system was determined by her husband's status – a woman only drew independent benefits for childbirth or in the event of his absence or death. The legal construction of a social security system assuming the male maintenance of women and children has so far stymied women's achievement of full social citizenship.

The post-war model of social security has been changed beyond recognition, yet the contemporary system still fails to reflect the multifaceted and often complex and diverse lives of women.[18] The crystallisation of the unfair treatment of women in the law creates a legal bind for those seeking to assert their rights and perpetuates greater reliance on legal enforcement routes to secure equality and public law redress.

Women and benefit administration

Generally, women receive a higher proportion of their income from social security benefits, partly because of their lower incomes and more frequent breaks in employment related to caring responsibilities in the private sphere.

[15] Gulland, J. (2019) *Gender, Work and Social Control: A Century of Disability Benefits*, Basingstoke: Palgrave Macmillan, 9; Lister, R. (2003) *Citizenship: Feminist Perspectives* (2nd edn), Basingstoke: Palgrave Macmillan.

[16] Beveridge, W. (1942) 'Social Insurance and Allied Services', Cmd 6404, London: HMSO.

[17] Bennett, F. (2018) 'Gender and Social Security', in J. Millar and R. Sainsbury (eds) *Understanding Social Security* (3rd edn), Bristol: Policy Press, 100.

[18] See, for example, Lister, R. (1994) '"She Has Other Duties": Women, Citizenship and Social Security', in S. Baldwin and J. Falkingham (eds) *Social Security and Social Change: New Challenges to the Beveridge Model*, Hemel Hempstead: Harvester Wheatsheaf, 31–44; Orloff, A.S. (2010) 'Gender', in F.G. Castles, S. Leibfried, J. Lewis and C. Pierson (eds) *The Oxford Handbook of the Welfare State*, Oxford: Oxford University Press, 252–64.

Contributory benefits (social security benefits provided on the basis of a sufficient National Insurance record), as exemplified by the post-war system, ingrain the traditional view of a working man who is in long-term, full-time and uninterrupted employment. They do not adequately reflect work patterns that are more typical of women's lives (and increasingly often men's lives), which is more often part-time, low-paid and interrupted by childbirth and caring responsibilities.[19] Therefore, the design reflects labour market inequalities. Men are eligible to receive higher absolute amounts and higher status contributions than women in the UK.[20] This has a knock-on effect on women's pension levels. Contributory benefits as social insurance against risk were viewed as the cornerstone of the Beveridge scheme. This has been greatly eroded over the last 75 years, to the point of non-existence in the contemporary social security system – with contributory unemployment and sickness benefit limited to six months of entitlement. Rather, the main form of social security provision is now means-tested benefits with the objective of providing 'basic sufficiency', whereby the state intervenes as a matter of last resort.[21]

Means-tested support in couple households cements women's financial dependency on their partner as entitlement is based on their partner's resources and presence – and increasingly on behaviour.[22] Means-tested benefits are paid as an income replacement, as top-ups to those on low incomes, or to help meet additional costs (for example, due to disability). Many women, and some men, are often ineligible to claim benefits, as their partner's earnings and resources take them beyond the threshold for entitlement. Furthermore, the means-testing system does not consider the division of resources within the household. The benefits/tax credits system has been criticised for creating a 'couple penalty' that discourages cohabitation and marriage, as they receive less living together than they do separately.[23] More recent research has also found that means testing itself, the

---

[19] Bennett, F. and Daly, M. (2014) *Poverty through a Gender Lens: Evidence and Policy Review on Gender and Poverty*, Oxford: Joseph Rowntree Foundation. Available from: www.spi.ox.ac.uk/sites/default/files/Gender_and_poverty_Bennett_and_Daly_final_12_5_14_28_5_14.pdf [Accessed 8 February 2023], 48.

[20] Bennett, F. and Sutherland, H. (2011) 'The Importance of Independent Income: Understanding the Role of Non-means-Tested Earnings Replacement Benefits', *Barnett Papers in Social Research 2011, No 1*, Oxford: Department of Social Policy and Intervention, University of Oxford.

[21] Esping-Andersen, G. (1990) *The Three Worlds of Welfare Capitalism*, Cambridge: Polity, 27–8.

[22] Bennett and Daly (n 19) 48.

[23] Adam, S. and Brewer, M. (2010) 'Couple Penalties and Premiums in the UK Tax and Benefit System', IFS Briefing Note (BN2012) Institute for Fiscal Studies. Available from: www.ifs.org.uk/bns/bn102.pdf [Accessed 17 June 2021]; Hirsch, D. (2012) 'Does the Tax and Benefit System Cause a "Couple Penalty?", *Joseph Rowntree Foundation*

removal of access to an individual income, has influenced decisions around cohabiting and more generally partnering decisions.[24] This draws out the issue of 'hidden poverty' in households, which recognises that there can be an unequal distribution of income within the household, and women will experience poverty when their husband does not, or women will suffer the impact of poverty more intensely.[25] A number of qualitative[26] and quantitative[27] studies show that income is not always shared fairly within the family and that women have less access to personal income. The development of UC provided an opportunity to address these legacy issues. However, the legislation enshrining the policy maintained much of the status quo, and indeed created further distinct barriers for women in accessing social citizenship rights, as will be explored in the next section.

The administration of Universal Credit, gender and social citizenship

From a public law perspective, there are two standout features of the Welfare Reform Act 2012 (which provides for the administration of UC) that are worth noting. First is the skeleton nature of the legislation, whereby most of the detail on how UC is to be administered is contained in secondary legislation, in this case the Universal Credit Regulations 2013. This effectively provided scope for the Secretary of State for Work and Pensions to dictate the legal parameters of the new system, as secondary legislation is not subject to the same level of parliamentary scrutiny as primary legislation.[28]

Closely linked to this is the second feature, which is the significant increase in the scope for discretionary decision making by 'street-level bureaucrats'[29] – those 'work coaches' who will be assigned UC claimants to manage. The

[online], 18 June. Available from: www.jrf.org.uk/report/does-tax-and-benefit-system-create-couple-penalty [Accessed 17 June 2021].

24 Griffiths, R. (2017) 'No Love on the Dole: The Influence of the UK Means-Tested Welfare System on Partnering and Family Structure', *Journal of Social Policy*, 46(3): 543–61.

25 Lister (n 12) 66.

26 Pahl, J. (1989) *Money and Marriage*, Basingstoke: Macmillan; Goode, J., Callendar, C. and Lister, R. (1998) 'Purse of Wallet? Gender Inequalities within families with Benefits', London: Policy Studies Institute; Bennett, F. (2013) 'Researching Within-Household Distribution', *Journal of Marriage and Family*, 75(3): 582–97.

27 Vogler, C. (1994) 'Money in the Household', in M. Anderson, F. Bechhofer and J. Gershuny (eds) *The Social and Political Economy of the Household*, Oxford: Oxford University Press, 225–66.

28 McKeever, G. (2016) 'Legislative Scrutiny, Co-ordination and the Social Security Advisory Committee: from System Coherence to Scottish Devolution', *Journal of Social Security Law*, 23(3):126–49.

29 Lipsky, M. (2010) *Street-Level Bureaucracy: Dilemmas of the Individual in Public Services*, New York: Russell Sage Foundation.

Coalition government at that time sought to introduce 'greater flexibilities into Jobcentre Plus, so that advisers have more discretion about the nature of the support, guidance and advice that they provide for individuals'.[30] However, it impinges upon the exercise of ensuring claimants' legal rights are put on a statutory footing. This discretionary approach to the provision of social rights represents a much compromised approach to T.H. Marshall's emphasis on the value of social integration provided by a defined legal right to entitlement.[31] Indeed, Boyle et al note that the increase in discretionary services and decision making in the social welfare arena indicates broader concerns over social rights that, due to their perceived lack of justiciability, are not promoted as rights, but rather as commodities.[32]

Both of these features have distinct consequences for women's access to social citizenship rights. The lack of detail in primary legislation was a missed opportunity to ensure that women's role in the private sphere is acknowledged as making an important contribution to the functioning of society. In addition, the prioritisation of a discretionary approach has compounded the erosion of ensuring greater equality through the provision of statutory rights in secondary legislation. Early evidence shows that work coaches are focused on the government's activation agenda and are showing little flexibility in the claimant commitment to account for caring responsibilities, and there is little that claimants can do to dispute the terms of the contract, particularly as receipt of payment depends on acceptance of the commitments.[33] This section of the chapter will examine design features of UC which pose particular barriers to women's individual social citizenship rights, including the administration of a single payment and the effect of welfare conditionality.

---

30 Minister of State for Work and Pensions, Chris Grayling, 29 March 2011, Public Bills Committee (Bill 154), col 196.

31 Fitzpatrick, C., McKeever, G. and Simpson, S. (2019) 'Conditionality, Discretion and TH Marshall's "Right to Welfare"', *Journal of Social Welfare and Family Law*, 41(4): 445–62.

32 Boyle, K., Camps, D., English, K. and Ferrie, J. (2022) 'The Practitioner Perspective on Access to Justice for Social Rights: Addressing the Accountability Gap', Research Report, May, University of Stirling and the Nuffield Foundation. Available from: https://www.nuffieldfoundation.org/wp-content/uploads/2019/11/Final-report-The-practitioner-perspective-on-access-to-justice-for-social-rights-1.pdf [Accessed 6 February 2023], 94.

33 Dwyer, P. (2018), 'Final Findings: Overview, Research Report', Available from: http://www.welfareconditionality.ac.uk [Accessed 4 June 2021]; Department for Work and Pensions (2018) 'Universal Credit: In Work Progression Randomised Control Trial', September, Research Report 966, London: Department for Work and Pensions; Andersen, K. (2020) 'Universal Credit, Gender and Unpaid Childcare: Mothers' Accounts of the New Welfare Conditionality Regime', *Critical Social Policy*, 40(3): 430–49; Wright, S. and Dwyer, P. (2022) 'In-Work Universal Credit: Claimant Experiences of Conditionality Mismatches and Counterproductive Benefit Sanctions', *Journal of Social Policy*, 51(1): 1–19.

A single payment

Section 2 of the Welfare Reform Act 2012 requires couples to make a single application for UC. A couple must nominate a single or joint bank account in which the payment is to be deposited. Supplementary legislation, in the form of the Universal Credit Regulations, allows for this default position to be circumvented in prescribed circumstances.[34] During the passage of the Welfare Reform Act 2012 and as UC continues to be 'rolled out', civil society organisations in the women's sector, feminists and politicians have consistently communicated their concern that a single payment threatens women's financial autonomy. The Equality and Human Rights Commission noted that the administration of a single payment could represent a drastic shift in household income from women to men, which would have serious implications for gender equality.[35] Research with couples on UC published in 2020 found that opinions on the administration of a single payment were 'split', with a 'small minority' expressing that the single, integrated payment made no difference, as they already pooled their income in a joint bank account. However, many preferred 'multiple payments paid at intervals through the month, and different sources and amounts going to each partner meant women having a personal income'.[36] Interestingly, Lister pointed to the fact that the single payment decision was made by ministers; rather than being positioned as an operational or a technical issue, it was framed as a 'political' decision.[37] This is critical, as it reveals the extent of power provided to the executive in determining the terms and conditions of the new social contract under UC.

The efforts of the devolved governments in Northern Ireland and Scotland to deviate from the default position of making a single payment provide evidence of its political connotations. As part of a package of measures to mitigate the worst impact of welfare reform in Northern Ireland (NI), the

[34] Universal Credit Regulations 2013, reg 3.

[35] Equality and Human Rights Commission (2018) 'The Impact of Economic Reform Policies on Women's Human Rights: To Inform the Next Thematic Report of the Independent Expert on Foreign Debt and Human Rights'. Available from: https://www.equalityhumanrights.com/sites/default/files/consultation-response-ohchr-impact-of-austerity-on-women-30-march-2018.pdf [Accessed 29 June 2021].

[36] Griffiths, G., Wood, M., Bennett F. and Millar, J. (2020) 'Uncharted Territory: Universal Credit, Couples and Money'. Available from: https://www.bath.ac.uk/publications/uncharted-territory-universal-credit-couples-and-money/attachments/Uncharted-Territory-Universal-Credit.pdf [Accessed 15 June 2021], 11.

[37] Lister, R. (2011) Written Evidence Submitted to the Work and Pensions Committee on the White Paper for Universal Credit, 7 March. Available from: https://publications.parliament.uk/pa/cm201011/cmselect/cmworpen/743/743we13.htm [Accessed 29 June 2021].

NI Executive put in place flexible arrangements whereby a UC claimant could request to have the payment 'split'. The take-up of UC split payments in NI is extremely low. The NI Affairs Select Committee concluded 'that offering split payments on request is not enough to encourage and enable uptake by those who most need it'.[38] Moreover, devolved administrations face operational barriers to implementing a distinct payment system due to both utilising the Department for Work and Pension's IT systems, and the huge cost attached to divergence from it.

Welfare conditionality

The government's political decision to treat couples who apply for UC as interdependent extends to conditionality requirements. Both members of a couple must sign a personalised claimant commitment in order to satisfy the eligibility conditions for UC. If one member of a couple refuses to sign the claimant commitment, neither partner will be entitled, which is an indicator of the government's reinforcement of interdependency and presents a barrier to an individual's realisation of social rights.

When UC is completely rolled out, about half of those households claiming will be in work; with one million likely to be subject to 'in-work conditionality' requirements, which means people in part-time, low-paid work will be bound to 'earn more and progress in work'.[39] Prior to UC, conditionality requirements ended when an individual worked 16 hours under the Working Tax Credit (WTC) regime which was introduced by the Labour government in 2003. This policy was beneficial to lone parents and to mothers, as it helped to increase women's participation in the labour market, while facilitating flexibility for women with caring responsibilities.[40] Under UC this threshold is abolished and claimants can claim support for any number of hours (based on household income thresholds). In order to counteract the possibility that in-work claimants will maintain part-time, low-income work supplemented by UC, the government will extend the reach of sanctions to all those in low-paid work, including (for the first time) both members of a couple. Fitzpatrick and Chapman found that

[38] Work and Pensions and Northern Ireland Affairs Committees (2019) 'Welfare policy in Northern Ireland': First Joint Report of the Work and Pensions and the Northern Ireland Affairs Committees, HC2100, 2019. Available from: https://publications.parliament.uk/pa/cm201719/cmselect/cmniaf/2100/2100.pdf (Accessed 4 May 2023].

[39] Department for Work and Pensions (2018), 'Universal Credit Programme Full Business Case Summary', June, London: Department for Work and Pensions.

[40] Haux, T. (2012) 'Activating Lone Parents: An Evidence-Based Policy Appraisal of Welfare-to-Work Reform in Britain', *Social Policy and Society*, 11(1): 1–14; Hick, R. and Lanau, A. (2019) 'Tax Credits and In-Work Poverty in the UK: An Analysis of Income Packages and Anti-Poverty Performance', *Social Policy and Society*, 18(2): 219–36.

the outworking of the policy will be more acute for women, due to the inequitable division of labour in the private sphere and the corresponding necessity for flexible working patterns to be accommodated.[41]

Work conditionality is extended to both partners in couples with dependant children (based on the age of the youngest child), which replicates established work requirements for lone parents. The couple is required to nominate a 'lead carer' and conditionality requirements are adjusted accordingly.[42] In research published by Griffith et al in 2020, 27 out of 30 couples with children who were interviewed nominated the woman as the 'lead carer', based primarily on the fact that she was at home more, although some worked part-time. Some couples opposed this 'enforced designation of differing roles' because they perceived it as reinforcing the male breadwinner model.[43] They were cynical of the resulting imbalance in work conditionality, with no recognition of the other parent's role in child-rearing or the realities of modern, more equal families. As asserted by Andersen, where previously women were excluded from social citizenship or were forced to derive such rights through their husband, now their access to social citizenship is predicated on 'entering the paid labour market on the same terms as men'.[44] This model of citizenship is situated as gender-neutral, yet it exemplifies a 'male standard masquerading as universalism'.[45]

UC intensifies conditionality and sanctions for lone parents. It lowers the age of the youngest child (from five to three) at which lone parents are required to actively seek and secure paid employment. Furthermore, the previous lone parent flexibilities have been downgraded to guidance and their application is at the discretion of the work coach.[46] Although the government has stated that work coaches will consider an individual's circumstances and adapt work requirements accordingly, Andersen's study and others found that caring responsibilities were not taken into account and seen as a personal barrier to employment.[47] Furthermore, the government's system of support for formal childcare has not proved effective at mitigating the tension between work-related requirements and unpaid labour,[48] with case law highlighting that it is inaccessible, impractical and even 'irrational'.[49]

[41] Fitzpatrick, C. and Chapman, A. (2021) 'From Working-Tax Credit to Universal Credit: Is the Older Workforce Ready? Perspectives from Employees and Employers in Northern Ireland', *Journal of Poverty and Social Justice*, 29(3): 297–315.

[42] Griffiths et al (n 36) 9.

[43] Ibid.

[44] Andersen (n 33) 443.

[45] Lister (n 15) 197.

[46] Cain, R. (2016) 'Responsibilising Recovery: Lone and Low-Paid Parents, Universal Credit and the Gendered Contradictions of UK Welfare Reform', *British Politics*, 11(4): 488–507.

[47] Andersen (n 33) 440; Department for Work and Pensions (n 33) 78.

[48] Griffiths et al (n 36) 16.

[49] *R (Salvato) v Secretary of State for Work and Pensions* [2021] EWHC 102 (Admin) [178]. In the 2023 Spring Statement, the Chancellor announced that the payment of the child

This further emphasises that while it is claimed that legislation for responsible carers is gender neutral, the outcome of the policy will be gendered due to the context in which it is enacted – one that overlooks women's primary responsibility for childcare and, for lone parents, the additional need to ensure that the most basic material needs of their children are met.[50] This has been frustrated further by the benefit cap and the two-child limit, which go beyond attempting to force women into the labour market through the use of conditional contractualism and sanctions by constructing a narrative of 'welfare decadence' where women and families were portrayed as being rewarded for having more children than they can 'afford'.[51] This narrative and the subsequent case law will be explored next.

The benefit cap

The benefit cap, introduced via the Welfare Reform Act 2012, places a limit on household income that can be received through the social security system (excluding disability benefits) in line with 'estimated average earnings'.[52] The amount was subsequently set in regulations at £18,000 for a single claimant (without dependant children) and £26,000 for all other claimants.[53] This has since been reduced to £13,400 and £20,000 per year respectively.[54] Those who earn £617 per month or more (after National Insurance contributions) are exempt from the policy.

During the debate on the Welfare Reform Act 2012, the then Secretary of State for Work and Pensions, Iain Duncan Smith, told Parliament that:

> The [benefit cap] principle is that people who are unemployed and on benefits should not be receiving more than average earnings. It is a matter of fairness, so that those who are working hard and paying their taxes do not feel that someone else will benefit more by not playing a full part in society.[55]

care element of UC would be paid upfront, rather in arrears, which was the basis of the *Salvato* case. Available from: https://assets.publishing.service.gov.uk/government/uploads/system/uploads/attachment_data/file/1144441/Web_accessible_Budget_2023.pdf [Accessed 20 April 2023].

50 Cain (n 46); Andersen (n 33).

51 O'Brien, C. (2018) '"Done Because We Are Too Menny": The Two-Child Rule Promotes Poverty, Invokes a Narrative of Welfare Decadence and Abandons Children's Rights', *International Journal of Children's Rights*, 26(4): 700–39.

52 Welfare Reform Act 2012, s 96(6).

53 Benefit Cap (Housing Benefit) Regulations 2012, SI 2012/2994.

54 Welfare and Work Act (Commencement No 3) Regulations 2016, SI 2016/910) and the Benefit Cap (Housing Benefit and Universal Credit) (Amendment) Regulations 2016, SI 2016/909.

55 HC Deb 9 March 2011, vol 524, col 922.

This reasoning was central during the passing of the legislation and was consistently used to ward off challenges from the opposition – such as the fact that some of those 'hard-pressed taxpayers' from working households may also be receiving benefits and would be impacted by the cap, and that larger families would be disproportionately affected and as such the cap should exclude child benefit. The government claimed that keeping the rule 'simple' and broadly applicable was preferable, particularly in pursuit of behaviour change, which would seek to push more people into the formal labour market.[56] This is despite the fact that it was estimated by the Department for Work and Pensions that 61 per cent of those impacted by the reduction would be lone parents.[57] Yet, the gendered impact of the policy has been minimised in public discourse and also by the courts due to the 'neutral' status of social security law and the pre-eminence of the government's economic objectives, despite the clear and disproportionate impact on women and their children.

The benefit cap provides no rights of appeal and so the only mechanism of legal challenge is via judicial review. Two unsuccessful judicial reviews progressed to the UK Supreme Court (UKSC): the *SG* case in 2015,[58] which challenged the original premise of the policy; and the *DA* case in 2019,[59] which challenged the reduction of the benefit cap amount. In *SG*, two lone parents, both victims of domestic violence and subject to the benefit cap, argued that the measure was indirectly discriminatory against women on the basis that they maintained overwhelming responsibility for the care of children. The claim was made under the Human Rights Act 1998. The mothers argued that the benefit cap interfered with their peaceful enjoyment of their possessions under Article 1 of Protocol 1 (A1P1) to the European Convention on Human Rights (ECHR) in a discriminatory manner contrary to Article 14 ECHR. The UKSC sought to determine whether there had been indirect discrimination in the application of the cap, which the ECHR determines as a 'difference in treatment [that] may take the form of disproportionately prejudicial effects of a general policy or measure, though couched in neutral terms'.[60] Campbell asserts that in theory, the Court's evaluation should have been 'highly contextual' and considered a wide range of prejudicial

56 HC Deb 17 May 2011, vol 528, cols 54, 952 and 975.

57 Department for Work and Pensions, 'Equality Analysis for the Benefit Cap (Housing Benefit and Universal Credit) (Amendment) Regulations 2016 (2016)'. Available from: www.legislation.gov.uk/uksi/2016/909/pdfs/uksiod_20160909_en.pdf [Accessed 24 December 2022].

58 *SG and Others v Secretary of State for Work and Pensions* [2015] UKSC 16.

59 *DA* (n 11).

60 *DH v Czech Republic* (2008) 47 EHHR 3 [184] (ECtHR).

impacts.[61] Yet, the disproportionate impact of the cap was subject to a single train of analysis based on its economic effect, which fundamentally limited the scope of scrutiny applied to the government's justification for the policy.[62] Lady Hale outlined that the 'effect of the cap is stark as it breaks the link between benefit and need',[63] and Lord Reed in the leading judgment explicitly recognised that the cap will disproportionately burden lone parents and 'the great majority of lone parents are women'.[64] However, a majority of the UKSC concluded that such treatment was justified based on the government's prerogative to determine economic policy, with Lord Reed explaining: 'It is not the function of the courts to determine how much public expenditure should be devoted to welfare benefits'.[65] In short, the Court failed to understand how in this case, the neutrality of the law and the continued reliance on women's capacity to maintain the burden of care, coupled with structural socioeconomic barriers such as insufficient childcare, exacerbate women's economic disadvantage. A failure to recognise the wider sociolegal context is interpreted by Campbell as a missed opportunity to reveal discriminatory impacts which go beyond poverty.[66]

In the 2019 *DA* case, the appellants (lone mothers and their children) argued unsuccessfully that the cap and the attached welfare conditionality indirectly discriminated against them contrary to A1P1, Article 8 and Article 14 ECHR, together with Article 3 of the United Nations Convention on the Rights of the Child (UNCRC). The judges accepted that the regime 'will strike at family life' and thus the claim fell within the ambit of Article 8.[67] The law failed to recognise that the main responsibility for childcare fell upon lone parents, which was indirectly discriminatory in relation to the enjoyment of private life under Article 14. Again, the UKSC acknowledged that the vast majority (92 per cent) of lone parents were women and furthermore that 65 per cent of individuals affected by the cap are women. However, the court simultaneously failed to undertake a gendered analysis of the impact of conditionality – some of which is outlined earlier – preferring to look at it through the same lens adopted in the *SG* case, that is, in purely economic/material terms. It was acknowledged that removing social security provision to address need set at below subsistence level would push people below the poverty line; however, there was no recognition that lone mothers are impacted to a greater extent due to caring responsibilities. Rather, the majority applied the concept of

[61] Campbell, M. (2021) 'The Austerity of Lone Motherhood: Discrimination Law and Benefit Reform', *Oxford Journal of Legal Studies*, 41(4): 1–30, at 8.

[62] Ibid.

[63] *SG and Others* (n 58) para 180.

[64] Ibid, para 61.

[65] Ibid, para 72.

[66] Campbell (n 61) 9.

[67] *DA and Others* (n 11) para 37.

formal equality to the economic inequality imposed by work conditions.[68] Lord Kerr's dissenting judgment (supported by Lady Hale) stood out in this case, as it explicitly recognised the failure of the government to address the criticisms levelled at the policy, particularly those which impinged upon the best interests of the child: 'There is simply no warrant for the claim that refusal to extend exemption from the cap to the DA and DS cohorts (lone mothers) will improve the fairness of the social security system or increase public confidence in its fairness. That sweeping statement partakes of a declamation for which no tangible evidence is proffered.'[69] Lord Kerr is here reminding us that the Supreme Court's constitutional role in scrutinising legislation includes consideration of the impact of the benefit cap, over and above the government's justification for it (particularly where the basis is lacking in evidence).[70] Yet Kerr's dissent represented a minority voice in the UKSC chamber, and the judgment in the two-child limit case in 2021 discussed in the next section further demonstrates the panel's complete deferral to the power of Parliament to justifiably undermine women's socioeconomic and equality rights by dismantling the concept of providing a social minimum on the basis of affordability of social security benefits.

The two-child limit

The two-child limit is a policy that is similar in form to the benefit cap, in that it seeks to moralise the receipt of benefits by dictating that low-income families require additional measures to control their reproductive behaviour – both the two-child limit and the benefit cap can impact a family at the same time. The legislation, introduced by the Welfare Reform and Work Act 2016, limits benefits to those on a low income (those unemployed and in low-paid work) and in receipt of UC or Child Tax Credit (which will eventually be phased out) to the first two children born on or after 6 April 2017.[71] There are a number of administrative exemptions to the policy, one of the most controversial being for children born as a result of 'non-consensual intercourse' – more commonly known as the 'rape clause', which requires the victim to provide evidence to support such an exception.

The act of having too many children is perceived by some policy makers as encumbering labour market attachment. Gulland points to a social

[68] Campbell (n 61) 9.

[69] *DA and Others* (n 11) para 189.

[70] McKeever. G. (2021) 'Scrutinising Social Security Law and Protecting Social Rights: Lord Kerr and the Benefit Cap', in *The Judicial Mind: A Festschrift for Lord Kerr of Tonaghmore*, Oxford: Hart Publishing, 119–38, 128.

[71] Child Tax Credit (Amendment) Regulations 2017; Social Security (Restrictions on Amounts for Children and Qualifying Young Persons) Amendment Regulations 2017.

history of the means-tested benefit system's incorporation of 'moralising assumptions of deservingness'.[72] The legacy of previous rules around 'sexual misconduct' remains strong and has created a tendency to stigmatise low-income claimants as being more likely to shirk their responsibility to work by having too many children. Thus, sanctions are required to punish misconduct and deter welfare dependency. McKeever argues that it is a further manifestation of the notion of ensuring 'fairness to taxpayers' in that it overlooks the importance of objective need enshrined in the concept of social citizenship, in favour of prioritising 'society's tolerance to support particular circumstances' which are viewed as socially responsible.[73] The British Association of Pregnancy Advice (BPAS) published research which showed that 57 per cent of women who were aware of, or likely to be affected by, the two-child limit took the reduction in support into consideration when opting for an abortion. Women who participated in the study communicated 'significant regret because they felt unable to continue what was a wanted pregnancy due to the policy'.[74] Further research has shown that in a similar way to the benefit cap, the two-child limit is not achieving its policy aims; rather, it is responsible for driving up child poverty.[75]

Two lone mothers (SC and CB) unsuccessfully challenged the two-child limit in the UKSC,[76] following an unsuccessful challenge in the Court of Appeal (CA).[77] The mothers' claim was on the basis that the two-child limit breaches Article 14 ECHR rights read in conjunction with A1P1 and Article 8 (the right to private and family life) and Article 12 (the right to found a family), as the policy directly interferes with choices about sexual relationships, family planning, contraception use and abortion. The appeal was unanimously dismissed in the UKSC, with Lord Reed giving the sole judgment. Gearty argues that Reed used the opportunity to provide a clear indication that the UKSC would not engage in debate on issues of social

72 Gulland, J. (2020) *Gender, Work and Social Control: A Century of Disability Benefit*, Basingstoke: Palgrave Macmillan, 156.

73 McKeever (n 70) 122.

74 British Pregnancy Advisory Service (2020) 'Forced into a Corner: The Two-Child Limit and Pregnancy Decision Making during a Pandemic'. Available from: https://www.bpas.org/media/3409/forced-into-a-corner-the-two-child-limit-and-pregnancy-decision-making-during-the-pandemic.pdf [Accessed 15 July 2021].

75 Reader, M., Portes, J. and Patrick, R. (2022) 'Does Cutting Child Benefit Reduce Fertility in Larger Families? Evidence from the UK's Two-Child Limit'. Available from: https://largerfamilies.study/publications/does-cutting-child-benefits-reduce-fertility-in-larger-families-evidence-from-the-uk-s-two-child/ [Accessed 8 April 2022].

76 *SC and Others* [2021] (n 10).

77 *SC and Others* [2019] (n 10).

and economic policy, a step change from his predecessor Lady Hale.[78] Reflecting on the approach by the CA, Campbell asserts that the judicial outlook was similar to *SG*, as the CA based its analysis purely on economic inequality, failing to consider the impact of the reform on the lives of lone mothers.[79] Justice Leggatt accepted that there was indirect discrimination against women, as women were more likely to be lone parents and the limit on benefits had a greater impact on women's finances.[80] However, there was no engagement with the prejudicial intentions of the policy that has been used to impose social control on the reproductive autonomy of women and more specifically on lone mothers who are increasingly unable to meet the basic needs of their children.[81] Lord Reed steadfastly maintained this narrow approach in his UKSC judgment. He stated pointedly that 'more women than men are affected because more women than men are bringing up children. That is an objective fact. There is no suggestion that that is itself the result of discrimination on the grounds of sex'.[82] This leads Reed to conclude that 'the differential impact on women is not, therefore, a special feature of this measure'[83] because, in short, any measure which seeks to limit social security expenditure on child-related benefits will have the same effect.[84]

In accepting 'as an objective fact' that hardship is inevitable for lone mothers who are affected by the two-child limit, the Supreme Court is prioritising the government's economic prerogative to ensure 'fairness to the taxpayer' over the need to protect women's access to a 'modicum of economic welfare', which is essential in accessing social citizenship rights.[85] In this case, Lord Reed firmly situates the Supreme Court as unwilling to override indirect gender discrimination in favour of a steadfast commitment to the doctrine of parliamentary sovereignty, based on the economic 'importance of the objectives pursued'.[86] As emphasised by Gearty and other public law commentators, the UKSC has taken a sharp turn towards

78 Gearty, C. (2022) 'In the Shallow End', *London Review of Books* [online], 27 January. Available from: https://www.lrb.co.uk/the-paper/v44/n02/conor-gearty/in-the-shallow-end [Accessed 4 April 2022].

79 Campbell (n 61) 8.

80 *SC and Others* [2019] (n 10) para 126–7.

81 Bloom, D. (2021) 'DWP Two-Child Benefit Cap Hits 1.1 Million Children as Universal Credit Cut Bites', *Daily Mirror* [online], 15 July. Available from: https://www.mirror.co.uk/news/politics/breaking-dwp-two-child-benefit-24539873 [Accessed 15 July 2021].

82 *SC and Others* [2021] (n 10) para 197.

83 Ibid, para 198.

84 Ibid.

85 Marshall T.H. and Bottommore, T (1992) *Citizenship and Social Class*, London: Pluto, 8.

86 *SC and Others* [2021] (n 10) paras 199, 204.

exercising a restrained approach to reviewing government policy.[87] This is particularly concerning for women. This chapter's analysis of the benefit cap and two-child limit cases reveals a worrying trend in public law: towards the complete dismissal of structural inequality on the basis of gender, whereby the realisation of women's social rights, and indeed their equality, is completely dependent on the economic objectives of Parliament.

Conclusion

This chapter has considered the administration of the UK's social security system from a gendered perspective. From the formation of the post-war social security system, women's labour in the private sphere, including their disproportionate role in childcare, has excluded them from claiming full access to social citizenship rights. Since then, the system has gone through multiple 'welfare reform' processes and despite the changing role of women in society, many remnants of the male breadwinner model introduced by the post-war social security system remain – for example, the single household payment, which subordinates women's financial independence.[88] Simultaneously, there has been a neutralisation of the law, whereby men and women are construed as equal participants in both the domestic sphere and in the labour market. This is despite evidence which shows that women persistently maintain equilibrium in the home. Moreover, it remains the case that a majority of lone parents are women.[89] However, women, particularly lone parents, are increasingly coerced into the formal labour market under threat of sanctions. Their caring role is devalued by the government, which asserts that their only route to claiming social citizenship rights is by engagement in full-time employment.

Those on a low income have been further stigmatised by the introduction of legislation which seeks to control the labour market behaviour and reproductive autonomy of women. The UKSC has unequivocally failed to recognise the disproportionate impact of caring responsibilities on women and instead has accepted their greater role in the private sphere as an inherent

[87] Gearty (n 78). See also Graham, L. (2022) 'The Reed Court by Numbers: How Shallow is the "Shallow End"?', *UK Constitutional Law Blog* [online], 4 April. Available from: https://ukconstitutionallaw.org/2022/04/04/lewis-graham-the-reed-court-by-numbers-how-shallow-is-the-shallow-end%EF%BF%BC%EF%BF%BC [Accessed 4 April 2022].

[88] Women's Budget Group (2022) 'Spring Budget 2022: Social Security and Gender'. Available from: https://wbg.org.uk/analysis/spring-budget-2022-social-security-and-gender [Accessed 4 April 2022].

[89] Gingerbread estimates that 90 per cent of lone parents are women. See Gingerbread (2019) 'Single Parents Today'. Available from: https://www.gingerbread.org.uk/what-we-do/media-centre/single-parents-facts-figures [Accessed 4 April 2022].

feature of society rather than fully interrogating the gendered consequences of the government's officious pursuit of austerity measures. Instead, the judiciary have unanimously accepted this serious erosion of social rights as a matter of parliamentary prerogative, despite increasing poverty, which is disproportionately affecting women and children.

Further reading

Andersen, K. (2020) 'Universal Credit, Gender and Unpaid Childcare: Mothers' Accounts of the New Welfare Conditionality Regime', *Critical Social Policy*, 40(3): 430–49.

Bennett, F. (2018) 'Gender and Social Security', in J. Millar and R. Sainsbury (eds), *Understanding Social Security* (3rd edn), Bristol: Policy Press, 99–117.

Campbell, M. (2021) 'The Austerity of Lone Motherhood: Discrimination Law and Benefit Reform', *Oxford Journal of Legal Studies*, 41(4): 1–30.

Lister, R. (2003) *Citizenship: Feminist Perspectives* (2nd edn), Basingstoke: Palgrave Macmillan.

O'Brien, C. (2018) '"Done Because We Are Too Menny": The Two-Child Limit Promotes Poverty, Invokes a Narrative of Welfare Decadence and Abandons Children's Rights', *International Journal of Children's Rights*, 26(4): 700–39.

11

Administrative Violence: First-Instance Decision Making in Sexual Diversity Asylum Claims

Alex Powell

Introduction

Public law scholarship has a tendency to focus on the high-profile and the precedential. We have embedded this into our legal education systems, encouraging students to analyse appellate cases and focus on moments that make law. As a result, the experiences of people coming face to face with the administrative state – and the ways in which these experiences impact their lives, rights and realities – are given limited consideration in academic and student-facing literature. A snapshot of the life-changing consequences these interactions can have was brought to light in some of the harrowing tales that emerged from the Windrush scandal, where ill-conceived administrative policy decisions resulted in people, who were lawfully resident in the UK, being denied fundamental rights such as access to healthcare.[1] To remedy some of the omissions of previous scholarship, this chapter focuses on first-instance decisions – that is, decisions which initially decide whether or not a claimant is able to rely on a given legal entitlement – with a view to shedding light on how administrative decision-making systems promote or deny access to legal rights.

This chapter argues that, in a context where the realisation of rights is dependent on recognition by administrative institutions, greater analysis

[1] See generally Gentleman, A. (2019) *The Windrush Betrayal: Exposing the Windrush*, London: Guardian Faber.

of how people experience first-instance decision making is required.[2] In order to highlight the significance of first-instance decision making for the operation of public law, I draw on a case study of asylum claims by sexually diverse people.[3] This case study is informed by eight semi-structured interviews with sexually diverse people who secured refugee status in the UK based on their sexual diversity. Interviews explored how participants understood their own sexual diversities, as well as how they had experienced the UK asylum process. These self-understandings were then compared and contrasted with the 2016 'Asylum Policy Instruction: Sexual Orientation in Asylum Claims'[4] in order to understand the extent to which UK asylum policy and practice corresponds to the heterogeneous lived realities of sexually diverse asylum seekers.[5] Narratives also reflected on the forms of violence the UK asylum process itself produces. These examples of violence form the subject matter of this chapter. The chapter is divided into three sections. The first section sets out a working definition of administrative violence by building on the work of Arendt.[6] The second section sets out the law and policy framework of asylum in the UK. Finally, the third section explores examples of first-instance decision making through the framework outlined in the first section.

Administrative violence

Administrative justice literature has thought through both the nature and quality of decision making regarding state entitlements.[7] As Halliday argues, research of this nature focuses on the challenges and issues that lead to poor

2 Wade and Forsyth effectively chronicle the huge expansion of the administrative state over the past two centuries. See Wade, W. and Forsyth, C. (2014) *Administrative Law* (11th edn), Oxford: Oxford University Press, 4–13.

3 For discussion of the term 'sexually diverse', see Powell, A. (2021) 'Sexuality through the Kaleidoscope: Sexual Orientation, Identity and Behaviour in Asylum Claims in the United Kingdom', *Laws*, 10(4) 90: 1–20.

4 Home Office (2016) 'Asylum Policy Instruction: Sexual Orientation in Asylum Claims', 3 August, London: Home Office. Available from: https://assets.publishing.service.gov.uk/government/uploads/system/uploads/attachment_data/file/543882/Sexual-orientation-in-asylum-claims-v6.pdf [Accessed 31 August 2021].

5 See generally Powell, A. (2021) 'Queering Refugee Law: A Study of Sexual Diversity in Asylum Policy and Practice in the United Kingdom', PhD thesis, City, University of London.

6 See generally Arendt, H. (1963) *Eichmann in Jerusalem: A Report on the Banality of Evil*, New York: Viking University Press; Arendt, H. (1970) *On Violence*, New York: Harcourt Press.

7 See further Adler, M. (2004), 'A Socio-legal Approach to Administrative Justice', *Law and Policy*, 25(4): 323–52; Adler, M. (2010) *Administrative Justice in Context*, Oxford: Hart Publishing.

decision making.[8] Because such research focuses on the idea that decision makers are rational, it proposes solutions that are premised on the provision of better information and skills. This is useful, but it leads to a failure to recognise the role of emotions and other irrational factors in decision making.[9] I offer a supplement of administrative violence to provide a language within which harms caused to claimants can be articulated.

Administrative violence is marked out by manifesting in the form of 'daily, mundane, business as usual acts'.[10] To fully understand this, it is also worth noting that violence can encompass psychological injury as well as restrictions to freedom and goes far beyond the simple idea of physical harm that is most frequently associated with the term 'violence'. As Arendt argued, one of the most unsettling things about violence is its mundanity.[11] Indeed, the form of government most often permitted to dispense violence is 'bureaucracy or the rule of an intricate system of bureaus in which no men … can be held responsible, and which could properly be called rule by nobody'.[12] Bauman and Butler have insightfully explored how bureaucratic mindsets contribute to unjust distributions of violence.[13] For our purposes, it is enough to say that by putting process, objectivity and efficiency above human needs, bureaucracy causes forms of harm and violence. The concept of administrative violence draws on multiple strands of Arendt's[14] work to be defined as 'injury sustained through the implementation of instrumental, formal processes which are justified as a social necessity, and operating at a level of abstraction, where attribution of individual responsibility is obscured or entirely denied'.[15]

Bureaucratic processes such as refugee status determination involve multiple sites at which administrative violence may be enacted. As Halliday has argued, '[b]ureaucracies are central to the delivery of law in modern society'.[16]

8 Halliday, S. (2021) 'Administrative Justice and Street-Level Emotions: Denial in Entitlement Decision-Making', *Public Law* 727–46, at 727–32.

9 Ibid.

10 Spade, D. (2015) *Normal Life: Administrative Violence, Critical Trans Politics, and the Limits of Law*, Durham, NC: Duke University Press, 151.

11 Arendt, H. (1963) 'Eichmann in Jerusalem – I' *The New Yorker* [online], 8 February. Available from: https://www.newyorker.com/magazine/1963/02/16/eichmann-in-jerusalem-i [Accessed 6 April 2020]. See also Powell, A. (2018) 'Officials Working within Hostile Government Departments are Not Free from Blame', *The Conversation* [online], 6 July. Available from: https://theconversation.com/officials-working-within-hostile-government-departments-are-not-free-from-blame-98741 [Accessed 23 March 2021].

12 Arendt (1970) (n 6) 38.

13 See Bauman, Z. (1988)'Sociology after the Holocaust', *British Journal of Sociology*, 39(4): 469–97; Butler, J. (2009) *Frames of War: When Is Life Grievable?*, New York: Verso.

14 See generally Arendt (1970) (n 6).

15 Powell (n 5) 347.

16 Halliday (n 8) 727.

Drawing on the work of Arendt, it becomes clear that within bureaucratic administrative systems, violence is frequent. Indeed, 'the relationship between legal interpretation and the infliction of pain remains operative even in the most routine of legal acts'.[17] The very function of administrative determinations as authoritative, purportedly objective acts often leads to the coercive infliction of force on people.[18] Think, for example, of the legal process of assigning a sex to a baby. This initially appears harmless, yet may later present life-changing consequences, some of which are rightly described as violent, in adulthood.[19]

The potential of public law issues to enact violence is well explained in the description of modern administration as revolving around '[p]recision, speed, unambiguity, knowledge of the files [or processes] … a discharge of business according to calculable rules and "without regard for persons"'.[20] As this suggests, the administrative state seeks to produce 'objective' outcomes from human interactions. Such issues become a concern for public law scholarship when they impact people's ability to access their rights. Central to this conception of administrative violence is a recognition of how the day-to-day processes of the contemporary administrative state figure as acts of harm. The asylum system can enact administrative violence because it is a formal process justified on the basis of a need to detect and deny 'false claims'.[21] This process operates at a high level of abstraction, with decisions being rendered as the view of the Home Secretary.[22] The result of this abstraction is that no individual who interacts with a claimant is required to recognise the full consequences of their role. This is despite the fact that, in possessing the power to deny an asylum claim which may result in the deportation of the claimant, decision makers are able to enact forms of power which can push the claimant into what Agamben called 'bare life'.[23] Indeed, as Agamben suggests, 'the refugee causes the secret presupposition of the

---

17 Cover, R. (1986) 'Violence and the World', *Yale Law Journal*, 95: 1061–629, at 1607. See also Butler, J. (2020) *The Force of Nonviolence*, New York: Verso, 122–41.

18 See further Powell (n 5).

19 See further Spade (n 10). See also Baars, G. (2019) 'Queer Cases Unmake Gendered Law, or, Fucking Laws Gendering Function', *Australian Feminist Law Journal*, 45(1): 15–62.

20 Gerth, H. and Mills, C.W. (eds) (1970) *From Max Weber: Essays in Sociology*, London: Routledge, 214–15.

21 See Jubany, O. (2011) 'Constructing Truths in a Culture of Disbelief: Understanding Asylum Screening from Within', *International Sociology*, 26(1): 74–94.

22 Bauman explored how processes of abstraction and moral distancing distorted and disarmed the moral objections of civil servants assigned to administer the Holocaust in Nazi Germany. See further Bauman, Z. (1988) 'Sociology after the Holocaust', *British Journal of Sociology*, 38: 469–97, at 485–97.

23 See, for a definition, Agamben, G. (1998) *Homo Sacer: Sovereign Power and Bare Life*, Stanford: Stanford University Press 1998, 1–12.

political domain – bare life – to appear for an instant within that domain'.[24] Essentially, that the refugee, in needing to prove their entitlement to status and its associated rights, shows the reality that anyone can fall outside of the protective framework of rights at any time if they lose the protection of a state. It is for this reason that the potential for administrative violence – the ticking of the box literally a withdrawal of protection – should be a central concern of public lawyers.

In the case of asylum claims made due to a fear of being persecuted on the basis of sexual diversity, administrative violence often includes symbolic violence. Bourdieu defines symbolic violence as being a 'gentle, invisible violence, unrecognised as such'.[25] He situates it as relating to the issue of 'mis-recognition'.[26] This issue of misrecognition is appropriate for understanding decision makers' expectations of what sexually diverse identities look like.[27] In this sense, one of the forms of violence within the asylum system arises from the imposition of dominant ways of being on marginalised people.

The law, policy and politics of refugee status determination in the UK

The UK is a signatory to the 1951 Refugee Convention[28] and its 1967 Protocol.[29] The Convention defines a refugee at Article 1A(2) as: 'A Person who owing to a well-founded fear of being persecuted for reasons of race, religion, nationality, membership of a particular social group or political opinion, is outside the country of his nationality and is unable, or owing to such fear, is unwilling to avail himself of the protection of that country.'[30] The Convention definition of a refugee was brought into UK law by the Refugee or Person in Need of International Protection (Qualification) Regulations 2006. Accounting for this, the Home Secretary has obligations in both domestic and international law to recognise as refugees – who are entitled to all the protections provided for under the Convention[31] – all people

---

[24] Ibid, 131.

[25] Bourdieu, P. (1992) *The Logic of Practice*, Cambridge: Polity, 127.

[26] Ibid.

[27] For an interesting discussion, see Topper, K. (2002) 'Not So Trifling Nuances: Pierre Bourdieu, Symbolic Violence, and the Perversions of Democracy', *Constellations*, 8(1): 30–56.

[28] Convention Relating to the Status of Refugees, 28 July 1951, 189 UNTS 137.

[29] Protocol Relating to the Status of Refugees, 31 January 1967, 606 UNTS 267.

[30] Convention Relating to the Status of Refugees, 28 July 1951, 189 UNTS 137, Article 1(A)2.

[31] See further Hathaway, J. (2010) *The Rights of Refugees under International Law*, Cambridge: Cambridge University Press.

meeting the definition outlined earlier.[32] However, the rights of refugees have become a deeply political issue. Maley argues there is often no connection between the Convention definition and common language invocations of the term.[33] The impact of political discourses on the administration of refugee law in the UK is further enhanced by the alarmist interventions of politicians and the press regarding the numbers of refugees and other migrants entering the UK.[34]

Yeo has charted how policies such as the net migration cap have contributed to the further politicisation of refugees by failing to distinguish between immigration and asylum.[35] This unhelpful conflation was at its most clandestine in August 2020 when a Home Office Twitter account posted a video that referred to lawyers representing asylum seekers who had come to the UK – often by unlawfully crossing the Channel[36] – as 'activist lawyers'.[37] This suggested that lawyers functioned only to delay

---

32 Note that since this chapter was written, the Nationality and Borders Act 2022 has come into law, resulting in reasonably significant, but as yet undefined, changes to the legal process. This includes the repeal of the Refugee or Person in Need of International Protection (Qualification) Regulations 2006. See Prabhat, D., Rifath, R., Singleton, A., Ziegler, R., Powell, A. and Sedacca, N. (2022) 'Reconsidering Asylum: Is it for Those Who Need Protection?' Available from: https://blogs.law.ox.ac.uk/research-subject-groups/centre-criminology/centreborder-criminologies/blog/2022/05/reconsidering [Accessed 21 July 2022].

33 Maley, W. (2016) *What is a Refugee?*, Oxford: Hurst & Company, 37–42. See also Campbell, J. (2017) *Bureaucracy, Law and Dystopia in the United Kingdom's Asylum System*, New York: Routledge, 16–98.

34 See further Gabrielatos, C. and Baker, P. (2008) 'Fleeing, Sneaking, Flooding: A Corpus Analysis of Discursive Constructions of Refugees and Asylum Seekers in the UK Press 1996–2005', *Journal of English Linguistics*, 36(1): 5–38.

35 Yeo, C. (2020) *Welcome to Britain: Fixing Our Broken Immigration System*, London: Biteback Publishing, 15–27, 109–45. See also Dustin, M. (2018) 'Many Rivers Still to Cross: The Recognition of LGBTQI Asylum in the UK', *International Journal of Refugee Law*, 30(1): 104–27, at 107–9.

36 The Refugee Convention protects the rights of those needing asylum from prosecution or detriment suffered as a result of unlawful entry, provided that certain other conditions are met. See Convention Relating to the Status of Refugees, 28 July 1951, 189 UNTS 137, Article 31.

37 See Hyde, J. (2020) '"Activist" Tweet Deleted – As Number 10 Targets "Loudmouthed Lawyers"'. Available from: https://www.lawgazette.co.uk/news/activist-tweet-deleted-as-number-10-targets-loudmouthed-lawyers/5105445.article [Accessed 4 May 2022]. In the spirit of *Diverse Voices in Public Law*, I argue, it is increasingly important that analysis of social media posts by government agencies and politicians is taken seriously. Social media has taken on exceptional power to affect law and politics. In another context, I have argued that the framing of Brexit discourses may come to undermine accepted conceptions of the UK constitution, such as the sovereignty of Parliament. See further Powell, A. (2019) '"The Will of the People": The UK Constitution, Parliamentary Sovereignty, and Brexit', in T. Ahmed and E. Fahey (eds), *On Brexit: Law, Justices and Injustices*, Cheltenham: Edward Elgar, 81–95.

the government's legitimate efforts to remove the claimants. This kind of communication gives the impression that all asylum seekers coming to the UK are illegitimate and that the government is simply being obstructed by lawyers.

The same attitude to claims is present in one immigration judge's suggestion that sexual diversity claims are 'easy to make and impossible to disprove'.[38] On the contrary, sexual diversity asylum claims have a higher rejection rate than claims made on other grounds.[39] Prior to the 2010 *HJ (Iran) and HT (Cameroon)* judgment, Rainbow Migration (formerly known as the UK Lesbian and Gay Immigration Group) identified a 98–99 per cent rejection rate for claims based on sexual diversity.[40] This was the result of 'expected voluntary discretion',[41] which meant that decision makers could find that an asylum claimant could be returned to their country of origin and keep their sexual diversity a secret in order to avoid persecution. This expectation was put by one Australian immigration judge as being a 'reasonable expectation that persons should, to the extent that it is possible, co-operate in their own protection'.[42] In the UK, the key test was whether the claimant 'would … adapt his behaviour so as to avoid persecution in … a way which was reasonably tolerable to him'.[43] As Dustin points out, this test could be viewed as a catch-all excuse for rejection.[44] The idea of discretion was vociferously criticised and was eventually recognised by the Supreme Court as being incompatible with a 'fundamental characteristic and an integral part of

---

38 *Krasniqi v Secretary of State for the Home Department* [2001] UKIAT 01TH02140, para 2.

39 'Experimental statistics' released in 2020 covering LGBT asylum claims indicated a grant rate of 46 per cent for claims involving sexually diverse asylum seekers. This represents a significant improvement from the 22 per cent grant rate recorded in 2017, but was still below the 52 per cent grant rate for claims where sexual diversity was not a relevant factor. Home Office (2020) 'Asylum Claims on the Basis of Sexual Orientation: National Statistics', updated 26 August 2021, London: Home Office. Available from: https://www.gov.uk/government/statistics/immigration-statistics-year-ending-june-2021/asylum-claims-on-the-basis-of-sexual-orientation-2020#:~:text=There%20were%201%2C012%20asylum%20applications,%25)%20over%20the%20same%20period [Accessed 3 October 2020].

40 UK Lesbian and Gay Immigration Group (2010) 'Failing the Grade', London: UK Lesbian and Gay Immigration Group – now Rainbow Migration. Available from: https://www.rainbowmigration.org.uk/wp-content/uploads/2022/03/Falling-the-Grade-April-10_1.pdf [Accessed 4 May 2023].

41 Chelvan, S. (2011) 'Put Your Hands up (If You Feel Love): A Critical Analysis of HJ (Iran) and HT (Cameroon)', *Journal of Immigration, Asylum and Nationality Law*, 25(1) 56–66, at 58.

42 V95/03527 [1996] RRTA 246 para 247.

43 *J v Secretary of State for the Home Department* [2006] EWCA Civ 1238, para 13.

44 See further Dustin (n 35) 110.

human freedom'.[45] Thus, requiring an asylum seeker to return to their country of origin and be discreet was held to be contrary to the UK's obligations under the Convention.[46] The Supreme Court also provided a three-stage test to be applied by decision makers in sexual diversity claims.[47]

Under the new test a decision maker must first 'ask itself whether it is satisfied on the evidence that he is gay?'[48] If they are satisfied the claimant is a sexually diverse person, then the next stage of the test calls for them to consider whether they are 'satisfied on the available evidence that gay people who lived openly would be liable to persecution in the applicant's country of nationality?'[49] If they are satisfied of this, then the third stage calls for them to determine 'what the individual applicant would do if he were returned to that country?'[50] If the claimant would be open about their sexual diversity, they are a refugee.[51] If they would conceal[52] their sexual diversity to avoid the potential of persecution, they are a refugee.[53] However, if the claimant would be discreet as a matter of personal preference, then they are not a refugee.[54] The core change lies in decision makers now being unable to decide that discretion would be reasonably tolerable; instead, they determine what the claimant would actually do and why. Millbank expressed concern that this test would lead to a shift from discretion to disbelief, with an increased focus on whether or not the claimant was a sexually diverse person.[55] In light of findings that, between 2011 and 2013, 86 per cent of rejected sexual diversity claims were based on a lack of credibility, it appears that Millbank's predictions have turned out to be accurate.[56]

---

45 *HJ (Iran) and HT (Cameroon) v Secretary of State for the Home Department* [2010] UKSC 31, para 33.

46 Ibid.

47 Ibid, para 82–3.

48 Ibid, para 82.

49 Ibid.

50 Ibid.

51 Ibid, para 83.

52 See further Equality and Human Rights Commission, '*HJ (Iran) and HT (Cameroon) v Secretary of State for the Home Department* – Case for the Equality and Human Rights Commission' cited in Wessels, J. (2013) '*HJ (Iran) and HT (Cameroon)* – Reflections on a new test for sexuality-based asylum claims in Britain', *International Journal of Refugee Law* 24(4): 815–39, at 825–26.

53 *HJ (Iran) and HT (Cameroon)* (n 45 para 83).

54 Ibid.

55 See Millbank, J. (2009) 'From Discretion to Disbelief: Recent Trends in Refugee Determinations on the Basis of Sexual Orientation in Australia and the United Kingdom', *International Journal of Human Rights*, 13(2–3): 391–414.

56 UK Lesbian and Gay Immigration Group (2013) 'Missing the Mark', London: UK Lesbian and Gay Immigration Group. Available from: https://www.rainbowmigration.org.uk/wp-content/uploads/2022/03/Missing-the-Mark-Oct-13_0.pdf

As such, one impact of this change has been to shift the main area of dispute towards determining whether or not the claimant is – or would be perceived as – a sexually diverse person. Despite the new test, some have argued that 'decision-makers still have no idea what claimants need to do to prove their sexual orientation'.[57] Indeed, as Juss argues, the test itself provides no guidance for how decision makers should determine whether a claimant is sexually diverse, or what constitutes evidence in this regard.[58] As I have argued elsewhere, this often leads to decision makers focusing on tropes common to the development of sexual identities within the UK.[59] Guidance on how to approach asylum claims by sexually diverse people is provided by the 'Asylum Policy Instruction: Sexual Orientation in Asylum Claims'.[60] However, the way in which this policy is applied in practice often reflects the tropes referred to previously.[61] Accordingly, decision makers' interpretations often come to be based on factors that might rightly be regarded as stereotypical.

These problems are exacerbated by the lack of viable appeal routes. In the context of asylum decisions, access to an appeal is difficult because the system is being overwhelmed.[62] As Thomas has charted, there was an increase in the average time for an asylum appeal to be resolved from nine weeks in 2013 to more than 35 weeks in 2016.[63] Such delays have been exacerbated by the COVID-19 pandemic. Thomas further identifies that the delays seen prior to the pandemic arose from both a limited number of tribunal judges and a rising number of cases.[64] Combining these factors, a picture emerges of poor access to appeals in an environment with extensive delays and poor first-instance decisions.

[Accessed 6 February 2023]. See also Powell, A. (2020). 'Normative Understandings: Sexual Identity, Stereotypes, and Asylum Seeking', in C. Ashford and A. Maine (eds), *The Research Handbook on Gender, Sexuality and Law*, Cheltenham: Edward Elgar, 149–63.

57 Lewis, R. (2014) '"Gay? Prove it": The Politics of Queer Anti-Deportation Activism', *Sexualities*, 17(8): 958–75, at 963.

58 Juss (n 78).

59 See generally Powell (n 3).

60 Home Office (n 4).

61 Powell (n 5) 279–344.

62 Thomas and Tomlinson have also noted substantial issues regarding limited access to legal aid. See Thomas, R. and Tomlinson, J. (2019) *Immigration Judicial Reviews: An Empirical Study*, London: Nuffield Foundation.

63 See Thomas, R. (2017) 'Immigration Appeals and Delays: On the Verge of a Crisis', UK Administrative Justice Institute. Available from: https://ukaji.org/2017/05/18/immigration-appeals-and-delays-on-the-verge-of-a-crisis [Accessed 24 December 2022].

64 Ibid. See also Independent Chief Inspector of Borders and Immigration (2021) 'An Inspection of Asylum Casework (August 2020–May 2021)', November, London: The Stationery Office. Available from: www.gov.uk/official-documents [Accessed 19 April 2022].

Bureaucracy, chaos and delay at first instance

Given that those who are claiming asylum are likely to have experienced trauma and may be vulnerable to retraumatisation, it is vital that refugee status determination is undertaken in a sensitive manner. The process of making an asylum claim needs to be humane and offer claimants the opportunity to put forward their experiences and be heard. In this regard, it should be noted that overly adversarial approaches, while common,[65] are not supported by the guidance given to decision makers.[66]

This section explores some of the issues arising within first-instance decision making. I document how these issues lead to potential administrative violence emerging within contemporary state decision-making bodies. In exploring these experiences, it should be recognised that – irrespective of the international framework – recognition as a refugee is dependent on being recognised by the state.[67] The question of refugee status is therefore fundamentally one of recognition. So, in a context of declining access to justice, it is important to interrogate the process through which recognition as a refugee is achieved in the UK. That process currently relies on the decisions made by Home Office decision makers. Therefore, potentially life-and-death decisions are being made by the first-instance decision makers administering the UK asylum system. Further, it should be noted that various forms of harm below the level of life and death are caused by the misrecognition and trivialisation of refugee narratives.[68]

The first stage of the asylum process is a screening interview. This is when the claimant gives a brief outline of their claim. These are intended to be a short, formal part of the claim process. Despite this, participants noted significant flaws in this screening stage. Adroa[69] reported that there was a lack of privacy where he had to give his screening interview, explaining that:

> 'I went there for the screening and that is the first time I put my case forward and it was a very very difficult time. I remember one of the most challenging things was the lack of privacy. It was just an open

---

65 Schuster, L. (2020) 'Fatal Flaws in the UK Asylum Decision-Making System: An Analysis of Home Office Refusal Letters', *Journal of Ethnic and Migration Studies*, 46(7): 1371–87.

66 Home Office (n 4) 22.

67 Hardy, C. (2003) 'Refugee Determination: Power and Resistance in Systems of Foucauldian Power', *Administration & Society*, 35(4): 462–88, at 467–8.

68 See, for example, Honkala, N. (2022) '"An Unhappy Interlude": Trivialisation and Privatisation of Forced Marriage in Asylum-Seeker Women's Cases in the UK', *Refugee Survey Quarterly*, 41(3): 472–97.

69 All participants' names have been changed to protect their anonymity.

building, there was no kind of little space where you could speak to anybody. You could just speak to someone behind a screen with a microphone and you just have to shout. I'm apply [sic] for asylum. … And there was no tick for sexuality. And then I have to say it is because I am a gay man and there are people there that are listening, because you have to shout so that you could be heard. Otherwise, she can't hear, and she was asking and asking. So, then I was expected to just give that kind of information … and I didn't want to express myself because for the first time I am standing in front of someone and expressing my sexuality.'[70]

Adroa's experience calls attention to the fact that first-instance decisions in the UK are undertaken on a mass scale.[71] This can often lead to a kind of conveyor belt system that is neither sensitive nor conducive to eliciting the deep, carefully articulated and well-developed narratives that the asylum process itself demands of claimants.[72] In Adroa's case, the first issue that arose was being asked to openly proclaim his sexual diversity in a semi-public setting to a uniformed official. Given that Adroa had previously experienced threats and arrest after his sexual diversity had become known, this will have risked causing him substantial distress.[73]

Babu also found the screening experience distressing. One cause of this distress was the fact that he was forced to sit in a waiting room for the entire day after his interview had taken place. He was then moved to a detention centre, even though his visa had not yet expired. In his words:

'I waited for around six hours … to meet with the immigration officer and then the immigration officer asked me to wait for another few hours. And then after waiting that long time, I think it was around 3:30 in the afternoon or 4. They decided that … on the basis of deception … that I didn't claim asylum at the borders that they are going to detain me.'[74]

As Babu's example demonstrates, being forced to wait an extended period after the screening interview with the threat of detention hanging in the air can cause distress. Babu's distress at this experience was made clear by the

70 Adroa, Ugandan refugee, speaking to the author.

71 Cwerner has usefully explored the issues of time and scale within the UK asylum system. See Cwerner, S.B. (2004) 'Faster, Faster and Faster: The Time Politics of Asylum in the UK', *Time and Society*, 13(1): 71–81.

72 Ibid.

73 Adroa, Ugandan refugee, speaking to the author.

74 Babu, Egyptian refugee, speaking to the author.

profound discomfort his body language displayed while he was recounting this experience.

Connected to this, two participants, including Babu, recounted the distress they felt at being detained in similar terms to the traumatic experiences that had led them to leave their countries of origin. Babu explained:

> 'It was very unlawful of them to detain me and there was nothing that I had done wrong. You know, I just claimed asylum. But then I was put in a detention centre and I had to wait another six or seven hours before I was actually transferred from Croydon to that detention centre. … And you're only allowed one phone call, and then they take your phone away from you so you can't call your family. You can't call anyone.'[75]

Babu situated the confusion and distress caused by being detained as having a lasting impact on his mental health. He also expressed that, even after his claim was granted, he was anxious that when the time came to renew his status after five years, he would be returned to detention. This demonstrates the significance and continuing nature of administrative violence, because it is not just the immediate issues that were affecting Babu, but also the continuing need to re-apply for status and the idea of having to interact with these same administrative processes again.

Babu's scenario is an example of how administrative violence can arise within a system designed to protect those fleeing persecution. His experience meets all three of the articulated criteria for administrative violence. The harm he suffered – mental health trauma – was caused by an institutional (Home Office) formal process justified by the need to ensure that individuals without proper legal status are prevented from remaining in the UK. Additionally, the process operates at a level of abstraction whereby no individual can be properly held to account for the experiences Babu endured.

Babu's own interpretation of this was that the operative hearing his screening interview did not believe he was gay. While it is difficult to say that Babu's experience was a direct result of the person who conducted his interview not believing he was gay, even his subjective perception that this was the case demonstrates the potential of the process to trigger and exacerbate the trauma of applicants. Babu's immediate detention should also be examined against the principle that, regardless of the legal power under which someone is subject to immigration detention, there must be a

[75] Ibid.

reasonable prospect of removal from the UK.[76] This has a longstanding basis in the *Hardial Singh* principles, which established that detention can only be used when there is a reasonable prospect of removal within a reasonable timeframe.[77] Thus, the use of immigration detention during the early stages of the claim, when there is not a reasonable prospect of removal, is of questionable compatibility with the relevant legal framework. As this suggests, such issues at first instance can even point towards deficiencies with regard to the rule of law.

Not all participants found the screening to be a distressing process. Three out of eight found the screening interview to be very straightforward. Nonetheless, these issues within the screening process should be taken as building a picture of how the processes adopted within first-instance decision making can lead to enactments of administrative violence which undermine both the UK's ability to comply with its international obligations under the Refugee Convention, and the UK's ability to ensure that it offers appropriate protection to vulnerable claimants.

Another element of the refugee status determination process that caused distress to claimants was the substantive interview. The substantive interview process is a crucial part of the asylum claim. It is the opportunity for the claimant to present their narrative. However, numerous researchers have documented the practice of decision makers repeatedly asking similar questions with a view to finding, or producing, contradictions and inconsistencies.[78]

While formally, discrepancy questioning is not a policy employed by the Home Office, participants documented this practice, with Abeo telling me that:

> 'she had to ask these questions again and then she started those questions and I remember that … the interview that was supposed to take a few hours took almost two days because … I just kept breaking down. I just couldn't be able to talk about those things and, you know, everyone keep telling me that they can still deport me and the whole idea that I could be deported kept nagging at the back of my head.'[79]

This shows that discrepancy questioning adds to the trauma faced by asylum seekers by leading to longer and more stressful interview encounters. In this

---

76 See further Home Office (2021) *Detention: General Instructions*. Available from: https://assets.publishing.service.gov.uk/government/uploads/system/uploads/attachment_data/file/992285/detention-general-instructions-v1.0.pdf [Accessed 24 December 2022].

77 *R (Hardial Singh) v Governor of Durham Prison* [1983] EWHC 1 (QB).

78 See generally Juss, S. (1997) *Discretion and Deviation in the Administration of Immigration Control*, London: Sweet & Maxwell, 62–7.

79 Abeo, Nigerian refugee, speaking to the author.

regard, it could even be understood as a form of secondary victimisation, forcing claimants to experience further distress. Abeo's experience also draws attention to the ongoing distress that can be caused by interacting with an organisation which presents a continuing threat to return the claimant to the country from which they have fled.

While it is recognised that some form of questioning is necessary to establish the validity of a claimant's narrative, it is submitted that, in line with the Home Office's 2016 Asylum Policy Instruction (API) on Sexual Orientation in Asylum Claims, decision makers should avoid searching for discrepancies in a claimant's narrative and should instead focus on creating a comfortable environment for claimants to put forward their narratives.[80] Or, preferably, the Home Office should move towards adopting a model for assessing asylum claims that focuses on the self-definition of claimants.[81] Such a model would leave space for the experiences of asylum seekers to be examined, but would mean statements that the claimant was, for example, lesbian or gay would be taken at face value.

This sheds light on the significance of first-instance decision making because, when the processes themselves are producing harmful consequences for claimants, the fact that an appeal or reconsideration may be possible is no longer an adequate safeguard.

Prior expectations and experiences of decision makers regarding the nature of sexual diversity can also produce forms of administrative violence. Decision makers often bring expectations regarding what constitutes sexual diversity to their analysis of claims.[82] These expectations are often founded on UK tropes. Even the 'Asylum Policy Instruction' reproduces tropes such as the idea of people moving through different stages in their sexual development.[83] This manifests in expectations that claimants will have 'realised' their difference from others during their teenage years and will then have gone through a process of development before eventually embracing their 'identity'. In other work, I have problematised this focus on identity and the expectation for

---

80 Home Office (n 4) 22–5.

81 Jansen and other associates of the Sexual Orientation and Gender Identity Claims of Asylum (SOGICA]) project have put forward a compelling case for giving a greater role to self-definition within the asylum claims of sexually diverse people. See Jansen, S. (2019) 'Pride or Shame? LGBTI Asylum in the Netherlands Following the XYZ and ABC Judgments', *COC Netherlands* [online], January. Available from: www.coc.nl/wp-content/uploads/2019/01/Pride-or-Shame-LGBTI-asylum-in-the-Netherlands.pdf [Accessed 6 February 2023].

82 Powell (n 56).

83 Best, K. (2018) 'What is the Reasonable Way for UK Asylum Seekers to "Prove They are Gay"?', *The Independent* [online], 14 October. Available from: https://www.independent.co.uk/voices/comment/what-is-the-reasonable-way-for-uk-asylum-seekers-to-prove-they-are-gay-8879686.html [Accessed 2 August 2020.]

sexual diversity to manifest in simple or easily identifiable ways by exploring the more culturally specific ways in which refugees experienced their own sexual difference.[84]

The deployment of these tropes can lead to significant distress for asylum claimants who face both a denial of their asylum claims and the symbolic violence of having their lived experience as sexually diverse people denied. Far from making the objective decisions administrative bodies are expected to make, particularistic criteria are applied, undermining the quality of decision making. For example, Abdullah told me that:

> 'Their [the Home Office's] understanding of homosexuality was that of a gay person. To me, gay is so different than homosexual. I mean homosexual is your sexual attraction, full stop. But when you are gay it is not just your attraction, it is also how you express your attraction and the slogans which you use to express that attraction and the way that you conduct yourself in relation to that attraction. So, basically, you have to reculture yourself in accordance with that attraction and if you haven't recultured yourself yet, then you are not gay yet. You are just homosexual.'[85]

Abdullah felt that the decision makers had not understood his sexual diversity and that he had therefore been forced to modulate his self-presentation in line with their expectations. This is a form of administrative violence, as the need to categorise claimants such as Abdullah in terms intelligible to the decision maker results in claimants being dehumanised by a tick-box approach. Similar forms of administrative violence have been recognised within the context of decision making by the Department for Work and Pensions, particularly in reference to the provision of the Personal Independence Payment.[86] Such tick-box approaches instrumentally result in claimants being exposed to formal processes that lead to them being refused access to something they materially need. Often such processes adopt a rigidity that is of at least questionable compatibility with the legal framework under which these administrative bodies operate.

Some participants linked this denial of their lived experience to colonialism. For example, Babu recounted that:

> 'One of the most interesting things is like how gender identity and sexuality, all of these things, like you know homosexuality and on

84 See further Powell (n 3).

85 Abdullah, Omani refugee, speaking to the author.

86 Alldridge, P. (2019) 'On Being Able to Walk Twenty Meters: The Introduction of Personal Independence Payments', *Journal of Law and Society*, 46(3): 448–75.

> the broader scale in these countries such as Egypt were influenced by colonialism. Because prior to colonialism sexuality was not an issue. Like a lot of Arabic literature actually talks about men falling in love with other men and how absolutely fine it was hundreds of years before colonialism. And then once colonial powers overtook those countries, they changed the laws and these regulations that they put in place to make them perceive the things that Europe was perceiving at the time and among them was the idea of sexuality, that homosexuality was wrong. This was only imposed from a European perspective and now it has become what it is today.'[87]

Being expected to discuss their sexual diversity in terms of sexual identity, to articulate their experiences in a manner recognisable to decision makers, itself featured as a source of discomfort for some claimants. This can rightly be understood as a form of symbolic violence as discussed, in the first section. This is because claimants are required to speak in a certain language – determined by the normative experiences of decision makers – in order to make their narratives intelligible. Correctly understood, this symbolic violence contributes to the wider administrative violence of the process as claimants are forced to represent themselves in ways that do not correspond to their lived experiences and may invoke feelings of discomfort or erasure.

Other claimants felt discomfort at being forced to articulate their experiences in fixed terms which did not account for why sexually diverse people may have behaved in a manner which the decision maker perceived as incompatible with their expectations. For example, Masani told me:

> 'I was forced to marry. I had no choice, because if I had refused then my sexuality would have been suspected. But when I came here, they said I was not a lesbian because I had been married. The letter made it sound so simple, you had a husband back in Uganda, therefore it is not credible that you are a lesbian.'[88]

As this suggests, Masani had her first-instance claim denied – though she was later successful on appeal – on the basis that her heterosexual marriage meant that her claim to be a lesbian was not credible. This example is particularly concerning, given that, as Giametta has identified, heterosexual marriage within the country of origin can often be a key strategy for preventing

[87] Babu, Egyptian refugee, speaking to the author.

[88] Masani, Ugandan refugee, speaking to the author.

one's sexual diversity from becoming known.[89] Further, the standpoint that someone who had been in a heterosexual marriage could not be a lesbian represents a fixed – and limited – way of understanding sexual diversity that does not correspond to the lived experiences of many sexually diverse people.

This denial of someone's self-defined identity based on the adoption of an overly essentialised conception of sexual diversity can be understood as a form of administrative violence. Once again, it arises as an injury – denial of identity can be a very painful and injurious experience[90] – as the result of a formal process, in the form of the Home Office interviews and decisions. This injury is justified on the basis of a need to ensure false asylum claimants are identified and refused. Finally, the process, as Masani identifies, ends with a letter from the Home Office, in this case directly informing Masani that they have determined that she is not a lesbian. As Sen has argued, violence often will, and does, take the form of forcing people to adopt and conform to institutionally valorised identities.[91] Thus, the humiliation, denial of lived experience and pain brought about by such an official declaration should not be underestimated.

A further relevant theme of administrative violence arises as a result of the delays that are so common within refugee status determination in the UK. These delays arise both from slow decision making on the part of the Home Office and the difficulties that many asylum claimants face when seeking appeals and reconsiderations of previous decisions. For example, Adroa told me of how isolated, disconnected and disempowering his days were before gaining refugee status. He said that before gaining status he waited:

> 'Five years. From 2005 until 2010 … Christmases could just come and pass by. Summer comes, winter comes, and I was just living, just surviving. Every single day was different. There was not any kind of particular time when things were consistent. It was very very difficult. Time just passed away.'[92]

The significance of delays such as this is well articulated in Arendt's argument that:

> What makes a man a political being is his faculty of action; it enables him to get together with his peers, to act in concert, and to reach out for goals and enterprises that would never enter his mind, let alone

[89] Giametta, C. (2017) *The Sexual Politics of Asylum: Sexual Orientation and Gender Identity in the UK Asylum System*, New York: Routledge, 45.

[90] See generally Sen, A. (2006) *Identity & Violence: The Illusion of Destiny*, London: Penguin

[91] Ibid, 1–40.

[92] Adroa, Ugandan refugee, speaking to the author.

> the desires of his heart, had he not been given this gift – to embark on something new.[93]

Each of these factors is denied to asylum seekers who are awaiting a decision on their asylum claim due to the continuing ban on employment.

Conclusion

This chapter has explored how factors such as delays, the perspectives and preconceptions of decision makers, and the use of tactics such as attempting to elicit contradictory responses, all result in forms of administrative violence. These incidents of administrative violence can, in turn, have an impact on the UK's ability to comply with its obligations under the Refugee Convention of 1951, and may at times even undermine the strength of the rule of law in the UK.

This chapter has drawn attention to the impact first-instance decisions can have on the lives of asylum claimants and has presented an argument for why first-instance decision making and the results it can have should be given greater consideration within public law scholarship. Although it has only directly looked at issues relating to refugee status determination, it is argued that these issues are present in relation to other administrative decision-making bodies such as the Department for Work and Pensions.[94] Research into the issues arising in the context of decisions relating to disability support has been included as one of the five further reading entries that accompany this chapter. In a context of declining access to justice, increasing delays and an inevitable backlog of cases resulting from the global COVID-19 pandemic that began in March 2020, it is important the researchers and policy makers within the field of administrative law pay greater attention to the significance and potential impacts of first-instance decision making.

Further reading

Alldridge, P. (2019) 'On Being Able to Walk Twenty Meters: The Introduction of Personal Independence Payments', *Journal of Law and Society*, 46(3): 448–75.

Burridge, A. and Gill, N. (2017) 'Conveyor-Belt Justice: Precarity, Access to Justice, and Uneven Geographies of Legal Aid in UK Asylum Appeals', *Antipode*, 49(1): 23–42.

Heimer, R.D.V.L. (2020) 'Homonationalist/Orientalist Negotiations: The UK Approach to Queer Asylum Claims', *Sexuality and Culture*, 24: 174–96.

[93] Arendt (1970) (n 6) 82.

[94] Alldridge (n 86).

Schuster, L. (2020) 'Fatal Flaws in the UK Asylum Decision-Making System: An Analysis of Home Office Refusal Letters', *Journal of Ethnic and Migration Studies*, 46(7): 1371–87.

Spade, D. (2015) *Normal Life: Administrative Violence, Critical Trans Politics, & the Limits of Law*, Durham, NC: Duke University Press.

A More Diverse Public Law: Suggested Further Reading

Decolonising public law in legal education

Adebisi, F. (2020) 'Decolonising the Law School', *Law Teacher*, 54(4): 471–577.

Cullen, A. (2021) 'Decolonizing Public Law', in D. Tran (ed) *Decolonizing University Teaching and Learning: An Entry Model for Grappling with Complexities*, London: Bloomsbury, 139–43.

Jivraj, S. (2020) 'Decolonising the Academy – Between a Rock and a Hard Place', *Interventions*, 22(4): 552–73.

Colonial legacies in public law

El-Enany, N. (2020) *(B)ordering Britain: Law, Race and Empire*, Manchester: Manchester University Press.

Lino, D. (2016) 'Albert Venn Dicey and the Constitutional Theory of Empire', *Oxford Journal of Legal Studies*, 36(4): 751–80.

Prabhat, D. (2020) 'Unequal Citizenship and Subjecthood: A Rose by Any Other Name ... ?', *Northern Ireland Legal Quarterly*, 71(2): 175–91.

Scott, P.F. (2020) 'The Constitutional Legacies of Empire', *Northern Ireland Legal Quarterly*, 71(2): 99–330.

Allocating power

De Mars, S. and O'Donoghue, A. (2021) 'Beyond Matryoshka Governance in the Twenty-First Century: The Curious Case of Northern Ireland', in O. Doyle, A. McHarg and J. Murkens (eds) *The Brexit Challenge for Ireland and the United Kingdom: Constitutions under Pressure*, Cambridge: Cambridge University Press, 64–85.

Grez Hidalgo, P., de Londras, F. and Lock, D. (2022), 'Parliament, the Pandemic, and Constitutional Principle in the United Kingdom: A Study of the Coronavirus Act 2020', *Modern Law Review*, 85(6): 1463–503.

Horne, A., Thompson, L. and Yong, B. (eds) (2022) *Parliament and the Law*, Oxford: Hart Publishing.

McEwen, N., Kenny, M., Sheldon, J. and Brown Swan, C. (2020) 'Intergovernmental Relations in the UK: Time for a Radical Overhaul?', *Political Quarterly*, 91(3): 632–40.

Public law and gender

Hunter, R. and Rackley, E. (eds) (2022) *Justice for Everyone: The Jurisprudence and Legal Lives of Brenda Hale*, Cambridge: Cambridge University Press.

Lammasniemi, L. (2017) 'Welfare, Anti-austerity and Gender: New Territory and New Sources of Hostility for the Human Rights Act', in F. Cowell (ed) *Critically Examining the Case against the 1998 Human Rights Act*, Abingdon: Routledge, 151–65.

O'Brien, C. (2019) 'What Is the Point of Social Security? Discriminatory and Damaging Effects of the Two-Child Limit Justified by the "Lottery of Birth"', *Journal of Social Welfare and Family Law*, 41(4): 479–82.

Public law and race

Atrey, S. (2021) 'Structural Racism and Race Discrimination', *Current Legal Problems*, 74(1): 1–34.

Bowling, B. and Westenra, S. (2018) 'Racism, Immigration, and Policing', in M. Bosworth, A. Parmar and Y. Vasquez (eds) *Race, Criminal Justice, and Migration Control: Enforcing the Boundaries of Belonging*, Oxford: Oxford University Press, 61–77.

El-Enany, N. (2020), *Bordering Britain: Law, Race and Empire*, Manchester: Manchester University Press.

Olatokun, M.A. (2021) 'Does the Law Think That Black Lives Matter? A Reflection upon the Role of the Public Sector Equality Duty in Promoting Racial Equality before the Law', *Theory and Practice of Legislation*, 9(1): 83–95.

Public law and persons with disabilities

Lawson, A. and Orchard. M. (2021) 'The Anticipatory Reasonable Adjustment Duty: Removing the Blockages?', *Cambridge Law Journal*, 80(2): 308–37.

Machin, R. (2017), 'Made to Measure? An Analysis of the Transition from Disability Living Allowance to Personal Independence Payment', *Journal of Social Welfare and Family Law*, 39(4): 435–53.

McColgan, A. (2015) 'Litigating the Public Sector Equality Duty: The Story So Far', *Oxford Journal of Legal Studies*, 35(3): 453–85.

Public law and social rights

Cowan, D. (2019), 'Reducing Homelessness or Re-ordering the Deckchairs?', *Modern Law Review*, 82(1): 105–28.

Meers, J. (2022) 'The "Cumulative Impact" Problem in Social Welfare: Some Legal, Policy and Theoretical Solutions', *Journal of Social Welfare and Family Law*, 44(1): 42–64.

Simpson, M., McKeever, G. and Fitzpatrick, C. (2023) 'Legal Protection against Destitution in the UK: The Case for a Right to a Subsistence Minimum', *Modern Law Review* 86(2): 465–97.

Index